The **Great** |Mutual Fund |**Trap**

The Great
|Mutual Fund|Trap

AN INVESTMENT RECOVERY PLAN

GREGORY BAER AND GARY GENSLER

Broadway Books | New York

Broadway Books titles may be purchased for business or promotional use or for special sales. For information, please write to: Special Markets Department, Random House, Inc., 1540 Broadway, New York, NY 10036.

PRINTED IN THE UNITED STATES OF AMERICA

BROADWAY BOOKS and its logo, a letter B bisected on the diagonal, are trademarks of Broadway Books, a division of Random House, Inc.

Visit our website at www.broadwaybooks.com

First edition published 2002

Designed by Chris Welch

Library of Congress Cataloging-in-Publication Data

Baer, Gregory Arthur, 1962–
The great mutual fund trap : an investment recovery plan / Gregory Baer and Gary Gensler.
p. cm.
Includes bibliographical references and index.
ISBN 0-7679-1071-0
1. Mutual funds—United States. 2. Investments—United States. 3. Investment analysis—United States. I. Gensler, Gary. II. Title.

HG4930 .B33 2002
332.63'27—dc21
2001056666

1 3 5 7 9 10 8 6 4 2

For the women in our lives
Francesca, Shirley, Anna, Lee, and Isabel
and
the three baers
Jack, Matt, and Tommy.

They give us purpose.

Contents

Acknowledgments

We were only able to write *The Great Mutual Fund Trap* with the assistance of many other people. In particular, we have one institution, two companies, and a lot of people to thank.

The institution is the U.S. public library, in particular the Library of Congress and Fairfax County Library, George Mason branch. If you haven't visited a library recently, you may be unaware that on-line databases now allow you to access practically any newspaper or periodical, going back decades.

Morningstar, Inc.'s comprehensive Principia Pro database is the source for much of our research on mutual fund performance. Much of this data is also available on the Morningstar website.

RiskMetrics Group, Inc., is a company dedicated to the measurement of risk, believing as we do that "return is only half the equation." At RiskMetrics, Ethan Berman and Greg Elmiger provided great help, particularly in analyzing the *Wall Street Journal*'s Dartboard Portfolio.

Daniel Greenberg at James Levine Communications was an able guide through the maze of publishing, and good company to boot. Jim

Levine was good enough to pluck our proposal from the "slush" of unsolicited manuscripts. For that alone we'll be forever grateful.

At Broadway Books, Suzanne Oaks, our editor, recognized immediately what this book was all about. Suzanne and Claire Johnson provided helpful edits and gentle nudges. When Suzanne moved on to greener pastures, Trish Medved became our guide, and helped us negotiate the end stages of the process. Rebecca Holland, our production editor at Broadway, maintained her professionalism and sense of humor in the face of a barrage of last-minute edits by nervous first-time authors.

We are indebted to our research assistant, Nataliya Mylenko. While working on her Ph.D. in finance, she spent countless hours researching historical performance data on hundreds of stocks. Her work provided the foundation for Chapter 10 on the *Wall Street Journal*'s stock picking contests.

Many people, not all of whom are eager to be named, have been kind enough to review the book and give us comments. Steven Schoenfeld was an informed and patient guide to the world of exchange-traded funds and indexing more broadly. Leslie Buckland, Doug Carroll, Stan Crock, Ed Demarco, Jane Gensler, Bill Grace, Bob Grusky, Bill Lang, Joe Minarik, Eric Mogilnicki, Peter Orszag, Ronni Rosenfeld, Paul Sagawa, Alan Summers, Larry Summers, Steven Wallman, and Leslie Woolley presented valuable review. Arthur Baer reviewed the early drafts and provided much-needed encouragement. At the earliest stages, Anna Gensler convinced her dad that he simply had to write this book. Rob Gensler, a very successful money manager, provided important support even as his identical twin brother's project questioned the very nature of his industry.

We are both fortunate to have married women smarter than ourselves. Francesca Danieli and Shirley Sagawa were, aside from their many other contributions, invaluable editors and sounding boards.*

At this point in most acknowledgments, you'll see the authors note

---

* Any reader who may happen to be considering establishing a corporate-nonprofit partnership should consider *Common Interest, Common Good: Creating Value Through Business and Social Sector Partnerships* by Shirley Sagawa and Eli Segal (Harvard Business School Press, 2000).

that, despite the myriad contributions of others, they are solely responsible for the contents and solely to blame for any errors. Having spent a few years in politics and government, we aren't about to fall into that trap! To anyone wishing to point out mistakes or assign blame, we say, "Haven't we had enough of the politics of personal destruction? Have you no decency?" That and, "We're sorry."

You may wonder why two guys like us would write a book about personal investing. We don't have any business to promote. We're not financial planners or brokers. Furthermore, given the things we have to say about the current state of money management, we're unlikely to make a whole lot of new friends. So why?

Initially, the reason was frustration. While serving at the Treasury Department during the Clinton administration, we undertook a review of the investment performance of the Pension Benefit Guaranty Corporation. The PBGC is the federal government entity that stands behind the corporate pensions of millions of American workers. It had been actively investing in stocks—that is, hiring managers to beat the market—since 1976. The performance was remarkably poor. A dollar invested by PBGC in 1976 would have returned 44 percent more by 2000 if it had simply tracked the market. Moreover, the PBGC earned these below-market returns while investing in stocks that were more risky than those in the broad market.

While the size of the lost earnings surprised us, the nature of the problem did not. While at Goldman, Sachs, Gary would often be asked for stock-picking advice. He always responded that passive investment was the best option, though his friends and family mistakenly thought he was being coy. While working at the Federal Reserve, Greg had some of the nation's best economists explain to him the folly of trying to beat the market. To our chagrin, though, we discovered that not everyone was inclined to see it this way. Our efforts to effect reform at the PBGC were successfully blocked by those with a vested interest in the existing system.

We therefore felt the urge to alert consumers to the traps awaiting them in financial markets. We knew that the average individual investor was probably paying more for active fund management than the PBGC and faring even worse. That said, we wouldn't have written this book if there were not good alternatives to the current system. Fortunately, we knew of wonderful new opportunities for investors to improve returns and diminish risks—opportunities that we believe most investors don't yet fully appreciate. So, we offer *The Great Mutual Fund Trap* as both a revealing look into the current system's failings and a promise of a better way.

We hope that as you read on, you'll have a few laughs and enjoy the everyday examples we use to illustrate complex financial concepts. We think investing books should be fun and interesting. That does not mean, though, that we believe investing itself should be fun. Interesting, yes, fascinating maybe, but to us "fun" is finishing work on your finances in time to throw the ball with your kids or read a good novel or call an old friend on the phone. Here's a good rule of thumb: if you're having fun investing, then there's a good chance that you're not properly diversified, you're trading too much, and you're taking too much risk.

—Greg Baer and Gary Gensler

The Great |Mutual Fund| Trap

Rediscovering Your Common Sense

The meek may inherit the earth, but they won't get the ball from me.—*Charles Barkley, professional basketball player*

This book is written for the millions of Americans who invest in the stock or bond market to help achieve their long-term financial goals—a home, a college education for their children, a secure retirement. We believe that the vast majority of these investors are investing the wrong way—paying billions of dollars in unnecessary costs and running needless risks in a quest to outperform the market.

Why are so many people wasting so much money? By making the perfectly understandable mistake of trusting the experts.

The Trap

As Americans, we have the benefit of expert advice in almost all aspects of our lives. Thanks to the wonders of capitalism, we can find a cardiologist to advise us on our hearts, a computer consultant to advise us on our computer, or even a wedding planner to advise us on how and where to get married. We take for granted that for almost any decision, major or minor, we can obtain and benefit from expert advice.

Therefore, as individuals decide how to invest, they naturally look to the experts. Investors cede control of their investments to mutual fund managers, brokers, or financial planners. They pick their own stocks after hearing the latest advice from Wall Street analysts and economists. They trust that the fees they are charged are fair and that the advice they obtain is sound.

In the great majority of cases, however, expert money management advice simply leads investors to underperform the market and enrich Wall Street. Investors should pay nothing for it, either directly or indirectly.

For example, Americans currently have over $3 trillion invested in actively managed stock mutual funds—that is, funds whose managers pick stocks in an attempt to beat the stock market's overall performance. They have another $800 million invested in actively managed bond funds. These mutual funds are held by investors directly or in brokerage accounts, 401(k)s, IRAs, or variable annuities. *Experience clearly shows that fund managers' stock and bond picking abilities usually fall short of their considerable fee-imposing abilities.* That's entirely predictable, given that the mutual fund companies run up at least $70 billion per year in costs for investors in their attempts to beat the market.

Other investors are buying stocks on their own or through investment clubs, frequently turning over their entire portfolios each year as they jump from one investment to another. Their reasons may include recommendations from brokers and the media or an interview or report about a "hot" new sector. *These are poor ways to choose stocks and great ways to increase risk unnecessarily.*

So, why do so many people keep investing in ways the evidence shows is counterproductive? We believe that there are four simple answers.

First, we are by nature optimistic and confident. We are all too willing to believe that poor past experience will reverse itself or in the future apply only to other people.

Second, our optimism and overconfidence are reinforced by a constant, consistent message from the financial industry and the financial media: try to beat the market. The message can be direct, even crass, as when a TV commercial promises that frequent stock trading will earn

you a Caribbean island of your own. More effective, though, is the subtle message conveyed by a constant parade of money managers and analysts, all promising that they have identified a winning stock that is
sure to outperform the market. To seize this opportunity, of course, you
must buy their fund or trade with a broker.

Third, we tend to focus on returns and ignore the costs of investing.
You probably know about how much you pay each month for electric-
ity, housing, and other services. If you're like most people, though,
you've never totaled up your costs of investing—all of them, including
management fees, transaction costs, and taxes.

There's a reason you don't consider the costs of investing, of course.
Mutual funds and brokers have constructed a system where the costs
are practically invisible. You had to write a check to your electric utility
or mortgage company, but you've never paid a bill for brokerage or mutual fund management. Such costs are simply deducted from your annual mutual fund returns or taken off the top when a broker executes
your trades. You don't notice when 1 percent disappears here, 2 percent
there, particularly when your investments are making money. How else
can you explain the fact that many Americans react furiously to the
$1.50 ATM surcharges they pay, on average, fifty times per year ($75),
yet don't utter a peep when they pay a 5 percent sales load on a $10,000
mutual fund investment ($500)?

Fourth, investors do not understand how markets work, and how
very difficult it is to beat them consistently, *even by a little bit.* The best
analogy we can think of is about betting on sports. Don't worry, even if
you don't care about sports or betting, we promise you'll be able to follow it.

Every fall weekend, there are about three hundred college football
games. Picking who will win those games unquestionably involves skill.
Those who have the time and ability to research the recent records and
players of each team will do better than those who do not. While some
games will be hard to pick, others will not. A little research will show,
for example, that Notre Dame has always beaten Navy, and Florida
State has always beaten Duke. In other cases, even where the teams historically have been more evenly matched, one team may have far better
athletes in a particular season. Because there are a lot of lopsided games

like these each weekend, the average fan can probably pick winners about, say, 60 percent of the time. Someone who does it full-time can probably get 70 percent or more right.

When individual investors think about picking stocks, this is how most imagine it. They believe that they can do research on the past performance and current management of companies and pick winning companies a majority of the time. Or they believe they can give their money to an expert money manager who probably can do even better, in exchange for a fee.

Here is the reality. Every fall weekend, sports handicappers in Las Vegas establish a point spread for each college football game. To reduce their risk, bookies need equal amounts bet on each team. Giving "points" to gamblers who bet on the underdog is the best way to accomplish this goal. Otherwise, no one would bet on Navy or Duke. In reality, then, sports gamblers do not have the option of simply picking Notre Dame or Florida State to win. They must pick them to win by more than twenty points or some similar spread. That's the price of Notre Dame's or Florida State's past performance and current talent. Because handicappers know their business well, someone who bets on college football games over time will rarely pick more (or less) than 50 percent of games correctly. And because bookies charge gamblers a percentage of any winnings—requiring them to pay $11 to bet $10—the average gambler is almost certain to be a long-term loser. (The bookies, of course, make money whether you win or lose.)

The reality for individual investors who pick stocks or have money managers pick for them is much the same. They do not get to buy a popular stock at the price at which it was originally issued and share in all the earnings. Rather, they must pay something akin to a point spread—most frequently expressed as a price-to-earnings ratio. Just as bettors must often give twenty points to bet on Florida State, investors often must spend $30 or more to buy $1 of projected earnings for a company that is a proven winner. The market has already priced the company's past performance and managerial talent into the price of the stock. And of course investors have to pay Wall Street to execute the trade or manage their money. That means that over time most investors underperform the market. (The fund managers and brokers, like the bookies, make money whether you win or lose.)

Here's a wonderfully self-serving explanation of how sports betting works, taken from an on-line gambling site.[1]

> Just by flipping a coin you will be right 50 percent of the time. At odds of 10/11 [the standard odds with a bookie], only 52.4 percent of your bets have to win for you to overcome the bookmaker's profit and break even, so you only need a very small edge to become a winner. Do your homework, bet selectively and 55 percent winning bets is definitely achievable. Even 60–65 percent is a realistic target. At those levels you will have an extremely profitable, as well as enjoyable hobby.

The ad's promise is preposterous. Sports betting is not an "extremely profitable" hobby for Americans. At best, it's moderately expensive entertainment. At worst, it's a self-destructive addiction. But notice how easy it is to say that you have to be right "only 52.4 percent" of the time. *With average annual costs not far from 2.4 percent, the mutual fund industry is sending a very similar message.*

In the chapters that follow, we will take a look at just about every market-beating strategy you can think of, including:

- buying mutual funds with good past-year performance
- buying mutual funds with good past-decade performance
- buying stocks with consensus "buy" recommendations from analysts
- buying stocks recommended by investment newsletters
- buying the Dogs of the Dow
- buying Morningstar five-star funds

The bottom line: they just plain don't work. Moreover, there are good reasons why you should never have expected them to work.

Managing Escape

So, what's an investor to do?

You *cannot* improve your returns by spending more time or money trying to pick funds or stocks. Double the time you spend researching funds and stocks, and your returns will not change. Add a financial adviser, a subscription to an investment newsletter, or a high-load fund, and your returns will shrink by the amounts you pay for the service.

You *can,* however, significantly improve your returns by improving the vehicles through which you invest. You can improve your returns by choosing vehicles that offer the lowest possible costs and the greatest tax efficiency. You can reduce your risk by choosing vehicles that diversify your portfolio.

The good news is that financial products have emerged that allow you to achieve these goals through passive investing. By passive investing, we mean attempting to duplicate the returns of the market at the lowest possible cost. For stock investors, passive investing means buying and holding a broad array of stocks in their proportion to the overall market, rather than buying only those stocks you believe are likely to outperform the market.

- The first product was the invention of **index mutual funds.** Index funds allow you to invest in the broad stock market at low cost. Index funds for large, institutional investors have been around since 1971, but they have only started to capture the attention of individual investors in the past ten years. They are still underappreciated and underutilized as a tool for individual investors. For most investors, they represent the best way to avoid the trap and achieve higher returns with lesser risk.
- The second innovation is the very recent emergence of **exchange-traded index funds,** which hold the same assets as stock index funds but trade like stocks. ETFs can offer marginally lower costs and substantially better tax consequences than index funds.
- The third innovation is what we'll call **discount portfolio investing.** For those who feel they must buy stocks directly, this vehicle allows them to buy baskets of stocks at costs close to those of an index mutual fund.
- The fourth innovation is the **democratization of the bond market.** You can now buy many types of bonds without incurring the substantial, and generally undisclosed, transaction costs that have made direct purchases difficult in the past.

- The fifth innovation is the **democratization of risk management,** allowing individual investors to manage their risks using some of the same sophisticated tools as brokerage firms.
- The sixth innovation, courtesy of the federal government, is the creation of genuinely **tax-free education savings accounts.** Starting in 2002, you can invest in a so-called "529 plan" and *never pay taxes on any of the earnings.*

Considering the Stakes

Embarking on a cost-reduction program may not seem as exciting as the latest market-beating strategy, but do not underestimate the stakes. A lifetime of monthly investments in a passive account can yield nearly twice as much as the same amounts actively invested. Assume, for example, that you're investing $250 per month ($3,000 per year) and that you can expect to earn 8 percent annually after the cost of passive investing. You end up with a retirement nest egg of about $872,000. Actively pursue the same goal and you'll end up earning at least 2 percent less per year on average, or $497,000 in all. Because of costs and compounding, you will have forgone fully 43 percent of your potential future retirement money. (As we'll see, the reality of fees and costs is actually a little worse.)

The Bite of Active Investing

Forgone Earnings
($375,000)
43%

Your Retirement
Money After Active
Investment
($497,000)
57%

Getting Started

Improving your returns and reducing your risk will require you to question a lot of what you know, tune out a lot of what you hear, and reinvigorate your common sense. Now seems like a good time to start.

Part I

Investors in Wonderland

What upsets me is not that you lied to me, but
that from now on I can no longer believe you.
—*Friedrich Wilhelm Nietzsche*

W e intend for this part to serve as a quick eye opener. In Chapter 1, we'll take a look at how actively managed mutual funds and individual stock pickers actually perform as opposed to how you may think they perform. In Chapter 2, we will examine the financial media and see how their reporting shapes our investing strategies. Finally, in Chapter 3, we'll acquaint you with three concepts that are fundamental to modern finance but that few individual investors fully appreciate.

Chapter 1

Money Management in a Nutshell

Finance, *n.* The art or science of managing revenues and
resources for the best advantage of the manager.
—*Ambrose Bierce,* The Devil's Dictionary

An Analogy

Every day there is a parade of money managers interviewed on
CNBC or featured in *Money* or similar magazines. Every time we
see them, we can't help but think of flipping coins.

Imagine that, instead of picking stocks, these scores of men and
women each flipped one hundred coins per day, with the goal of producing the maximum number of "heads" possible. Viewers tune in to
see who's doing well and bet on their favorite flippers.

Over time, the flippers' task is essentially hopeless: statistics doom
them to an average performance of 50 percent heads. If you observe
them on only one day, though, there will be winners and losers. While
most will have around 50 heads, some will have 57 or 43.

Now suppose that some of the coin flippers are permitted to raise the
stakes of each given flip by taping up to five coins together. For example, if one tapes four coins together, each flip will yield either four heads
or four tails. Now, we might expect some of our flippers to produce 60
or 64 (or 40 or 36) heads in one day. By taping the coins, they are tak-

ing on risk (the possibility of four tails at once) in return for the possibility of reward (four heads).

Imagine, then, the Coin Flipping News Network (CFNN), giving us twenty-four-hour-a-day coverage of the flipping market. In comes coin flipper Lee with 56 heads, touting her latest tactic—say, many revolutions of the coin, with three taped together. Long forgotten is last week's guest, who had favored the few-revolution, one-coin-at-a-time tactic that worked so well during the last 500 flips but is now seriously out of favor. "Momentum" viewers favor those who have recently had more heads, while "value" viewers favor those who have recently had more tails.

Above all, viewers are assured that they are not capable of flipping the coins themselves—that they must rely on the experts to do it for them. *And they are convinced that they should never be satisfied with just 50 percent heads—that is, "market" performance.*

The Reality

The current state of money management is similar to this example—only worse. The returns for money managers are like those of our coin flippers. Most tend to stay close to the mean, while riskier funds tend to produce more volatile returns that balance out over time. The difference, though, is that whereas coin flipping is free, money management is not.

For that reason, the chances of your money manager beating the market are small. Evidence suggests that the average actively managed mutual fund underperforms the market three years out of five. According to data at Morningstar (which maintains a comprehensive database on fund performance):

- Through the end of 2001, there were 1,226 actively managed stock funds with a five-year record. Their average annualized performance trailed the S&P 500 Index (a measure of the U.S. stock market) by *1.9 percentage points per year* (8.8 percent for the funds, and 10.7 percent for the index).[1]

There were 623 actively managed stock funds with a ten-year record. Their average annualized performance trailed the S&P 500 by *1.7 percentage points per year* (11.2 percent for the funds and 12.9 percent for the index).*

- These figures include the sales loads charged by many funds. Loads are akin to brokerage commissions and come straight out of your returns. They are charged by many funds when you either buy or sell shares of the fund. Even with those loads excluded, however, the average five-year return trailed the S&P 500 by 1.4 percentage points per year, and the average ten-year return trailed by 1.4 percentage points per year as well.

  Looking over a longer period of time yields a similar result. Excluding sales loads, the 406 actively managed stock funds that had been around for fifteen years or more trailed the S&P 500 Index by 1.5 percentage points per year.

- None of these aggregate numbers includes failed mutual funds, which would tend to have poorer performance and bring the averages down significantly. The exclusion of these mutual funds is called survivorship bias. The most comprehensive study of survivorship bias concluded that it inflates industry returns by 1.4 percent over a ten-year period and 2.2 percent over a fifteen-year period. *With returns corrected for survivorship bias, the average actively managed funds trail the market by about 3 percentage points per year.*

How can such a clever, hardworking group of fund managers trail the market by 3 percentage points per year? It's actually rather simple. The collective performance of stocks held by actively managed mutual

---

* Throughout this book, we will compare the performance of stock mutual funds to the stock market as a whole. We will use two measures of the market. The first is the Wilshire 5000 index, which includes over 6,500 stocks and covers 99 percent of the assets of the U.S. stock market. The second is the S&P 500, which consists of 500 stocks chosen to represent the broad market and represents 77 percent of the market's total assets. While the S&P 500 Index tends to include larger companies in greater proportion than they appear in the overall market, it is the index that most actively managed mutual funds consider their benchmark.

funds, prior to any direct or indirect costs, generally will equal the performance of the market as a whole. With around $3 trillion in stock holdings, these funds basically represent the market.

But then along come management fees, trading costs, and sales loads. All of these costs weigh heavily on actively managed funds. The failure of almost all money managers to earn back their costs does not make them crooked or stupid. The problem is that their direct and indirect costs severely handicap their performance.

Nonetheless, each year some money managers will outperform the average fund, and even the market as a whole. The question is, can you identify these managers in advance of their market-beating performance? There is no reason to think so. As an individual investor, you have no comparative advantage in choosing those managers. In other words, there is no reason to believe that you will do any better a job picking *stock pickers* than you would picking *stocks*. If you can't do the latter, why would you expect to do the former?

Humorist Tony Kornheiser illustrated this point in a column about the trauma of the 2000–01 bear market.

> My friend Tom, who has all of his money in mutual funds, panicked when somebody on the *Today* show said: "Your mutual fund is only as good as the manager investing the money. If your fund changes money managers, you need to check out the new manager." Tom pointed out, "If I was smart enough to check out my money manager, I wouldn't *need* a money manager."[2]

Exactly!

Most investors simply choose funds based on past performance, but past performance truly is no guarantee of future results. The fact that a fund has outperformed the market for the past year, five years, or even ten years turns out to be a very poor predictor of whether it will outperform the market in the future. Funds that are above average for a time tend to regress to the below-market performance of the average fund.

Let's go back to our coin-flipping example. There were about 1,100 stock funds in 1991, and we know that each year about two out of five such funds (40 percent) have outperformed the market. If the identity of those 40 percent is just like coin flipping—that is, produced by random chance—how many funds would we expect to outperform the market each and every year over the next ten years? (In other words, how many beat the market in 1991, 1992, 1993, all the way to 2000?) Simple statistics tell us that by random chance between 0 and 1 fund should outperform the market each and every year.

That probably seems an improbably low number to you. But what has happened in reality? Over the ten years 1991–2000, only one fund (Legg Mason Value Trust) outperformed the S&P 500 every year. While we are happy for Legg Mason and its manager, Bill Miller, we view that outcome as roughly in line with random chance and as an indictment of active fund management. To the financial media, that outcome is a vindication of active fund management, and profiles of Bill Miller are everywhere. We'll let you decide.

The story is no better when it comes to picking individual stocks. Over a lifetime, the average individual's stock picks should return something close to the market, before costs. Sadly, the research shows that individual investors tend to churn their portfolios in an attempt to beat the market, incurring trading costs and taxes that radically diminish their returns. Investors also fail to construct broadly diversified portfolios, thereby running risks for which they do not receive commensurate rewards. In the end, they wind up trailing the market almost as badly as actively managed funds.

The rise and precipitous fall of Enron—once the seventh largest company in America—has provoked public debate on accounting practices, corporate responsibility, and numerous other issues. But for individual investors, Enron should provide two humbling lessons about the folly of trying to beat the market by picking stocks. First, in October 2001, less than two months before Enron declared bankruptcy, nineteen of the twenty-two analysts who covered the stock rated it a "buy." Critics have charged that these ratings were motivated by the investment banking business that Enron dangled before the analysts' firms. Wall Street has vigorously denied those charges. In fact, Wall Street should have welcomed the allegations as a distraction from an even more embarrassing alternative. The alternative, of course, is that analysts simply don't know a lot more than the rest of the market about the stocks they cover. Enron analysts who testified before Congress claimed that they couldn't be expected to discover problems that the company was deliberately hiding, but we suspect that many investors are relying on them to do exactly that.

The second, greater, lesson of Enron is the value of diversification. Some investors have reacted to Enron by expressing outrage with the accounting profession, corporate governance, and Wall Street; they have questioned whether they ought to invest in a market where Enron-like abuses can go undetected. We can certainly understand investors being outraged, but part of the risk of stock investing has always been that you might end up holding an Enron. Every year, some well-known companies are going to fail. Some will fail because of incompetence. Some will fail because of greed or over-ambition. Some will fail because of bad luck. Some, like Enron, will fail spectacularly because of what appears to be malfeasance. But the cause of the failure shouldn't matter to you as an investor; your money is still just as lost.

What should matter to you as investor is the ability of diversification to protect you against this risk. Diversification insulates you from the failure of any one company or even any one sector. Millions of Americans held Enron stock—but only as part of an S&P 500 or broad-market index fund. They suffered inconsequential damage from the affair, even as those who held Enron as their only investment were wiped out. That's the lesson most worth remembering from Enron.

September 2001

The terrorist attacks of September 11, 2001, were a horrible tragedy for our nation. They also triggered a crisis in financial markets, as markets closed for the week, reopened, plunged, plunged some more, and then recovered by the end of September.

In order to connote the idea of crisis, the Chinese combine the characters for danger and opportunity. Consistent with that view, proponents of active management must have considered the tragic month of September 2001 as holding substantial opportunities for smart money managers. With the airlines and tourist industries in free fall, the mobile phone and defense industries rising, and untold ripple effects emanating from the crisis, there should have been innumerable opportunities for profit in individual stocks. Furthermore, looking at the broader market, active managers could have avoided the general panic selling in the week the market reopened, bought at the bottom, and cleaned up on the recovery.

The actual results for September 2001 refute that idea. The average active manager did not profit. As a group, actively managed stock funds lost more than the market, underperforming the S&P 500 Index by two percentage points (-11.0 percent for the funds and -9.0 percent for the Wilshire 5000 Index, the broadest measure of the U.S. equity market). The largest stock index fund, the Vanguard 500 Index Fund, outperformed 69 percent of all actively managed stock funds for the month.[3]

As expected, some actively managed mutual funds did perform very well during September 2001. The best performing ones, though, were "bear" or "short" funds that were already betting that the market would go down. These funds didn't quickly internalize the events of September 11 and identify profitable opportunities. They simply continued betting—as they always do—that the market would go down. These types of funds may outperform the market when it's down, but tend not to do as well in the long term. In fact, the ten biggest winners of September 2001 had trailed the market by over 13 percentage points per year over the prior three years. Those that had been around for five years trailed by over 15 percentage points annually.

Many investors turn to active money managers because they want a steady hand on the wheel when markets are in upheaval. Beyond the many more important lessons September 2001 has taught us, it also includes a lesson about active management during a time of crisis: you do a lot better by leaving your investments on autopilot.

How You Can Do Better

"Okay," you say, "so what do I do instead?"

Here, in a nutshell, is how we see it. Everyone investing in the stock market now has a wonderful option. Claim the same returns as the broad market at remarkably low cost, with the ability to defer almost all capital gains taxes. This option exists through traditional open-end index funds and their younger cousins, exchange-traded index funds. It takes minimal effort. It also leaves you free to work more or play more, or a little of both.

We believe that the best analogy to index investing is the generic drug market. Brand-name drugs and their generic equivalents provide the same medicinal benefits. The brand-name drugs cost far more, however, because their owners must recoup the costs of research and development. The generic drug makers incur none of those development costs and instead free ride on the expertise of the "active" drug companies. Informed consumers buy generics. Consumers, however, must wait a few years for a generic drug, as the patent laws were designed to allow inventors (the active drug companies) a period of time without competition to help recoup their research costs by charging consumers high prices.

Index funds are the generics of investing. Because they needn't hire the highly paid stock pickers required for active investing, or pay the transaction costs their strategies impose, they are a bargain for investors. Moreover, "generic" mutual funds, or index funds, are available from the beginning of each market "invention." They adjust daily, even hourly, to track the market prices being established by active money managers. Thus, for stock investors, the free riding can start today.

The mutual fund and brokerage industries belittle indexing because it is deadly competition for their higher margin products. The financial media ignore it because it makes such lousy copy. Have you ever read anything more boring than a profile of an index fund manager? Can you imagine a cover story entitled "Ten Hot Index Funds to Buy Now!"?

We consider the indexing option a miracle. We consider it a testament to technological innovation, human imagination, and market capitalism. If you had told a Wall Street executive fifty years ago that individual investors would be able to purchase shares in five hundred of the largest U.S. companies at zero commission and with annual management fees of 18 cents per $100 invested, he would have fainted dead away. You should be equally impressed.

Attractive alternatives to expensive money management do not end with equity investing. Investors now have new ways to buy bonds more cheaply than ever before. Investors have on-line access to sophisticated asset allocation and risk management tools that were unavailable even a few years ago. And investors willing to do their homework can now legally shield more of their investments from taxation than ever before.

What it really takes to improve your returns and diminish your risks is a willingness to stop focusing exclusively on the movement of the markets. The more you focus on the structure of your investments—their costs, diversification, and tax status—the better you will do. If you end up sharing this view—a conclusion quite contrary to what money managers and the financial media tell you every day—you will begin investing very differently.

Chapter 2

And Lead Us Not into Temptation

He watched a very great deal of TV, always had done, years and years of it, eons of TV. Boy, did Keith burn that tube. And that tube burnt him, nuked him, its cathodes crackling like cancer. "TV," he thought, or "Modern reality" or "the world." It was the word of TV that told him what the world was. How does all the TV time work on a modern person, a person like Keith? . . . TV came at Keith like it came at everybody else; and he had nothing whatever to keep it out. He couldn't grade or filter it. So he thought TV was real.—*Martin Amis,* London Fields *(1989)*

With all that is known about the poor results of active stock picking, why do so many investors still buy high-cost mutual funds or churn their stock portfolios? One major reason is because they are told to do so, every day, explicitly or implicitly, by the financial media and Wall Street. The message of "trust the experts / trade frequently / beat the market" saturates the airwaves and fills the newsstands.

The overall impression investors receive is of an exciting, confusing market where the masters of money management rule. Markets are a place where you can make a lot of money if you just invest with the right people. Go it alone and be lost.

To break out of that mindset—to tell one's acquaintances, "I don't try to beat the market, I just try to match its performance"—will not be easy. It will be like a guy telling his buddies, "Sorry, but I just don't follow sports." In this chapter, we will prepare you for the battle by making you an informed, even cynical, viewer of financial news and advertising. We will teach you about the noise, so you can tune it out.

We're not saying you should stop watching CNBC, any more than we would suggest you stop watching ESPN's *Sports Center* or *Jeopardy*. It's fun. You can learn some interesting facts. It beats watching the Weather Channel or the grisly car wrecks, fires, and brutal crimes that all too often are the daily fare of the local news. But you need to watch with a critical eye, or you will fall back into the old investment traps for sure.

That's Entertainment

To a greater extent than ever before, investing has become entertainment for Americans. Analysts and other market experts are as revered for their skill as sports heroes. Like the sports media, the financial media is dedicated to glorifying winners, occasionally punishing losers, and generally ignoring the middle of the pack. They do so not to mislead or harm investors, but because that's what keeps readers and viewers coming back.

Thus, where Americans previously turned to soap operas or baseball games for midday entertainment, they now turn to CNBC. Where the barbershop used to feature *Playboy* magazine and sports talk, it now features *Money* magazine and investment talk. Bull market or bear market, tech up or tech down, the future of biotech—these have become the topics of conversation for Americans' idle moments. Even as tragedy and war dominated our airwaves in the fall of 2001, talk of which stocks would benefit or suffer from war followed close behind.

The greatest feat of the financial media has been to convey a constant sense of *urgency*. No one does this any better than CNBC. From shouted reports from the floor of the bustling New York Stock Exchange to instant updates on a two-cent change in the price of Microsoft, investors get the impression that big things are happening. Stop the presses: an analyst at a firm you've never heard of has just downgraded a company you've never heard of from "buy" to "market outperform." Brokers are telling David Faber that a major fund company is selling stock, though we don't know which fund or which stock. But CNBC does it in such a way that it is captivating. That's terrific production, direction, and talent. But it's the wrong message for investors who should be buying and *holding* rather than trading on each new report. They don't need captivation; they need patience.

The Kind of Coverage Anyone Would Love

Here's a good way to put the financial media in perspective. If you turn on the television at any point of the day, the serious nonfiction media are most likely talking about one of two subjects: politics or money. Celebrity trials and wars may come and go, but politics and money are here to stay. Each is now the focus of entire cable channels. Interestingly, though, this coverage has made Americans more cynical and distrustful of their government yet, until Enron erupted, increasingly trusting of their money managers. Why?

We're in This Together

Since Watergate and the Pentagon Papers, investigative reporting has been the highest form of political journalism. Since the explosion of cable television, paid political punditry has become a potent source of revenue for otherwise underpaid journalists. Combine these trends, and you have a force of journalists dedicated to first exposing and then lambasting any wrongdoing in government. Although some like to talk of a liberal bias in the media, the real bias is usually an antigovernment bias, a scandal bias. Furthermore, this bias is not tempered by concern about serious repercussions. Aggressive reporters are not banned from press conferences. Their sources do not dry up. Their company's advertisers do not go elsewhere.

Compare this state of affairs to the financial media. Whereas the *Washington Post* does not need to worry about offending the Democratic or Republican parties, the financial media are critically dependent on the companies they cover for both content and advertising revenue. The financial media have no right of access to Wall Street executives.

Even if financial reporters were inclined to operate with the cynicism of political reporters, they would still face a major structural obstacle.

Wall Street lacks the equivalent of the political two-party system. If a Wal-Mart executive states that store launches are going well, there is not a K-Mart executive there to denounce her statement as untrue or to subpoena a junior Wal-Mart executive to testify about the accuracy of the numbers. Because companies don't compete the way politicians do, one of the staples of the political media—the clash of opposing views—is unavailable to the financial media on a regular basis.

The Soft-Hitting Interview

The hallmark of financial reporting is what we call the "soft-hitting interview." While it looks as dynamic and confrontational as a political interview, it has all the punch of a *Parade* magazine profile. ("Imagine while walking the grounds of his Malibu home with Robert Downey, Jr., one can't resist the temptation to ask him . . . 'Where did you get your knack for landscaping?' ") The most important feature of the soft-hitting interview is to get the guest to *pick* stocks.

Indeed, in his book *The Fortune Tellers,* Howard Kurtz describes how CNBC producers make clear to every guest that, regardless of the subject of the interview, they must be ready to pick stocks. Mutual fund companies are of course always ready and eager to supply their hottest fund managers (the coin flippers of the month) to recommend a few stocks that they already own or recommend. Interviewer and guest work together.

To illustrate the vast difference between financial and political reporting, try to imagine money managers on CNBC treated not in the way to which they've grown accustomed but like politicians. Imagine a fictitious (the lawyers want us to emphasize that word) Jackson Ford from the fictitious Emerging Value Fund at Fidelity walking onto the CNBC set with Maria Bartiromo:

Jack: Hey, Maria, how ya doin'?
Maria: Fine, Mr. Ford, but let's get down to business. Although you've reported high returns this year, your risk-adjusted return badly trails the market over the past five years. How do you explain this?

Jack: Well, Maria, the market has been very skittish recently, and we think we've just about got this turned around. Right now, we really like a couple of stocks—

Maria: Mr. Ford, I don't think we want to hear you pick new stocks until we've heard why you've made mistakes with your past stocks. You do acknowledge that you've made mistakes, don't you?

Jack: Certainly, we've taken some hits, but that's the way it is in this market. We believe we're well positioned for some real positive growth.

Maria: Our sources tell us that some investors are suggesting you should resign. Will you resign?

Jack: Uh, no, I wasn't planning to.

Maria: Also, I understand that two years ago you received a Fund Manager of the Year medal. Do you think that accepting that award was right, given the risks that you ran for your investors and your poor subsequent performance? Will you return that medal?

Jack: Gee, I dunno, I mean I've never *worn* the medal—it just sits on a table at our place in the Hamptons. I only see it on weekends—

Maria: Mr. Ford, there are some reports circulating that there are problems in your personal life. Would you care to comment?

Jack: What? I mean that's hardly relevant . . .

Maria: Mr. Ford, if you have been unfaithful to your wife, shouldn't investors be concerned that you will be unfaithful to them? Can they really trust you?

Jack: Huh, what? I, uh, don't feel comfortable discussing this.

Maria: Well, we also have in our studio Thomas Arthur, who runs a very similar fund over at Janus. Tom, what are your views on the "mistakes" Mr. Ford has made?

Tom: Well, frankly, Maria, we believe that Jack's investing strategies are the strategies of the past and that, frankly, he ought to resign.

Jack: What? Tommy? C'mon buddy . . .

Tom: Investors want change, and they've seen that Jack's fund cannot deliver it. If investors choose our fund, we will restore honor and decency to their investments, and we will make them rich.

Maria: Well, we're out of time, so that will have to be the last word. In our next segment, we'll focus on a fund manager who was forced to resign in disgrace after falling short of her benchmark.

She's now mounting a comeback, which many observers have labeled pathetic.

We don't expect to hear that *fictitious* colloquy anytime soon, and that's probably a good thing. We wouldn't advocate the financial media becoming as cynical as the political media, or the political media becoming as warm and cuddly as the financial media. A happy medium, however, would be nice.

Stocks and the Running Man Syndrome

Another staple of the financial media is profiling an individual investor who has triumphed. The implication is that you, too, can win on Wall Street. This reminds us of the movie *Running Man,* starring the unlikely duo of Arnold Schwarzenegger and game-show host Richard Dawson. The movie centers on a futuristic game show run by Mr. Dawson, the tool of a corrupt government. On the show, convicted criminals are given a chance at freedom if they can avoid the deadly pursuit of a series of celebrity bounty hunters with names like Captain Freedom (Jesse Ventura) and Fireball (Jim Brown). Although the vast majority of convicts meet a grisly televised demise, each episode begins with pictures of the few lucky winners/escapees celebrating on a Caribbean atoll. The hero of the movie is Mr. Schwarzenegger, playing an unjustly convicted political prisoner turned Running Man. Midway through the movie, he discovers the decomposing remains of the supposedly Caribbean-dwelling "winners."

In the investing world, we see individual investors who are profiled because they have recently achieved tremendous returns on their investments. There are no follow-up stories if those returns should subsequently decompose. At the end of 2000, *Fortune* magazine published an article, "My Stocks Are Up 10,000%," highlighting individual investors who had achieved extraordinary results. The article notes, "Their investing styles couldn't be more different, though they usually combine an Olympian tolerance for risk with a penchant for unorthodox strategies that involve charts, options, margin and the like—not to mention insane luck." We agree with the insane luck point, but the rest deserves a closer look. Their tolerance for risk and use of options and margin is a given, as no one can achieve such returns without using leverage to assume tremendous risk. Their strategies are divergent and unorthodox because they are not real strategies.

Not surprisingly, the big winner, Richard Zanger, pronounces himself a technical analyst. This choice is by default, since he knows nothing of the companies in which he is investing. "I trade whatever the market is going to push up the most," Zanger says. "It doesn't matter what the company does, or what their earnings are." Later: "Stocks are my buddies," Zanger says. "I know when they feel good and when they feel bad." He bought Qualcomm because it was "acting a little frisky." He bought AskJeeves.com because it was headed into a "pennant" formation.[1]

To us this man is babbling, as the article's author manages to convey in a subtle way. And of course all of these returns came over a relatively brief period, in a bull market for technology stocks. But nonetheless, there he is, pictured in front of his mansion, along with all the other lucky winners. We are pretty confident that Mr. Zanger had a pretty hard time in 2001, but there is no way to know. *Fortune* hasn't run a follow-up article, and brokerage records are private.

The Beardstown Ladies offer a twist on Running Man syndrome. They became national celebrities after they claimed to have achieved a 23 percent annual return on their investments over a ten-year period, and their *Common-Sense Investment Guide* sold about a million copies. In the ordinary course, they would have then disappeared from view, with any subsequent lower returns buried away. But a challenge to their work by *Chicago* magazine and a subsequent Price Waterhouse audit revealed that their actual returns for the period were 9 percent (as compared with 15 percent for the overall market). Apparently, they were entering some of their data incorrectly.

We believe that the decline and fall of the Beardstown Ladies may have taught investors the wrong lesson. Originally, the public considered the Ladies insightful stock pickers. Post-audit, the public considered them frauds. We, on the other hand, originally considered them some nice ladies who got lucky. Post-audit, we considered them nice ladies who weren't so lucky after all. The point is that, even assuming no skill on behalf of investment club members, random chance will make some of the nation's thousands of investment clubs outliers, either significantly outperforming or underperforming the market. While 23 percent would certainly have been at the outer end of the old bell curve, it is not a shocking number. Yet the outliers are celebrated in the media as if their performance were inspired and easily duplicated.

Featured in countless articles and TV stories, people like Mr. Zanger and the Beardstown Ladies are held out to the investing public as examples of successful investing. In reality, they are akin to Lotto winners, and their "strategies" are equally likely to pay off for you in the future.

The Top Ten Whoppers You'll Hear on CNBC

The "trust the experts/trade frequently/beat the market" message that is so vital to the financial industry is often conveyed subliminally. It's done through a whole set of terms that suggest the need for expertise and the presence of endless profit-making opportunities. It's a bit dizzying.

We'd prefer that you tune out this noise and use your common sense. To that end, here are our "Top Ten Whoppers You'll Hear on CNBC." (Of course, you'll hear the same whoppers or worse lots of other places, but, hey, sometimes life isn't fair.)

1. "We're in a stock picker's market."

Turn on CNBC after a week of market declines, and you will hear a money manager make this statement. It is self-serving and misleading on a variety of levels.

First, just as a matter of common sense, why in the world would picking outperforming stocks be easier when the market is going down than when it is going up? We can't think of any reason.

Second, recognize that while some stock pickers will underperform and some will outperform the market, their average performance always will be, well, average—that is, the same as the market as a whole (before fees and taxes). So, the idea that stock pickers, *as a group,* can ever outperform the market as a whole is fundamentally flawed.

Third, it is not possible to have a market where stock pickers do well and passive investors do badly. Because indexers own the market, they will by definition achieve the average performance of the overall market. Garrison Keillor got a lot of laughs by saying that in Lake Wobegon all the students are above average. A money manager saying that we're in a "stock picker's market" is really implying that most actively managed funds are going to perform better than average. Viewers should laugh just as hard.

2. "That's one great chart!"

Any time a company is mentioned on CNBC, up pops the Chart, generally showing the company's stock price over the past fifty-two weeks. The commentators then say things like, "Look at that chart" or "Nice chart" or "That's a really bad chart." They fail to explain, however, why the chart should influence viewers' expectations about the future prospects of the charted company. Generally, a rising chart evokes favorable comment, but we've also heard a CNBC anchor say, "This chart may be getting people interested—the stock is down 58 percent from its high."

The use of charts is part of an investment strategy based on technical analysis. We'll explore that pseudoscience in more detail later. In essence, though, it relies on the assumption that a stock's future price movement can be predicted by research into its past price movements. There are two things you need to know about technical analysts: (1) the charts used on Wall Street are far more sophisticated than those shown to you on CNBC; and (2) even sophisticated charts have proven rather useless as a predictor of stock price movements.

This topic used to be a subject of somewhat greater debate. Those who insisted that price movements were independent events went to war with technical analysts who insisted that "resistance levels" and "support levels" had real meaning. Fortunately, modern computing speeds have largely resolved this matter. It is not too difficult to input all the price movements for a bunch of stocks into a computer and see if any patterns emerge. The result: no useful patterns emerge. Actually, lots of patterns emerge—sine curves, Vs, Us—but they appear and disappear randomly.

Moreover, even if technical analysis was good science, it's hard to see how the charts on CNBC could benefit you. Markets adjust rapidly to news. Professional traders can easily determine a stock's moving average or the shapes of its past movements and have the ability to trade quickly and cheaply. To the extent that such averages or shapes carried any predictive power, the pros would presumably buy or sell first, eliminating the profit potential for you as an individual investor. Furthermore, any strategy based on technical analysis necessarily involves frequent trading, which means high transaction costs, making it useless to individual investors.

Here's a practical test of technical analysis. Does anybody get rich doing it? For now, we'll rely on Burton Malkiel, a leading financial economist at Princeton University. Malkiel states that he, personally, has never known a successful technician but has seen the wrecks of many unsuccessful ones.

3. "This market is not going to turn around until we see capitulation."

"Capitulation" is such a great word. It carries drama. It rolls off the tongue. It makes the speaker sound important. Small wonder then that "capitulation" has become one of the favorite terms of market timers and CNBC interviewers during down markets ("Are we seeing capitulation here?"). The only problem is that it is meaningless.

What do analysts and interviewers mean by "capitulation"? According to David Futrelle of *Money,* "The idea here is that a bear market isn't really over until pretty much everyone has given up on stocks." Okay, so the bear market isn't over until the bear market is over. Is that it? He continues, "Basically if you still have optimists in the market there's a chance they could grow pessimistic and suddenly decide to sell their stocks. And the idea is when these people finally capitulate and become pessimistic themselves—that there's simply no one there left to sell stocks. And at that point the only place for stocks to go is up."[2]

Huh? We thought that for every seller there has to be a buyer. For everyone capitulating, someone else is on the other side of the trade, doing whatever the opposite of capitulating is (exulting?). At any price above zero, stocks can go up and stocks can go down.

"Capitulation" seems to be simply a fancy way of saying that the market has hit bottom. Sometimes commenters use another phrase, "the market is oversold." Obviously, with hindsight, every bull market starts somewhere, namely a bottom. That bottom is completely unpredictable, but analysts and journalists, always looking to personalize the market, have decided to personalize the bottom. They have decided that the point where a bull market begins must have been the point where investors "capitulated" and sold all their stocks, even though every seller must have found a willing buyer.

4. "There's a lot of money on the sidelines right now."

Translation: "Investors are holding money out of the stock market (the game) until a better time to invest comes along." In other words, investors are trying to time the overall stock market.

Market timing is a discredited concept—statistically and anecdotally. Statistically, studies show that major market movements are unpredictable (and generally go unpredicted). Anecdotally, it is almost comical how many analysts who have become famous for making a correct market timing call have fallen flat on their faces when the next major market move comes.

So, why do we read and hear so much about the market timers? First, whether the market is up or down is the simplest topic of discussion at the watercooler. Most folks don't tell their colleagues what stocks or mutual funds they hold, so you're not going to start a conversation with, "Hey, I saw your General Electric shares had a good week." Instead, the question is, "Have you seen what the Dow is doing today?" Everyone wants to know where "the market" or a given sector is headed next. The market timers are the ones who claim to know the answer.

Second, everyone has a 50 percent chance of calling the direction of the market. Call for a bigger rise or fall and your chances of being correct fall. But if you get it right, everyone remembers. Get it wrong and most people forgive or forget. That means there will always be at least a couple of "superstar" market timers ready to appear on TV.

Third, as noted, financial TV channels and magazines cover investing like sports. Calling for a big market move is the investing equivalent of football's 80-yard bomb, or Hail Mary. It may not be a high percentage play (Daryl Lamonica and Jeff George will never make the

Hall of Fame), but it sure is exciting! Once a market timer hits it big, no amount of failure seems to eliminate them from the airwaves. For example, Elaine Garzarelli correctly called the 1987 crash, but then missed the ensuing bull market. Ralph Acampora famously called the bull market that began in 1995, but then spent years issuing a series of bad, and frequently contradictory, predictions.[3] Both remained fixtures of the financial media.

We call this phenomenon "Clark/Darden Syndrome," for the O. J. Simpson prosecutors. They put on one of the most notorious losing cases in legal history, yet they now analyze legal issues on television.

So the next time you hear someone say that there's money on the sidelines, just ignore them, smile, and repeat to yourself, "Not my money."

5. "Don't fight the tape, and don't fight the Fed."

You hear this statement a lot on CNBC. You get the sense that the speaker believes himself to be imparting some deep, fundamental truth—sort of akin to "Neither a borrower nor a lender be" or "Plastics." From our days at the Federal Reserve and on Wall Street, you might think we'd have a special appreciation for this wisdom. To the contrary, we think that it's mindless.

"Don't fight the tape" means that you should sell stocks whose prices have recently been rising or buy stocks whose prices have recently been falling. This is akin to the idea of "momentum investing," which became popular during the bull market of the 1990s. It then became very unpopular with all the people who bought Amazon at $300 a share and Yahoo at $200. Over time, it's a strategy guaranteed to generate enormous trading costs and unlikely to produce better returns. The clear lesson is: don't fight the tape; don't hug the tape; *ignore the tape.*

"Don't fight the Fed" means that one should not buy stocks when the Fed is raising interest rates or sell stocks when the Fed is lowering interest rates. The thought behind this is that when interest rates go down, the stock market is likely to go up and vice versa. The problem with this strategy isn't any fault in the analysis, but rather the fact that *everyone in the world knows this to be the analysis.* And there is no shortage of information about which way rates might be heading. The Fed indicates after each meeting which way it is leaning with respect to future rate cuts or increases. Wall Street employs highly paid "Fed watchers" who try to anticipate the central bank's next move. When market events occur that are likely to provoke Fed action—a drop in consumer sentiment, a rise in new claims for unemployment—the market does not wait for the Fed's next meeting to adjust. It adjusts within moments, and the Fed's potential future action is "priced into the market." The Fed may even feel pressure at times to confirm that market price in its subsequent policies. In that sense, one could even say that at times, the Fed does not fight Wall Street.

For an individual investor, trying to trade on Fed policy is loony. How in the world is an individual investor supposed to make money second-guessing the market's view of what the Fed will do next?

6. Every Single Word Spoken About Day Trading

Day traders have been big business for brokerage firms fighting hard for their business. Firms like Datek Online, CyberTrader, Heartland Securities, and TradeScape aggressively compete to attract them, promising instant information, immediate execution, up-to-the-second research. They turn the day trader into a master of the universe, able to trade in the blink of an eye. We especially love the ads from CyberTrader (a Charles Schwab company), which feature the late martial artist Bruce Lee talking with great seriousness about how if you put water in a cup, the water becomes the cup (or does the cup become the water?). His cup-related musings are to us a perfect symbol of the stock charts that CyberTrader is peddling to day traders.

There is, however, one fact you will never, ever see included in any story, profile, or advertisement about day trading. What is it?

Think about it.

If you haven't guessed by now, here's the answer: *the average performance of those who day trade.* How well do CyberTrader's customers do when they implement the cup and water strategy? Don't know. How much does the ability to trade in three seconds, as opposed to three minutes, boost investor returns? A mystery. The largest day-trading companies must have aggregate numbers about how their clients do. Never seen them.

Every study we have ever seen on the subject shows that the more frequently individual investors trade, the worse they perform. They perform worse because they incur substantial transaction and tax costs (unlike the traders at investment banks, who have low marginal trading costs) and tend to trade poorly. We have never seen a study, or any other evidence, to show that more frequent trading by individual investors has brought greater profits. That's not to say that day traders didn't make money buying and selling technology stocks in the early to mid-1990s. It is to say that they would have made more money buying and *holding* technology stocks. Either way, they had lost most of it by 2001.

We challenge the folks at Datek and Power E*Trade and all the rest to post aggregate data on the performance of their clients. Although we are sensitive to issues of personal privacy, there should be no problem with posting aggregate returns, or even the range of individual returns, on an anonymous basis. We strongly urge you to disregard every word of their advertising unless they make such data available. *Until you can measure it, don't believe it.*

7. "We have that stock rated a buy."

You might wonder whether it's fair for us to classify a simple analyst rating as a "whopper." After all, analysts are smart people, and institutional investors pay quite a lot for their research. One can debate—as we later do—just how much use Wall Street research is to institutional investors. But this much is clear: recommendations are whoppers *when presented to individual investors through the financial media.*

When you see an analyst on television rating a stock as a buy, it pays to think about what the analyst is really saying. That is, "The market is wrong about the stock. All the managers at the major pension funds and mutual funds, and those who advise them, have gotten it wrong. They have underpriced this stock." In fact, there is even more going on. Usually the analyst has already given institutional clients this same recommendation days or weeks earlier, before appearing on the show. If those institutions accepted and traded on the recommendation, the stock has already risen accordingly, and you're buying at a higher price. If they all ignored it, then shouldn't you?

Suppose you learn that a stock is rated a "buy" not just by one analyst, but by almost all the analysts following a given company. What that means—and here it's getting a little like Alice in Wonderland—is that everyone believes the stock is undervalued, but no one is buying it!

Think of it this way: you arrive at an art auction that features a painting attributed to an apprentice of Rembrandt, with an estimated value of $10,000. In the hallway, however, you talk to a gallery owner who tells you that the painting is grossly undervalued. As he told his clients earlier in the week, the painting is in fact the work of Rembrandt himself! The bidding starts and the auction is jammed with noted collectors and representatives of all the world's major museums. The price, however, never rises above $10,000. Going once . . . Going twice . . . Do you still feel like bidding? Do you still believe it's a Rembrandt?

8. Any Reference to a "Hot" Fund

The "hot" fund is a fixture of the financial media. Numerous magazines run annual, quarterly, or even monthly reports on the hottest mutual funds. The story has innumerable variants: "Hot Funds to Buy Now," "Top Growth Funds," "Best Sector Funds to Buy Now." All, though, are based on the recent performance of the relevant mutual funds.

Here is a fundamental law of mutual fund investing: the hottest fund is almost always: (1) a fund in a sector that performed well over the relevant period; and (2) a risky fund. If, for whatever reason, financial services stocks are up and energy stocks are down, then only financial services funds will be able to turn in the high returns necessary to make the "hot" lists. An energy fund, no matter how well managed, has no chance. Diversified funds by definition will never qualify as "hot" because they are bound to include some stocks from both outperforming and underperforming sectors. Even within the "right" sector for that month or year, not all funds have a shot at being "hot." Only those that take on greater risk—generally by investing in relatively few stocks—will show up at the top.

Thus, employing an intelligent stock picker generally has nothing to do with a fund's obtaining "hot" status. An industry's most brilliant stock picker will never make the "hot" list if that industry is hitting hard times.

Let's return to our earlier coin-flipping example. Assuming a world where a flipper can take on more risk by taping coins together, who do you think will perform the very best over one hundred flips? The answer is one of the flippers who taped together all one hundred coins.

Consider the case of James McCall. Merrill Lynch hired him to run its new Focus Twenty Fund in November 1999. McCall was lured by big dollars from his previous post at Pilgrim Baxter funds, where he had been ranked as the number-one growth fund manager while running the PBHG Large Cap 20 fund. Based on his track record, Merrill was able to raise $1.5 *billion* for its Focus Twenty Fund in a short period of time. As its name suggests, the Focus Twenty Fund (and its predecessor) was highly concentrated, predominantly in technology stocks, and thus highly risky. In the year following its launch, that risk caught up with the Focus Twenty Fund. It achieved the quintuple crown of bad investing from Morningstar, which at one point ranked it in the lowest 1 percent of all funds for the past day, week, month, quarter, and year. Through third quarter 2001, the fund was down a load-adjusted 71 percent since inception, and Mr. McCall accepted a buyout package and left shortly thereafter. No such luck for the investors who bought this "hot" fund.

So, the next time you see "The Year's Hot Funds," you should mentally translate that headline to read "Funds to Avoid Now!" or "Risky Funds That Were Invested in Last Year's Hot Sector!"

9. "The traders on the floor are telling me that this market is looking for leadership."

This statement is another CNBC staple, generally intoned by one of the floor correspondents while the market is relatively stagnant. It used to mean that institutional investors were reluctant to buy until other large institutional investors were buying. Increasingly, though, we hear correspondents talking about individual stocks or sectors "leading" the market.

Stocks aren't people; they don't value leaders. Certainly, economic factors—interest rate cuts, declining energy costs—can "lead" the market higher, and within a given sector a favorable earnings report from one company can presage equally good news for similarly situated companies. But individual stocks and even individual institutional investors cannot lead the market higher by themselves.

The danger of the "market leadership" comment for individual investors is that it furthers the notion that something they don't understand is going on behind the scenes. Picture one stock gathering all the other stocks around it in a quiet corner of the exchange and giving the equity equivalent of a Knute Rockne halftime speech. "Let's go out there and win one for the Gap!"

It's just a bunch of stocks. They don't know each other. For every institutional investor who thinks it's time to buy, there's generally one who thinks it's time to sell. You don't need to hire someone to eavesdrop on their conversations.

10. "Salvador Dali is considered one of the most influential artists of all time. . . . His works are disappearing from the market."

Obviously, this quote doesn't relate directly to stock investing. It was taken from a television advertisement appearing on CNBC during the summer of 2001. The advertiser was an art gallery specializing in Dali's works. In fact, few, if any, serious people consider Salvador Dali one of the most influential artists of all time. Far worse, he was either a witting or unwitting participant in some of the greatest fraud in the history of art. He signed thousands of pages of blank paper, and others created artwork over his name. The comment about his works disappearing from the market is hilariously ironic. In fact, "new" works by Dali continued to appear on the market even after his death.

We offer this example simply to illustrate one point: *the advertisers on CNBC must be operating on the assumption that its viewers will believe just about anything.*

Show Me the Money

Mutual funds and retail brokerage firms certainly benefit from the soft-hitting interviews, the Running Man syndrome, and the whoppers, but they don't just leave it at that. They spend huge sums on advertising. The mutual fund industry spent over half a billion dollars on advertising in 2000.[4] That number pales, though, beside the advertising budgets of the biggest brokerage firms. According to *Advertising Age,* in 2001 Morgan Stanley spent $539 million; Charles Schwab, $379 million; Ameritrade, $287 million; and E*Trade, $218 million.

Let's return to the analogy of generic drugs. Just about any brand-name pain or cold medication you can think of—Tylenol, Contac, Nyquil—now sits on the drugstore shelf right next to a store-brand equivalent. That store brand—from CVS, Rite Aid, and the like—contains the same active ingredient in the same quantity. Yet most shoppers pay considerably more—often 50 percent more—to obtain a brand name they recognize ("Advil") rather than a bland, soulless chemical name they don't ("Ibuprofen"). They choose to pay more largely because advertising has made them very comfortable with the brand names. Shoppers may be fairly sure that the two products are the same, but they're not *completely* sure.

Advertisements keep brand awareness high for the mutual fund industry as well. A recent academic study, however, demonstrates that advertisements are a poor guide indeed for investors trying to decide on a mutual fund.[5] Writing in the *Journal of Finance,* Prem Jaij and Joanna Wu examined two years of mutual fund advertising in *Barron's* and *Money* magazine. In particular, they looked at advertisements by diversified (nonsector) domestic stock funds whose ads reported past performance as an inducement to purchase. In all, 294 funds were examined.

The study reached three conclusions.

- First, not surprisingly, the advertised funds had performed well in the year *before* the advertisement was run. The *pre*-advertisement returns of those funds over the past year were 1.8 percentage points better than the S&P 500 Index. In other words, funds with a happy story to tell tend to advertise, and those with a sad story don't.
- Second, the advertisements were extremely effective in attracting new money to the funds. Advertised funds were compared to a control group with similar funds, recent inflows, and of similar

size. Advertising appeared to increase inflows 20 percent over what one would otherwise have expected.
- The third conclusion, however, is by far the most significant. The *post*-advertisement performance of the funds was quite poor. The funds' *post*-advertisement performance *trailed the S&P 500 by 7.9 percentage points* over the next year.

Examples of the counter-cyclical nature of fund advertising are not hard to find. With tech stocks soaring in 1999 and 2000 the financial press was inundated with advertisements for technology and Internet funds. By 2001, with technology in the dumps, the technology funds had disappeared from the magazines. They were replaced by value funds, real estate investment trusts, and bond funds. In retrospect, the right move would have been to advertise (and buy) these value funds in 1999 and 2000. At that point, however, the industry was obsessively creating and advertising technology funds in order to lure the assets of tech-crazy investors. Those were the days when value funds were being pressured, both by market forces and fund management, to change their style and come to grips with the New Economy. Many did, to their considerable regret.

Wrapping Up

We don't mean to suggest that you tune out everything you hear in the financial media. There are a lot of wonderful writers and columnists out there giving extremely good advice. Jason Zweig, Jean Sherman Chatzky, and Walter Updegrave at *Money* and Suze Orman, who appears regularly on CNBC but seems to be omnipresent, do a terrific job for consumers. At the large daily newspapers, Jonathan Clements with the *Wall Street Journal,* Mark Hulbert with the *New York Times,* independent columnist Andy Tobias, and Jane Bryant Quinn at *Newsweek* are among those worth reading. Even though we include *Money* as one of the largest floats in the "you can beat the market" parade, we would list money.com as one of the first places to look for up-to-date information about exchange-traded funds, buying bonds, and many other investing topics. The problem, though, is while these wonderful features and articles are true pearls, they sit in an oyster of boosterism.

To appreciate the size of that oyster, consider this: when was the last time you read a profile of an investment club or individual investor who *underperformed* the market for the past year or decade? Imagine the story:

> Meet Brad Dunbar, whose portfolio has returned 6.2 percent over the past ten years. He has lost out through excessive full-service brokerage costs on his stock portfolio, paying front-end loads and excessive taxes on his underperforming mutual funds, and through feeble attempts at market timing. "I am a loser," says Brad.

Think that would sell a lot of magazines?

Chapter 3

Risk, Diversification, and Efficient Markets

The revolutionary idea that defines the boundary between
modern times and the past is the mastery of risk: the
notion that the future is more than the whim of the gods and that men
and women are not passive before nature. Until human beings
discovered a way across that boundary, the future was a
mirror of the past or the murky domain of oracles
and soothsayers who held a monopoly of knowledge
of anticipated events.—*Peter Bernstein,* Against
the Gods: The Remarkable Story of Risk

In order to understand why professional money management won't
work for you, there are three key concepts you need to appreciate:
risk, diversification, and efficient market theory.
Why are these concepts important?

- The only way for an investor to earn predictably higher returns
  over time is by taking on more **risk.** Risk is a difficult concept,
  though, and one frequently misunderstood by investors, who
  rarely evaluate their investments on a risk-adjusted basis. We'll see
  why that's a mistake.
- The best way to decrease risk without sacrificing returns is
  through **diversification.** Diversification is the free lunch of investing. Most investors, however, fail to construct a diversified
  portfolio.
- **Efficient market theory** states that the prices of stocks and bonds
  take into account all available information. The more efficient
  markets are, the harder it is for you to beat them. Most investors
  underestimate this fact.

As profound as these concepts are, you don't need an M.B.A. to appreciate their basic thrust. If you read to the end of the chapter, you should learn enough to start viewing your investments very differently.

Risk and Risk-Adjusted Returns

Risk is all around us. Should I go through the yellow light? Should I fold if I only hold a pair in poker? Should I ask the boss for a raise? Managing risk is part of living life. That's not to say, however, that we always do a good job of it.

Our ability to manage any particular risk is really a matter of practice and feedback. (Psychologists call this "calibration.") You may not think of yourself as having practiced your yellow-light running, but you have. Angry honks from behind, and you know you've been too cautious. Loud squeals of brakes and the occasional trip to the body shop, and you know you've been too aggressive. Through a dozen yellow light encounters a week, you've become a fairly good judge of the risks and rewards. By the same token, play a lot of hands of poker and eventually you'll notice that drawing to an inside straight rarely pays off. You'd love to play against someone who hasn't noticed.

Very few individual investors, however, practice financial risk management. They are therefore poorly calibrated financial risk takers. Of course, the financial industry doesn't go out of its way to make practice easy for you. Financial risk and financial return are two sides of the same coin, but when was the last time you received a statement from your mutual fund or broker quantifying your annual risk as well as your annual returns?

In fact, many in the financial services industry have a vested interest in keeping you in the dark about risk, for three reasons.

- First, you feel more dependent on them to manage risk. Financial advisers and brokers depend on your concern about risk. You tend to need them most when you're worried and uncertain.
- Second, money managers can run higher risks with your money than you might otherwise permit. The promise of high returns draws investors, and only the taking of high risk may allow it. They'd just as soon you didn't notice that last part.

- Third, the industry can convince you that it is possible to earn high returns without risk. Generally, in pursuing our life goals, we are able to substitute hard work or innovation for risk. You improve your chances of the boss giving you a raise by putting in extra hours or coming up with a cost-saving idea. The financial industry wants you to believe that stock picking is much the same. Do the research and trade frequently, and you can earn high returns without high risk. That's the promise, anyway.

The Nature of Financial Risk

Here is the reality. Risk and reward are inextricably linked in finance. Because financial markets are filled with thousands upon thousands of well-calibrated risk takers—traders, hedge fund managers, you name it—the risks and rewards are finely balanced. Just as no casino's roulette table will pay you $3 for a successful $1 bet on red, no one in the financial markets is going to pay you as high an interest rate for an investment-grade bond as for a junk-rated bond. People on Wall Street keep very good track of financial risk indeed.

So, what exactly is financial risk? In life, the types of risk we run vary with the endeavor. In mountain climbing, the risk is death; in basketball, a blown-out knee; in blind dating, a dull evening. With investing, you're probably aware that the risk is losing your money, or not earning as much as you expected, or when you expected it. You may be less aware that the accepted measure of financial risk is volatility. It is a measure of randomness—that is, the chance that rather than receiving the returns you expect, you will instead receive unpredictable returns. Along the path of a stock or bond's performance, volatility represents how much the price or return bounces around over a given period—be it daily, monthly, or annually. Because we count on having our money there when we need it—for a down payment or a tuition bill—randomness can be a big problem.

We'll illustrate how volatility can quantify risk with two examples.

Suppose that you generally ride the bus home at night, but occasionally rely on coworkers to give you a ride. In the past one of your coworkers, Anna, has obeyed the speed limit, taken the direct route, and gotten you home in thirty minutes every time. Another coworker,

Matt, drives fast, explores new shortcuts, and misses the occasional turn; your trips with him have averaged thirty minutes, but have ranged from fifteen minutes to forty-five minutes.

Tonight, your daughter's birthday party is starting in thirty minutes, and you cannot be late. Which driver do you choose? The clear answer is Anna. You are not tolerant of risk for this trip, and the volatility in Matt's trip times is unacceptable tonight. The higher chance of getting home early that Matt's driving affords is not worth the risk of getting home late.

Now let's move our example into the financial world. Consider two mutual funds (or stocks, for that matter) that exhibited the following annual performance over the past four years.

Fund	Beginning value	Year 1	Year 2	Year 3	Current value
A	$10,000	$13,000	$15,000	$17,000	$20,000
B	$10,000	$7,000	$30,000	$9,000	$20,000

Both funds begin and end at the same price. If you invested $10,000 in either, you ended up with $20,000 four years later. There is a major difference between the funds, however. Fund A, like Anna's driving, was much less volatile than Fund B, which shared Matt's volatile performance. Fund A was therefore a better investment, because it achieved the same returns with lower risk. In the language of finance, Fund A had higher risk-adjusted returns.

"But who cares?" you may still say. "Because in the end, they made the same amount of money!" True, but let's think about it a little more. Suppose that at the end of the first year, you wanted to use your investment to make an $8,000 tuition payment for your daughter's education. Suppose that at the end of the third year, you had the opportunity to start your own business if you could contribute $10,000. With Fund B, you would have missed the payment and the opportunity. The volatility of Fund B would have stood between you and your goals.

There's another potential downside to investing in Fund B. Suppose that at the end of the first year, you'd had *new money to invest*. With future tuition payments in mind, would you have felt comfortable continuing to invest in Fund B? Probably not. Consciously or subconsciously, you would have sought to diminish the volatility of your returns by investing the money in a less risky asset—perhaps even in cash. On the other hand, had you been a Fund A investor, you probably would have put the new money in Fund A. Because cash earned less than either fund over time, that means that you would have ended up with more money through Fund A, as it outperformed the returns you would have received through a portfolio that combined Fund B and cash.

Measuring Risk and Volatility

Now that we know that risk is important, we need to think about how to measure it. On the surface, financial risk doesn't seem that complicated. "Markets go up, and markets go down" was a favorite expression of former Treasury Secretary Robert Rubin, one he used so frequently that President Clinton used to kid him about it. He meant it to be reassuring in times of stress. For many investors, though, "Markets go up, and markets go down" is the sum total of their understanding about financial risk. They track the prices of their stocks or funds every day but never quantify the volatility, either individually or as a portfolio.

The most widely used measure of volatility is the standard deviation of an investment's return. Don't worry if you skipped or slept through your statistics courses: standard deviations simply measure how widely dispersed an asset's returns are. Put another way, they measure how far individual returns vary from average returns. Once you've identified a mean return for a given period, one standard deviation generally is the amount of variation from the mean (plus or minus) that covers about two thirds of the results; two standard deviations cover 95 percent of the results.

So what are some real-life standard deviations? For the ten years 1992–2001, the S&P 500 returned 12.9 percent annually with a standard deviation of 15.8 percent. What that means is that over that ten-year period, the S&P 500 Index fluctuated consistent with annualized returns between -2.9 and 28.7 percent a little more than two thirds of the time. Conversely, about one third of the time, the S&P 500 Index fluctuated consistent with annualized returns of less than -2.9 percent or more than 28.7 percent. Compare that relatively high volatility to the returns for the Lehman Brothers Aggregate Bond Index over the same period. It returned 7.2 percent annually for the period, but with a standard deviation of only 4.0 percent. In other words, two thirds of the time, its returns were consistent with annualized returns of between 3.2 and 11.2 percent. That's more of the predictability you'd look for if you were anticipating some upcoming tuition payments.

Case Study: Pro Funds

One family of mutual funds, ProFunds, helps to illustrate the importance of volatility and standard deviation as a measure of volatility. Through 2001, the profile of its twenty-nine domestic equity funds looked like a misprint.

	Average Monthly Standard Deviation (3 years)	Average Annual Turnover Ratio (3 years)	Average % of Assets in Top 10 Holdings
ProFunds	51%	1,569%	64%

Source: Morningstar Principia Pro

The standard deviation of 51 percent is almost triple the volatility of the S&P 500. One cause of this volatility is apparent from the funds' concentrated holdings: on average 64 percent of its assets invested in only ten stocks. Also, a turnover ratio of over fifteen times per year means that the fund is changing its bets every day—not necessarily a risky strategy, but a good hint.

But guess what? If you run twenty-three funds with an average standard deviation of 51 percent, you will occasionally generate some very high returns. In 1998 and 1999, one of those funds, Ultra OTC Investor Shares, returned 185 and 233 percent respectively. For that short time, it ranked near the top of all funds.

But if you run a fund with a very high standard deviation, then you will also eventually generate some very low returns. In the year 2000, Ultra OTC Investor Shares lost 76 percent of its value. Through 2001, it lost an additional 69 percent of its value. Thus, if you had invested

$10,000 in the Ultra OTC Fund at its inception in 1997, you would have had a wild ride, up to over $100,000 in early 2000, and back down to only $5,800 by 2002.

Here's the bottom line: anyone who looked at the returns of Pro-Funds Ultra OTC in 1998 or 1999 *but did not look at its standard deviation (or some other measure of volatility)* would have made a horrible mistake.* Without standard deviation or some similar risk measure included, any picture of a fund's performance is woefully incomplete. Anyone who understood standard deviation and volatility would have known that buying this fund was the equivalent of driving with your eyes closed. You can find standard deviations at morningstar.com and other financial websites.

The Equity Premium and Mrs. Muscleman's Social Studies Class

The tradeoff between return and risk is most obvious in the relative performance of stocks and bonds. Over time, stocks carry more risk and earn higher returns than bonds. That difference is known as the equity premium.

A share of stock represents an ownership interest in the future success of a company. Stock ownership makes you a partner with the firm, able to share in the company's future earnings. A bond, on the other hand, represents a company's promise to pay a fixed rate of interest over a period of years, and then to refund your principal at maturity. Stocks carry more risk because holders of bonds have first call on corporate assets in the event of trouble. Stockholders are first in line to absorb any loss, and bondholders begin to suffer losses only after the stockholders have lost their entire investment.

As a result, stocks tend to be more volatile than bonds. Good news about a company generally means more to stockholders (who can share in the higher earnings) than to bondholders (who need only worry about default). Bad news is more likely to endanger stockholders than bondholders, who continue to receive their fixed coupon payments.

---

* While the fund was going up at that time, standard deviation captures both upside and downside risk. And while we don't think of extraordinarily *high* returns as a "risk," generally they are a sign that extraordinarily low returns are equally possible.

Consequently, over the ten years ending in 2001, the stock market has been almost four times as volatile as the bond market.

Investors expect a higher return on stock to compensate them for the greater risk of loss. Put another way, if bonds and stocks carried the same returns over time, who would buy stocks? The prices of stocks and bonds diverge so that the higher returns of stocks balance the higher risks.

Historically, those willing to bear equity risk have earned a premium. From 1872 to 2000, stocks outperformed the lowest risk type of bonds by about 5.5 percent per year.[1] The gap actually widened during the last fifty years. From 1951 to 2000, the equity premium rose to 7.5 percent.

The equity premium has never been very predictable, though. Economists have scrambled to explain why the equity premium rose in the latter part of the twentieth century. Many believe that the rise may be only temporary. Special factors such as wider participation in the equity markets, changes in tax and pension laws, and the growth of the mutual fund industry may have explained a vast part of its recent increase. Many economists predict that it is more likely that the equity premium over risk-free securities will return to earlier levels of between 3 and 4 percent. Some economists even suggest that the premium will be close to zero.[2]

Gary received a very early introduction to the power of the equity premium in Mrs. Muscleman's ninth-grade Social Studies class. It was 1971, and Mrs. Muscleman assigned her ninth-grade class a stock market challenge. She gave each student a pretend $10,000 to invest in the stock market. Grades would depend on how well each student's investments performed. Each trade would be entered in a register and results posted along the way. Anyone who broke even would be assured a B-, but better grades were reserved for moneymaking returns.

Many of the students, however, were focused on the downside, worried that if they invested their money in the stock market, the market could go down, dooming them to a C or a D. Some decided that they wouldn't invest at all, hoping that Mrs. Muscleman would still give them a B-. Gary's father, however, had taught him that over time, one made more money investing in the stock market than in a savings account. With a confidence in what we now know as the equity premium, Gary offered the nervous students of the class an option. If they gave him their money to invest, he would issue a written note promising to return it in full at the end of the semester with a modest interest rate, ensuring that they received a B. In essence, he established a bank paying interest on deposits. (There was always the chance that if the market tanked, Gary would have been unable to refund the money. Even before the savings and loan bailout of the 1980s, though, he figured that his teacher probably would have bailed him out. He would have found out if the contest had been held a year later, when the market took a big dip.)

As it turned out, the plan worked very well. With control of a few hundred thousand dollars of pretend money, Gary invested both his own money and that of his depositors in the market, which earned positive returns over the semester. Gary received an A (and then some); his depositor classmates received their Bs, and everyone went home happy. Mrs. Muscleman was highly amused.

Managing Risk

Understanding and quantifying financial risk are the two first steps on the road to managing risk. Do not underestimate your ability to do so.

Observers often liken the stock market to a roller-coaster ride, noting simply that it has its ups and downs. In fact, the analogy goes further. In both cases, one tends to feel a little nauseated after the first big plunge, but getting off the ride at that point is a very bad idea. More important, you can take steps to avoid roller coasters, or investments, that carry more ups and downs than our constitutions will allow. (Greg knows this all too well, having spent high school summers working the Thunder Road roller coaster at Carowinds amusement park. His duties sometimes included mopping up when the ride left someone's constitution more than a little unsettled.) At an amusement park, diminishing volatility may mean riding the nice, smooth Scooby Doo roller coaster rather than the more volatile Thunder Road. In investing, it may mean buying Treasury securities or FDIC-insured certificates of deposit rather than stocks. In either case, *risk and volatility are within our control if we choose to manage it.* Later, in Part VI, we'll explore how you can use asset allocation to control the riskiness of your investments.

The Virtues of Diversification

We have seen the tradeoff between risk and return—that is, one generally cannot diminish the risk of a particular investment without sacrificing potential returns. As they say, there is no such thing as a free lunch. But wait! When it comes to assembling a *portfolio* of assets, you *can* reduce your risk without sacrificing returns. Sort of like a free bagel when you order a dozen. If we've whetted your appetite, please read on.

Modern Portfolio Theory

In the 1950s, economist Harry Markowitz developed an approach to investing that became known as modern portfolio theory. In 1990, he received the Nobel Prize in Economics for this work. Basically, modern portfolio theory is the economic equivalent of the old notion that a good team is worth more than the sum of each of its members. In modern portfolio theory, the team is a diversified equity portfolio and the members of the team are the individual stocks that make up that portfolio.

The reason a team of, say, football players is better than the sum of each individual player's talents is comparative advantage. The scrawny little kicker doesn't have to tackle anybody. The 350-pound lineman doesn't have to catch the football and run with it. If each player had identical size and skills, there wouldn't be a team benefit.

Stocks, too, have something akin to "skills." One stock may excel when oil prices rise, while others suffer or remain unaffected. Another stock may excel when it patents a new invention. A harsh winter may benefit some stocks, while leaving others out in the cold. While stocks generally tend to move in the same direction as the overall market (just as all football players tend to share the same morale, strength of schedule, and weather conditions), a team of stocks will have different offsetting attributes.

Markowitz observed that holding a group of stocks with dissimilar price movements allows an investor to reduce risk without sacrificing returns. When one stock in the portfolio falls, there are others that either rise or fall less. You can think of modern portfolio theory as a fancy name for the old expression "Don't put all of your eggs in one basket."

Here's an illustration. A recent study looked at the performance of the Russell 1000 Index (basically the 1,000 largest publicly traded stocks) over the seven-year period ending December 31, 1999.[3] The average annual return of those stocks was 17 percent per year, for a cumulative return of 201 percent over the entire period. Some stocks performed much better and some performed much worse but 201 percent was the average.

Suppose that at the beginning of the seven-year period, you'd wanted to make sure that you would earn *at least* half of the Russell 1000's total return—which ended up being 100 percent—over the seven years. How could you diminish your risk enough to feel pretty certain that you'd get half the total return?

Holding only one Russell 1000 stock over the period, you had only a 48 percent chance of earning at least half the average return—that is, 52 percent of individual stocks fell short of a 100 percent return. With a basket of five stocks, though, your chances of earning at least 100 percent went up to 69 percent. At twenty stocks, there was a 92 percent chance. With thirty stocks, you'd have had a 96 percent chance of earning your 100 percent, or more. Move to fifty stocks and you're up to 99 percent. That, in a nutshell, is the benefit of diversification.

Not All Risks Are the Same: The Capital Asset Pricing Model

A further refinement of modern portfolio theory is the capital asset pricing model, or CAPM. You may never have heard of the CAPM, but you've almost certainly seen evidence of it as you scan the financial media. Anytime you see a chart refer to "beta," then you're looking at an application of CAPM.

Economist William Sharpe developed the capital asset pricing model in 1964. In recognition of his achievement, Sharpe received the Nobel Prize, along with Markowitz, in 1990. Sharpe observed that stocks actually leave their holders with two types of risks. One type of risk—so-called "systematic" or "market" risk—relates to the market as a whole. That is, many economic and political factors affect all stocks, though some more than others. Other risk—so-called "specific" or "firm-specific" risk—relates to an individual stock rather than the market as a whole.

The distinction is important. According to Sharpe, an investor can eliminate specific risk by holding a diversified portfolio, but cannot eliminate systematic risk. Because you can readily reduce firm-specific risk, the market won't pay you for holding it. The market will compensate you, however, with higher returns for taking systematic risk.

To appreciate firm-specific risk, imagine a company operating exclusively in New England. Shareholders of that company run the risk of a downturn in the New England economy—say a banking crisis such as occurred there in the 1980s. If you were to hold only this stock, you would need to factor in this "New England risk," in addition to its other risks. Other investors with broader portfolios, though, aren't that worried about New England risk. They hold the stocks of companies whose fortunes are unaffected by New England's fortunes or, ideally, may even benefit from New England's misfortunes—say stocks of companies in the South. Because these other investors needn't demand a New England risk premium, *they can outbid you for the stock.* Or you can outbid them, *but only if you are willing to bear the New England risk without any compensation.*

In our example, the other investors have succeeded in reducing their specific risks with diversification. If you choose to hold, rather than diversify, that risk, then you're kind of a financial chump. (Sorry, but there's really no other way to put it.) You are akin to an NFL general manager who uses all of his draft picks on place kickers.

Systematic risk, however, cannot be diminished with diversification. Users of the capital asset pricing model often quantify this risk as "beta." Beta simply represents the correlation of a stock's historical price movements to that of the overall market. A stock with a beta of 2.0 tends to fall or rise by twice as large a percentage as the overall market. That is, if an interest rate cut pushes the market up 5 percent, then a stock with a beta of 2.0 will tend to be up 10 percent.

What lessons should you take from the CAPM? First, because some risks can be eliminated through diversification, assembling a portfolio of varied stocks can substantially reduce risk. Second, because some risks are systematic and cannot be reduced through diversification, a diversified portfolio cannot eliminate all risk.

For a time, some took an additional lesson from the CAPM. More specifically, they suggested using beta as an investment approach. Given that the market rewards holders of systematic risk, and beta measures systematic risk, investors willing to shoulder risk could simply buy high beta stocks and lock in those rewards. For a time, the nation's business schools and finance classes went beta crazy.

The enthusiasm dampened with the publication of a study by two finance legends, Eugene Fama and Kenneth French. Their study, published in 1992, demonstrated that between 1967 and 1990, high beta stocks had not outperformed low beta stocks.[4] What appeared obvious in theory had not worked in practice. Does this mean that risk and reward don't go together? No. Does it mean that you should buy low beta stocks, thereby earning market returns with lower risk? No. What it probably means is that beta is an imprecise measure of risk and may not reliably carry predictive value.

Efficient Markets and the Random Walk

As we discussed earlier, bookies are very good at their business. They know that the only way they can ensure themselves a relatively risk-free return is by setting the terms of the bet such that half of the money is bet on each side. If an initial point spread set by the oddsmakers attracts too much money to one team, bookies quickly adjust the spread to get the bets back into equilibrium. Thus, as we saw, the point spread comes to reflect the consensus view of the likely outcome of the game—initially the view of the oddsmakers but eventually of the entire gambling public as well.

As a gambler, you only make money when your team beats the spread. You only make money when half the betting public loses money. And, over time, you only make money if your team beats the spread frequently enough to offset what you pay the bookie.

Stock markets are much the same. It's never enough to be right about which companies make good products or which companies are about to grow rapidly. The price of a stock generally reflects that information. You need to predict whether the actual value of a company is higher or lower than the consensus price. You need to be right where other investors are wrong. And you need to be right more frequently than not, since the brokers and mutual fund companies will take their cut.

The efficient market theory, developed by Eugene Fama and other economists in the 1960s, captures this notion. Entire books and academic courses have been devoted to efficient market theory, so we will not do it full justice here. The basic thrust of efficient market theory, however, is relatively simple and extremely important: *information currently known about a company is reflected in the prices for its bonds and stock.*

In its simplest form, efficient market theory tells us that information about the U.S. stock market is so widely and quickly available that you cannot profit from trying to predict the future price of the overall market, any sector of the market, or any individual stock. In other words, the U.S. stock market is so liquid and transparent that stock prices quickly adjust to incorporate new information, and you can't make money second-guessing those prices. Any news about a stock that you see on television, discover through your investment club, or read about in a magazine is *by definition* old news, stale news, and thus *unprofitable* news.

Efficient market theory also implies that the past movement of a stock's price isn't useful in predicting its future movement. Maurice Kendall first examined the so-called "random walk" in 1953, explaining that stock prices take a random and unpredictable path. The term gained wider popularity from Eugene Fama's 1965 paper, "Random Walks in Stock Market Prices," and in 1973 when Burton Malkiel published the first edition of his classic book, *A Random Walk Down Wall Street.* The random walk means that stock prices take a random and unpredictable path, individually and collectively. Thus, technical analysis, based on charts of past performance, is not likely to help you second-guess an efficient market.

As you might expect, efficient market theory has proven to be controversial, particularly among those on Wall Street whose business it is to sell research or actively manage your money. Just about everybody agrees that the U.S. equity market—particularly the segment of the market that includes the large companies included in the S&P 500—is basically efficient. The question, of course, is how efficient. Over time,

there have emerged "strong," "semi-strong," and "weak" forms of efficient market theory, all with varying views about just how efficient markets are.

Most of this debate, however, is irrelevant to the decisions you must
make as an investor. We have no doubt that there are situations where
particular stocks are trading at prices that are out of line with their fundamentals. (Enron circa 2001 certainly fits this bill.) There are times
when the entire market is as well. The problem is that you, as an individual investor, must be able to identify and trade on such efficiencies
before the consensus price adjusts. The market price for a stock reflects
equal pressure to buy at that price and sell at that price. You as an individual investor need to be confident that you can profitably pick
whether the better bet is higher (buy) or lower (sell). You also need to
be correct a substantial majority of the time in order to pay your fees
and trading costs.

You've got another problem, as well. You must forsake the risk-
reducing benefits of a diversified portfolio in order to try to capitalize
on any inefficiencies in the market. If you hold a diversified portfolio,
the chances of finding multiple profitable opportunities are very small.
But focus on just a few stocks in an attempt to improve your chances
and you'll have to run large, uncompensated risks.

These same challenges confront the portfolio managers at Fidelity
and Dreyfus and all the rest. The average actively managed diversified
mutual fund holds more than one hundred stocks in its portfolio. Given
that such funds are costing you 3–4 percent in fees, transaction costs,
and taxes each year, they need to spot a whole lot of inefficiencies in a
whole lot of stocks in order to outperform the market. It turns out that
markets just aren't inefficient enough for active fund management to
make sense.

What does efficient market theory imply for index funds? Those
who advocate active management like to paint index funds as eschew-
ing sound judgment by picking companies blindly, based only on their
relative market capitalization.* But, in fact, efficient market theory

---

* A company's market capitalization is simply the price of its stock multiplied by its
total outstanding shares. Index funds buy each stock in its pro-rata share of the total
capitalization of the index.

teaches us how index funds *benefit* from the judgments of all of Wall Street's best and brightest. If the experts—analysts, fund managers, and other asset managers—like a stock, then that stock's market capitalization will rise. Index funds, which already held the stock, benefit from that rise and end up with a greater percentage of their assets invested in the now-more-popular stock—without having to buy a single share. Thus, passive investment does not disregard expert judgments. It incorporates all of them—without having to pay for them—as a *free rider*. Those billions of dollars of research aren't lost to the passive investor; they are just free to the passive investor.

Moving Forward

So what do we learn from these three key concepts? First, approach with skepticism those who claim they will be able to help you beat the market on a consistent basis. Second, evaluate all returns on a risk-adjusted basis. Third, reject any investment approach that does not allow you to dine on the free lunch of diversification. Fourth, recognize that the higher returns of stocks come with higher risks. Fifth, accept the fact that you are unlikely to beat a market where prices are set by the consensus of thousands of professionals and where you have to pay a steep price for every attempt.

Part II

The Great Mutual Fund Trap

The world's best putters (the golfers on the PGA Tour) make only about half of all their putts from six feet away. . . . There are good reasons for putting results to be uncertain and hard to understand. And those reasons don't change much over time. Once you understand them, they are easy to accept as part of the game. But putting is, was, and likely always will be difficult to comprehend for those who don't understand the true rules of the game.
—*Dave Pelz*, Dave Pelz's Putting Bible

M utual funds have become the investment vehicle of choice for more than 50 million American households. There are over 4,700 stock funds and 2,000 bond funds for sale to investors. Mutual fund assets have grown from $48 billion in 1970 to $158 billion in 1980; to $567 billion in 1990; to $5.120 *trillion* by the end of 2000.[1] Most of that growth has come in *actively managed stock* funds. Over $3 trillion is invested in these funds.[2]

Clearly, the stakes are large. Yet by any objective measure, mutual funds are failing their millions of devoted clients. Over a five-year period, only about 20 percent of actively managed stock funds perform well enough to earn back their fees and loads. Furthermore, five years later, the identity of the fortunate 20 percent will have changed. This point is crucial. It turns out that the government-mandated disclaimer that accompanies every fund's reported results—"past performance is no guarantee of future results"—is absolutely true.

So who really benefits from active fund management? Stock and bond funds alone impose costs on investors that conservative estimates put at $70 billion annually. Most of this money—in excess of $50 billion per year—goes directly to fund companies in the form of management fees and sales loads. The rest is paid to the brokerage industry, which happily executes the huge trading volume generated by active fund managers.

It's All Relative

A generation ago, before the development of mutual funds, people with small to moderate amounts of money did not have a realistic option for investing in stocks or bonds. Instead, their savings were relegated to either bank savings accounts or whole life insurance. The ability to own part of America's corporations was generally the province of institutional and wealthy investors who bought stocks and bonds from full-service brokers.

The advent of mutual funds offered all investors a chance at the superior long-term performance of equity investing, as well as a convenient way to buy bonds. Mutual funds offered liquidity, as they must by law be prepared to redeem an investor's shares at the end of each day. Mutual funds also brought diversification, as most owned a broad spectrum of the market. Finally, compared with the full-service brokerage commissions of the time, mutual funds' costs were relatively attractive.

Like most choices, however, financial choices are relative. One choice can be judged only in comparison with those forsaken. In the 1970s and 1980s, actively managed mutual funds were a good alternative for investors. In the twenty-first century, however, other options have emerged that make traditional mutual fund investing relatively unattractive.

Index funds now offer the choice of investing in the market as a whole—achieving broader portfolio diversification than the original mutual funds—at very low cost and with minimal taxes. Exchange-traded index funds offer the same diversification and similar cost advantages with even better tax consequences. The U.S. government, municipalities, and even some corporations now sell bonds directly to the public at reasonable prices. *In this century, any actively managed mutual fund must be measured against these alternatives.*

Exploring these alternatives means climbing out of the mutual fund trap. It means comparing your stock fund's performance not to the performance of your checking account but to a meaningful benchmark like the Wilshire 5000 or S&P 500. It means checking your records to see how much you're paying in fees, loads, and unnecessary taxes. It means viewing with a critical eye the blizzard of advice generated by the fund industry and a codependent financial media. It means finally coming to grips with the fact that past performance really isn't predictive of future performance. That's a lot to ask. Let's get going.

Chapter 4

The Grim Reality of Poor Performance

Does history repeat itself, the first time as tragedy, the
second time as farce? No, that's too grand, too considered a
process. History just burps, and we taste again that raw-
onion sandwich it swallowed centuries ago.—*Julian Barnes,*
A History of the World in 10½ Chapters

During the bull market of the 1990s, investors were generally satisfied with the returns of their mutual funds. The market was way
up. Their funds were way up. Why bother checking to see if they
were up by the same amount? So long as investors were more focused on
absolute performance—"My stocks are growing 10 percent per year!"—
rather than relative performance—"Wait a minute: the market is growing 15 percent per year!"—the mutual fund industry was sitting pretty.

We hope that the recent rocky ride in the stock market has caused
some investors to take a closer look at the performance of their investments. A central lesson of this book is this: your success as an investor
must be measured in relative terms, not in absolute returns. Once you
have allocated your assets to different asset types, you should judge each
investment against a relevant benchmark: that is, a measure of how the
overall market for such investments has done. For example, if your corporate bond fund earned 8 percent annually over the past ten years, you
should be delighted, because the bond market returned 7 percent annually. In the relatively low-risk world of bond investing, you did well.
If your stock investments earned 8 percent annually over the past ten

years, you should be distraught, because the overall stock market returned 12 percent over the same period. You took all the risks of stock investing and received a bond-like return.

The Sad Average

As a matter of simple arithmetic, it would not be logical for actively managed mutual funds to beat the market *on average*. It's the old "where all the children are above average" problem again. Thus, no matter how skillful individual managers become, broad market index funds are going to beat about half of them, even before costs.*

Here's how William Sharpe, one of the world's leading financial economists and a Nobel laureate, explains it:

> If "active" and "passive" management styles are defined in sensible ways, it *must* be the case that
> 1. before costs, the return on the average actively managed dollar will equal the return on the average passively managed dollar; and
> 2. after costs, the return on the average actively managed dollar will be less than the return on the average passively managed dollar.
>
> These assertions will hold true for *any* time period. Moreover, they depend *only* on the laws of addition, subtraction, multiplication and division. Nothing else is required.[1]

To echo the quotation that started this chapter, that's the raw onion taste in your mouth. Leave it to a Nobel Prize winner to make things simple.

But enough of this cold logic. Let's look at the data and see what happens in practice.

---

* Actually, to be more accurate, index funds will outperform active managers holding half of the assets. Although this may be a little more or less than half the managers, it will be close.

Things Are Not What They Seem—Survivorship Bias

Before we look at the numbers, we need to pause a moment to consider survivorship bias. Survivorship bias may be a new topic to you, but understanding it is crucial to judging any study on mutual fund performance. We believe it's also crucial to understanding how the fund industry operates and markets itself.

Survivorship bias is the tendency of reported aggregate returns to be biased upward because they exclude funds that went out of business. Funds generally go out of business due to poor performance. Dropping those funds from reported results therefore inflates the returns of the overall mutual fund industry.[2]

Remember the emerging market funds of the early 1990s and the Internet funds of the late 1990s? While those funds were soaring, their results boosted the industry average. Now that many of them have gone out of business, their poor subsequent performance is no longer reflected in industry averages.

Imagine a sales manager at an automobile dealer whose bonus depends on the average sales of all the salespeople employed as of December 31. Think some laggard producers may be fired in December to get the average up? Or imagine that you're anticipating heart surgery and ask prospective surgeons for the five-year history of their patients. They provide histories for only the patients who survived the period. Is that information useful to you?

Alternatively, you can think of this phenomenon as *Survivor*-ship bias, after the recently popular reality show. If someone asked a viewer how interesting the first group of *Survivor* contestants were, they would probably think of the last contestants, Rudy, Richard, Kelly, and Susan, and conclude that it was a pretty wild bunch. They'd probably forget the ones who were voted off in the first few weeks. Remember B.B. and Sonya?

Survivorship bias has a perfectly innocent explanation. When investors are deciding which mutual fund to choose, they want to see a list of their available choices. They don't want to see the records of dead funds, since they can't buy them anyway. As a result, any financial publication giving guidance to investors has good reason to include only live funds in its rankings. That's fair.

What is misleading is when publications (or industry representatives) total up the returns of all those funds and present an *average* return. That's not fair. That number suggests that if you had invested in the average mutual fund over the period being reported, you could have earned the average. Wrong. Now that we're looking retrospectively (examining past performance) rather than prospectively (evaluating choices for future investment), the performance of the least fit is highly relevant. We'd want to know, for example, about the Ameritor Industry Fund, which rather remarkably trailed the S&P 500 Index for eleven consecutive years, from 1989 to 2000. You won't see it in any recent studies, though, because that fund closed up shop in 2001.

The most comprehensive look at survivorship bias was conducted by Burton Malkiel. He found that for the ten-year period 1982–91, the average annual return of *surviving* general equity funds (a survivorship-biased sample) was *17.09* percent. For the same period, the average annual return of *all* general equity funds (including those that failed to survive) was only *15.69* percent.[3]

Thus, over a ten-year period survivorship bias was inflating average industry returns by 1.4 percentage points per year. Over a fifteen-year period, the bias increased (as more dead funds were excluded). Malkiel calculated that survivorship bias inflated returns *2.2* percentage points *per year* when looking at fifteen-year returns.

We believe that survivorship bias has probably grown since Malkiel's study. The number of liquidating funds is rising. From 1991 to 1995, the mutual fund industry liquidated 54 funds per year on average. From 1996 to 2000, the industry liquidated 185 funds per year on average, with 225 liquidations in the year 2000 alone.[4] So, in other words, about 4 percent of the funds is disappearing each year. At that rate, just under 20 percent of funds—and their records—should disappear over the next five years.

Thus, unless you're pretty sure that it's been corrected for survivorship bias, take any report about the average returns of mutual funds and mentally deduct about 2 percent per year.

The Average Fund

Here's the grim reality of mutual fund performance: the average stock fund trails far behind the market. Only a small percentage beat the market over a multiyear period. To recap the data we mentioned earlier:

**Performance of
Actively Managed Funds Versus the Market**

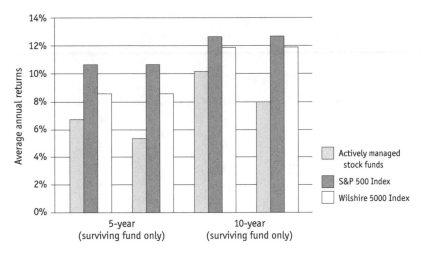

Source: Morningstar Principia Pro, data through September 30, 2001.

Consider these results from the point of view of an individual investor trying to select an actively managed fund that will beat the market (that would be you). The average actively managed fund trails the market considerably. Even an above-average fund only stays even, beating the market by enough to offset its fees and expenses. Only a few funds beat the market by a significant amount, and then not for long. More specifically:

- Over the five-year period ending December 31, 2001, only 33 percent of surviving actively managed stock funds beat the market. Only 25 percent beat it by more than 1 percent per year.
- Over the past ten-year period ending December 31, 2001, only 28 percent of surviving actively managed stock funds beat the S&P 500. Only 11 percent beat it by more than 2 percent per year.[5]

- Adjust for survivorship bias and those numbers drop even further. It's likely that fewer than 20 percent of all funds actually beat the market over a five-year period, and fewer than 10 percent over a ten-year period.

Risk and the Life of a Portfolio Manager

Not only have actively managed funds underperformed the market, *they have done so while running greater risk for their shareholders*. Actively managed funds are more volatile than the market. Have a look:

Relative Risks of Actively Managed Funds

	Standard Deviation (5-year)	Standard Deviation (10-year)
Actively managed funds	25.5%	19.4%
S&P 500 Index	19.9%	15.8%
Wilshire 5000 Index	20.4%	16.2%

Source: Morningstar Principia Pro, data through December 31, 2001.

The chart shows that the returns of actively managed funds were 20 to 25 percent more volatile than the broad market. Why are actively managed funds so much riskier? We have three explanations.

First, actively managed funds are not as diversified. Sector funds obviously are not fully diversified, but even *diversified* actively managed funds have considerably higher volatility than the market—a standard deviation of 24.9 percent for five years and 18.8 percent for ten years.

Second, a lot of money has flowed into growth funds, which tend to be more volatile than other funds. Still, even excluding growth funds *entirely*, the remaining funds still have higher risks than the broader market.

The third possible explanation has to do with the economics of mutual fund companies and the personal incentives of fund managers. Consider:

- The revenues of mutual funds depend on building up a large amount of assets under management. Fund companies derive most of their revenues from management fees, which are stated as a percentage of assets. A mutual fund can only generate inflows—that is, increase its assets—when its sector of the overall market is doing well. For example, if technology is hot, then most technology funds will see inflows. If technology is cold, then all technology funds—even the best ones—will stagnate or see outflows. The same is true of growth funds, large-cap funds, and even diversified funds.

- A mutual fund in a hot sector will see significant inflows only if it is ranked toward the top of its group. Generally, that means that a fund's past performance must put it in a sufficiently high percentile to qualify as a Morningstar four-star or five-star fund.
- *The most likely way for a fund manager to generate a high ranking is to take on additional risk.* A manager's greatest fear is to turn in mediocre performance during a bull market in his or her sector. In fact, some fund managers refer to this concept among themselves as the "fear of the upside."

Note the perverse incentives implied by that last point. Generally, our willingness to take on risk is tempered by our fear of the downside. But from the view of a fund manager, downside risk is much less important than upside potential. To individual investors, a portfolio that earned 3 percent higher returns in good times and 3 percent lower in bad times would be of little interest (assuming good times and bad times were equally frequent). To a fund manager, such a portfolio would be a dream come true. When the sector was hot, the fund would earn five stars and generate huge inflows. When the sector was cold, the fund would earn one or two stars, but no one would be investing anyway.

To illustrate the average fund manager's incentives, here's the only table in the book that doesn't have numbers in it.

The World of the Mutual Fund Manager

	Sector/Benchmark Doing Well	*Sector/Benchmark Doing Poorly*
Fund Outperforming Sector/Benchmark	Cash flows into fund; manager gets **big bonus, promotion**	Cash flow stagnant; manager **keeps job**
Fund Underperforming Sector/Benchmark	Fund misses opportunity to grow; manager gets **fired**	Cash flow stagnant; manager **keeps job**

Lesson: the risk-taking incentives of fund managers are likely to generate greater risk than you would choose for yourself.

From Bad to Worse: Sectors, Lies, and Tickertapes

To generate more business, the mutual fund industry has opened up three other tables in the great fund casino. These funds divide the stock universe in three ways: by industry (e.g., technology, energy), by size (e.g., large-cap, mid-cap), or by style (growth versus value). For convenience, we will call all of them sector funds.

It's tempting to pick a few slices of the market. In roulette, some gamblers don't like the risk of picking a single number and instead prefer to bet on red or black. The bet with sector funds is that you know more about what sector will outperform than you do about what stock will outperform.

Let's take a look at the average performance of the three main categories of sector funds.

Industry Funds

Industry funds offer investors the lure of specialization. These funds are based on the notion that a fund manager focused on just one area of the economy will use the resulting expertise to outperform fund managers investing in all areas of the economy. In reality, though, many of the large fund companies use such funds as a training ground for new fund managers. Only a couple of years out of business school, they're trying to move up the ladder to larger, diversified funds. Once they gather experience in one sector, they're usually transferred to a new one.

The record seems to show that, expert or not, sector fund managers cannot do any better against the market than any other active managers. Here are the returns of all actively managed funds focusing on a particular industry over the past five and ten years.

Performance of Actively Managed Industry Funds (load adjusted)

	Average Annual Performance (5-year)	Average Annual Performance (10-year)
Industry funds	7.5%	12.0%
S&P 500	10.2%	12.7%
Relative performance	-2.8%	-0.7%

Source: Morningstar Principia Pro, data through December 31, 2001.[6]

As poor as all these figures are, they don't tell the whole story. Industry funds are risky, with standard deviations significantly higher than those of the average actively managed diversified fund. Risk-adjusted returns therefore are far worse than absolute returns. Furthermore, if we were able to adjust for survivorship bias, these figures would be *much* worse. As noted earlier, survivorship bias has been estimated to be as much as 1.4 to over 2 percent per year when looking at the performance of all mutual funds. We believe that the upward bias for industry funds (which tend to close up shop when the next sector becomes hot) is significantly higher.

In light of these numbers, we wondered why anyone would invest in an industry fund. So we picked up the recent *Where the Money I$, How to Spot Key Trends to Make Investment Profits,* by Dr. Bob Froehlich. Since Dr. Bob has trademarked the word "sectornomics" and is the chief investment officer at a major fund company, we thought his book might be a good place to learn why to invest in sector funds.

The book argues persuasively that a company's sector will be the one factor with the greatest influence on the company's future stock price. He identifies the five sectors that he believes will achieve the best long-term performance: pharmaceuticals, technology, telecommunications, financial services, and energy. He then recommends investing in these five sectors for the long term, ignoring short-term "blizzards" along the way. In other words, he argues that, regardless of how well sector funds do on average, all you have to do is pick the right sectors—namely the five sectors he recommends.

We were with him until that final recommendation. The recommendation to invest in his five favorite sectors is puzzling because it includes *no recognition that the market prices of these sectors might already reflect his research or the data and sources upon which he relies.* It goes back to our college football analogy: Dr. Bob is telling you to bet on the top-ranked teams for each game of the upcoming college football season—without waiting to consider the point spread.

Size Doesn't Matter—and Neither Does Style!

If you don't want to invest in particular industries, companies can also be categorized by size. The fund industry now offers us large-, mid-, and small-cap funds focusing on companies with large market capitalizations, mid-sized capitalizations, and small capitalizations.

Another popular way to pick funds is by "style." The notion is that companies with higher potential growth in revenues and profits (so called "growth" companies) will trade differently from those with lower growth (so called "value" stocks). Wall Street uses many different definitions for growth stocks and value stocks. We find them all a bit arbitrary. As seen below, though, growth funds tend to have more volatility and risk than value funds.

For purposes of reporting returns, funds are generally grouped according to both size and style—hence, large-cap growth or small-cap value. You might assume that if, say, large-cap growth funds are underperforming the market, then small-cap value funds must be outperforming the market. You'd be wrong. Have a look.

Volatility of
Size and Style Funds (5-year)

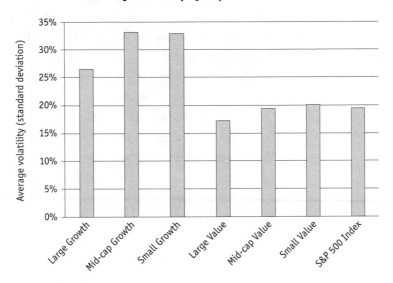

Performance of
Size and Style Funds (5-year)

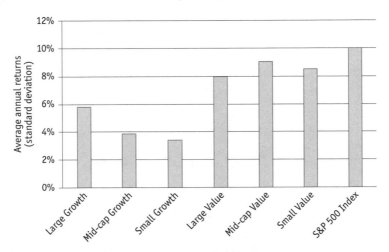

Source: Morningstar Principia Pro, as of September 30, 2001.

Results include all domestic stock funds of the given style, excluding index funds, exchange-traded funds, institutional funds, and multiple classes of the same fund.

As you can see, over five years and ten years *every* major size or style of fund underperformed the S&P 500, generally by significant amounts. All but mid-cap value underperformed the Wilshire 5000 as well.* Here, it's the anti-Wobegon—all the children really are below average. The reason is not difficult to understand. While in any year, growth may be up and value down, over time the performance evens out. The ankle weights of fees and costs, however, are a constant drag.

Looking at risk, the higher relative standard deviations for the funds mean they are *more* risky than the market. None was noticeably lower, so in every case, the risk-adjusted returns fall far short.

From the Horse's Mouth—
the Fund Managers for the Defense

The evidence against active fund management is formidable, but you won't often hear that case taken on directly. Instead, if an industry representative is confronted with the facts, you're more likely to get misdirection. (You're actually not likely to hear any industry representative confronted in the financial media, but you may work up the courage to ask your financial planner or broker a few tough questions.) Be prepared for the following arguments. We heard most of them during our attempts to reform the investing policies of the Pension Benefit Guaranty Corporation.

○ **RED HERRING 1**: "If passive investing is so good, why don't the major pension funds use it?"

The appeal to authority can be a very strong rhetorical device. For that reason, actively managed funds will stress to individual investors that professional money managers—insurance companies, pension funds, foundations—engage in active management.

One easy response to this argument is that the major pension funds

---

* While the mid-cap value funds outperformed the Wilshire 5000, they trailed their own benchmark (the S&P Midcap 400) by 4.3 percentage points over five years and 1.9 percentage points over ten years.

and other institutional investors *are* investing passively, in increasing amounts. They index far more, not less, than individual investors do. Corporations index close to one third of their equity assets. At the state level, almost half of equity pension assets is allocated to index funds. The state of Washington indexes all of its U.S. stock holdings, and California, Connecticut, and New York reportedly index more than 75 percent of their equity holdings.[7]

States that fail to index do so at their peril. Gary's home state of Maryland is in that unfortunate position. Happy with the bull market returns of the 1990s, Maryland continued to allow most of its pension assets to be actively managed. Chaired by a former Merrill Lynch stockbroker, the State Pension Board failed even to ask how its returns compared with those of other plans. The board, and the rest of the state, got a wake-up call when the local papers broke the story in October 2001 that Maryland's pension returns ranked thirty-eighth out of thirty-eight state plans with assets over $1 billion; over five years its U.S. equity investments trailed the market by $1.2 billion.

It's easy to understand why pension boards and other institutional investors might want to stop short of a 100 percent indexing strategy. They are as interested as the next guy in preserving their own jobs and those of their friends. A pure indexing strategy would not only mean firing a bunch of fund managers but also firing the people whose job it is to select and evaluate them. Consider the beauty, then, of indexing a large percentage of the portfolio—locking in close-to-market returns—and then continuing to employ people to select some active fund managers as well. That's what we experienced at the Pension Benefit Guarantee Corporation during our time at Treasury, and it is a preferred option for many state pension boards.

Moreover, institutional investors are no more immune to overconfidence and a desire to outperform than are individual investors. They like the spin of the wheel and the roll of the dice, particularly if enough of the portfolio is indexed so that they are shielded from really poor performance.

You can do better.

○ **RED HERRING 2:** "You're better off in an actively managed fund during bear markets."

The central thrust of the argument is that fund managers will time their cash holdings so that they can buy when the market falls and sell when it bounces back.

The hope that fund managers could time the market—building up cash as the market peaks and using it to buy stock at market lows—turns out to be false. As John Bogle, founder of Vanguard, has observed, since 1974, funds have "consistently tended to hold large amounts of cash at market lows and small amounts at market highs. For example, cash equaled only 4 percent of assets immediately *before* the 1973–74 market crash, but increased to about 12 percent at the ensuing low; at the beginning of the bull market in 1982, equity funds held cash equal to 12 percent of assets. Managers, in short, generally have been bearish when they should have been bullish and bullish when they should have been bearish."[8]

That said, there is a germ of truth to the argument. Actively managed funds always hold more cash than index funds. When the market drops, those cash holdings hold their value. Of course, when markets are moving up, these cash holdings are a significant drag on returns. Not exactly a big advantage for actively managed funds. And if you could predict a bear market, the better strategy would be to pull your money out of the funds and just hold more cash yourself. You don't need to pay someone 1 percent or more of your assets to manage cash.

○ **RED HERRING 3:** "The mutual fund industry is very competitive, with full disclosure of its costs."

Certainly, the mutual fund industry is competitive. There are thousands of funds and hundreds of fund companies. They disclose costs to the considerable extent required by law. That does not mean, however, that the mutual fund industry competes on cost. There are hundreds of casinos in Las Vegas, but that doesn't mean that you'll find one where the odds are in your favor. Casinos compete on glitz, and mutual funds compete on service and hope of outperforming the market. In both cases, cost is an afterthought for the customer.

Here's the acid test. With the exception of index-heavy Vanguard, have you ever seen an advertisement by a fund company that emphasized its expenses? We didn't think so.

○ **RED HERRING 4:** "If everyone invested passively, our capital markets wouldn't work. We need active management to allocate capital to the best companies."

This argument is actually very interesting (if ultimately specious). It is true that efficient capital markets require some investors to distinguish among companies based on their quality. For capitalism to succeed, good companies need to attract capital more easily than bad companies. Indeed, passive investment depends on the presence of active investors to determine a consensus market price for each security.

That said, the idea that an individual investor's decision to index could affect the overall economy is preposterous. First, your assets aren't likely to even be a drop in the multitrillion-dollar equity bucket. (Unless your name is Bill and you live in Redmond, Washington.) Second, even if a majority of mutual funds were indexed, that would still leave trillions that were actively managed, enough to ensure consensus market pricing. Finally, there is a self-correcting mechanism at work here. If index funds ever did come to dominate the market, then the remaining actively managed funds would be able to exploit market inefficiencies more profitably. If actively managed funds began to outperform index funds, money would flow back in that direction.

So don't feel guilty about destroying our American way of life. You won't.

Conclusion

Back in the 1980s, students at the Hurricane Island Outward Bound School concluded their experience by spending four days alone on one of the many deserted coastal islands of Maine. Before venturing out, they received wise advice about whether it was better to forage for food on those often-barren islands or simply to fast. Foraging was a good idea only if the energy gained from the food exceeded the energy expended to find the food. Deer, after all, are sometimes found with bellies full of berries but nonetheless dead of starvation. Therefore, on some more desolate islands, the unlucky solo camper (Greg, for example) might find fasting the most efficient strategy.

While the deer story may have been apocryphal, it leaves an enduring image. It's also one that should ring true to mutual fund investors. In pursuing market-beating returns, investors often exhaust themselves and their money paying money managers and brokers. They don't receive enough in return to make the effort worthwhile.

Chapter 5

The Triumph of Hope over Experience

Faith may be defined briefly as an illogical belief in the occurrence of the improbable.—*H. L. Mencken,* Prejudices

Faced with the grim statistics about the average actively managed mutual fund, many investors will naturally respond, "I'm not going to pick one of those average or below-average funds; I'm going to pick an above-average fund." If only it were that easy.

In general, individual investors will use two methods when trying to pick above-average mutual funds: (1) buying funds whose past performance is good, and (2) buying funds recommended by experts. You'll see that looking at past performance doesn't work as a strategy. Listening to experts doesn't either. We know that's hard to believe. That's why in this chapter we'll explore popular fund-picking strategies.

The Past Performance Trap

The first question most investors ask about any fund is how it performed in the past. Investors assume that strong past performance of a fund is evidence that its managers have stock picking skill and that such skill is likely to persist in the future.

Let's see whether that assumption is valid.

Looking at the Big Picture

Perhaps the most important study of the factors affecting mutual fund performance was conducted by a researcher named Mark Carhart, a former professor at the School of Business at the University of California.[1] The study is important for several reasons. First, it examined mutual funds over a very long period, from 1962 to 1993, through bull markets and bear markets. Second, it looked at a very large number of funds of the type in which we're most interested: 1,892 diversified (nonsector) equity funds. Finally, unique for a study of this size, the study is free of survivorship bias. Finding all the old, dead funds requires a lot of detective work. Carhart did that work.

What did he find? Basically there isn't much hope for those looking to use past performance to predict future performance. The winning funds of the past are unlikely to be the winning funds of the future. Carhart found that if you take the top 10 percent of funds in a given year, by the next year 80 percent of those funds have dropped out of that top 10 percent ranking. For the top 20 percent of funds, 73 percent drop out the next year. For the top 50 percent of funds, roughly 45 percent fall out the next year. That's not much different from what you'd expect from random chance.*

Moreover, some of the small amount of persistence in fund performance was attributable to risk and transaction costs. Higher risk funds tended to have slightly higher returns, as modern portfolio theory would teach us. Funds with lower transaction costs also tended to have higher returns. Those results are not good news for actively man-

---

* Carhart concluded, "Persistence in mutual fund performance does not reflect superior stock-picking skill. Rather, common factors in stock returns and persistent differences in mutual fund expenses and transaction costs explain almost all of the predictability in mutual fund returns. Only the strong, persistent underperformance by the worst-return mutual funds remains anomalous."

aged funds. Investors may not wish to run higher risks and can always get lower costs from an index fund.

Carhart also attributed some persistence to market momentum—that is, the tendency of last year's winning stocks to win again. Further analysis of the data, though, indicated that the funds that benefited from this phenomenon were not consciously following a momentum strategy; that is, they were not displaying stock picking skill. Rather, they simply happened to be holding on to last year's winners. As Carhart explains, "Since the returns on these stocks are above average in the ensuing year, if these funds simply hold their winning stocks, they will enjoy higher one-year expected returns and incur no additional transaction costs for this portfolio. With so many mutual funds, it does not seem unlikely that some funds will be holding many of last year's winning stocks simply by chance."[2]

Still, you might ask, "If funds that *accidentally* end up holding last year's winners outperform the ensuing year, why not invest in them anyway?" Carhart tested to see if such a strategy would work. In fact, any increased returns from such a strategy are offset by—we hope you guessed it—the transaction costs of implementing the strategy. In addition, any persistence he found was very shortlived. Other studies have reached similar conclusions.[3]

There is another reason to avoid a momentum strategy: it requires you to forsake diversification. Hot funds tend to come from the same sectors. Thus, buying them will likely produce a nondiversified, very risky portfolio.

A follow-up study by economist Russ Wermers attempted to gain further insights into the stock picking skills of fund managers. Starting with Carhart's fund database, he then examined the performance of the individual stocks held by the funds in addition to the performance of the funds themselves.[4] Thus, he was better able to focus on how much of a fund's persistence was attributable to stock picking skill, as opposed to other factors. The results of Wermers's study provide no comfort to investors in actively managed mutual funds. He found that the average mutual fund net return trailed the market by 1 percent per year. Risk adjusted returns were 1.6 percent worse.

Wermers's study does include some solace for fund managers. He found evidence of modest stock picking skill that the Carhart study had not. In particular, he found that the underlying stocks held by mutual funds outperformed the broad market when risk adjusted by 0.7 percent per year.[5] The problem, however, is that 0.7 percent of stock picking skill is woefully inadequate in the face of mutual fund costs.

What About "Hot" Funds?

We already took a brief look at the "hot" fund phenomenon. But the popularity of these lists, and their importance to the industry, is so great—even *Consumer Reports* is ranking mutual funds, for Pete's sake—that we believe a closer look is in order. "Hot" status says everything about the risk of a fund and its place in a hot sector. It says little about the skill of its manager or its *long-term* prospects.

Consider *Money* magazine's annual Mutual Fund Guide, where you can find the fifty top-performing funds for the preceding year. We looked at the lists for the years 2000, 1999, and 1998. Of the fifty top-performing funds in 2000, *not a single one appeared on the list in either 1999 or 1998.* There were seven mutual funds that appeared on the list in both 1998 and 1999, all in the Internet area, which had remained hot for two years. Heaven help you if you thought this was a sustainable trend. Here is the performance of those seven funds in 2000 and 2001.

Fund	*2000*	*2001*
ProFunds UltraOTC Investments	-76.3%	-69.1%
Munder NetNet A	-54.2%	-48.2%
Morgan Stanley Dean Witter Information B	-25.2%	-44.7%
Hancock Global Technology A	-37.2%	-43.1%
Northern Technology	-38.4%	-34.5%
Pimco Innovation C	-29.4%	-45.5%
Fidelity Select Technology	-32.5%	-31.7%

Source: Morningstar Principia Pro, data through December 31, 2001.

Talk about past performance not being an indicator of future results! What single factor best explains why some funds (and fund companies) end up on the list? It's the sector or style of the fund. In 2001, thirty-one of the top fifty were small company funds. Of the fifty best performing funds of 2000, half were in two business sectors, health care (20) and real estate (5). The same was true in 1999, where a majority were technology or Japan funds. In 1998, it was technology or communications.

This result is extremely significant. Investors looking at the top fifty might infer that these were the best managed funds over the past year—that their managers, at least for one year, had the magic touch. In fact, that's not the case. Yearly results reflect what economic sector outperformed the rest of the market that year. Almost any fund devoted to that sector is going to score well, regardless of the talents of its fund manager. Conversely, even the most brilliant fund manager cannot hope to crack the top fifty if he or she is in a "cold" sector. In the late 1990s, you never saw an energy, financial services, retailing, or aerospace fund ranked among *Money*'s winners. Did the fund managers in those sectors have lobotomies at the beginning of the year? No, they were just following the wrong sector.

The financial media and the fund industry are of two minds on this subject. They tout the winners of the top fifty, directly or indirectly suggesting that you should invest your money with them for the future. Yet the media and even the industry would *never* suggest that investors concentrate all of their assets in a single sector. In fact, they consistently (and responsibly) warn investors against doing so. But by buying multiple sectors, investors are effectively eliminating any hope for the top-fifty–type returns they seek. A diversified portfolio, while better in the long term, will never earn those types of short-term returns, because it will necessarily include cold sectors as well as hot sectors.

More Reasons to Distrust Hot Funds

There are other reasons you should be skeptical of hot funds. Mutual funds understand the rules of chance, and are not shy about using them to their advantage. And when chance doesn't yield good enough results, well, they may help it out a little. Welcome to the world of "incubator"

funds, and two strategies for generating the type of eye-popping performance that attracts fund investors: portfolio prospecting and selective attention.

Portfolio prospecting employs statistical chance to create the illusion
of stock picking prowess. Think of it as survivorship bias in action. A
fund company will start several small incubator funds and run them for
a year or two. These funds may start with only a few hundred thousand
dollars in assets. They are not widely held, and you will not see much
about them in the financial media. There's a reason for that: the fund
family is waiting to see how things turn out before deciding which fund
to promote.

When one of the funds outperforms the market, the fund company
markets the fund and its extraordinary performance aggressively. Those
funds that underperform the market are liquidated and disappear from
notice (and industry averages). The fund company suffers no embar-
rassment.

Portfolio prospectors tend to focus on aggressive growth funds.[6] Doing so raises the chances of achieving extraordinary returns through a
few fortunate picks. It's all a matter of probabilities.

With selective attention, a little less is left to chance. Fund companies can take active steps to boost the performance of their new funds.
A large fund family, for example, may allow its small funds to trade
ahead of its large funds, benefiting from the boost in price that a large
sister fund's purchase provides. A greater boost, however, can come
when the fund family steers its allocation of initial public offerings
(IPOs) to incubator funds.

Generally, in an IPO, the offering price is set at a discount to its expected trading price, which helps ensure interest in the offering. A discounted price means that those who are allowed to buy those shares at
the outset will generally end up with a quick, low-risk profit. This may
be a friend of the company going public, the investment bank under-
writing those shares, or those on whom the investment bank bestows
shares at the IPO price.

Mutual fund families are among investment banks' largest clients, so
they get their share of hot IPOs. The fund families, in turn, get to
choose which of their funds will be winners. Just given the arithmetic,
small funds can get more of a boost from such attention than the fund

companies' larger, more established funds. A little bit of juice shared with a very small fund can go a long way.

As far back as 1996, *Money* magazine noted that sixteen of that year's top-twenty performing portfolios were less than a year old.[7] In the year 2000, five of the top-ten domestic equity funds and seven of the top-twenty funds were less than a year old. None of the top ten were more than three years old. None of those top-ten funds had more than $100 million in assets, meaning that none was among the fifteen hundred largest funds.

The *Money* article explored why new funds were outperforming more established funds. When asked about the phenomenon, Michael Lipper of Lipper Analytical Services was quoted as saying, "Oh, you mean the IPO phenomenon." A remarkably candid representative from Twentieth Century funds was quoted as saying, "If there's an interesting IPO, maybe we can get 50,000 shares total. If it's a $20 stock, that's $1 million. In a $15 billion fund, $1 million is too small to make an impact, but in a new fund it could make a big difference. So we would allocate the IPO shares where they would make the biggest difference, given the charters of the funds."

If you are like most people learning about this phenomenon for the first time, you are probably wondering, "Isn't this unfair and deceptive? Isn't the SEC supposed to protect investors from this sort of behavior?" The answer is "Yes, and no."

The SEC does take action from time to time. In 1996, the Van Kampen Growth Fund posted a 62 percent gain. That performance had all the signs of selective attention. It had extremely high returns and the fund was new and very small (listed as only $200,000 to $380,000 in assets). Although more than half the gain was attributable to thirty-one IPOs, the fund's semiannual report and marketing materials failed to disclose the role of the IPOs, and Van Kampen officials told the media that the IPOs had not played a significant role. Predictably, the fund underperformed in the years following its debut returns. The SEC fined the fund and its chief investment officer for failure to disclose the role that IPOs had played.

Investors should take little comfort, however, from this case. But for the public misstatements, it might never have been brought. Companies remain free to use incubator funds and even IPOs to stimulate first year returns. (One thing holding them back of late has been the dearth of new IPOs.)

For an individual investor, the lesson is clear: regard new funds with extraordinarily good performance with skepticism, not enthusiasm.

What About Proven Funds?

Confronted with the poor record of the mutual fund industry as a group, many folks with whom we've spoken respond, "But I stick with the proven funds." So, does it work?

In his *Random Walk Down Wall Street*, Burton Malkiel took the top-twenty best performing equity mutual funds of 1978–87 and tracked them for the next ten years. His results showed that while those funds had beaten the S&P 500 by 5.8 percentage points a year, during the ten years they grew to fame, they trailed by 0.8 percentage points. We can look at those funds to see how they have performed for the ten years through 2001. In other words, if you'd read a profile ten years ago of the twenty very best mutual funds for most of the 1980s, and decided to buy them, how would you have done?

Fund	*10-year load-adjusted*
Fidelity Magellan	12.6%
Federated Capital Appreciation A	14.4%
AIM Weingarten A	5.9%
Van Kampen American Capital Pace A	8.4%
Alliance Quasar A	7.7%
AIM Constellation A	10.4%
Spectra	16.1%
IDS New Dimensions A	11.6%
Smith Barney Appreciation A	11.0%
Growth Fund of America	14.8%
MFS Growth Opportunities A	10.1%
Mutual Fund Shares Z	15.5%
American Capital (Exchange)	14.1%
Janus Fund	11.1%
Stein Roe Special	Closed

Fund	10-year load-adjusted
Van Kampen American Capital Comstock A	13.8%
AIM Charter A	8.5%
Van Kampen American Capital Enterprise A	9.7%
Fidelity Congress Street	11.9%
Van Kampen American Capital Emerg Growth A	15.0%
Average	*11.7%*
Vanguard 500 Index Fund	12.9%

Source: Morningstar Principia Pro, data through December 31, 2001.[8]

Here it is in a nutshell: if you'd bought and held a portfolio of the twenty best diversified mutual funds ten years ago, you would have trailed an S&P 500 Index Fund by 1.2 percentage points *per year.* The index fund outperformed twelve of the twenty funds for the period.

Moreover, results for the actively managed funds are inflated by one instance of survivorship bias. Because the Stein Roe Special Fund had ranked in the bottom 10 percent of all funds over the three years ending June 1999, its manager was dismissed, the style of the fund was changed, and the fund was renamed the Disciplined Stock Fund. Within a year, Liberty Funds acquired Stein Roe and merged the Disciplined Stock Fund out of existence. Thus, we can't report results for this fund.

A Closer Look at Two Favorites

Let's take a closer look at what are probably the two most famous of the big funds: Fidelity Magellan and the Janus Fund.

Fund Name	Net Assets $BB	Average Annual Return (5-Year)	Average Annual Return (10-Year)	Standard Deviation (10-Year)	Tax Efficiency (10-Year)
Fidelity Magellan	80	10.3%	12.6%	16.9%	80%
Janus	26	9.5%	11.1%	20.2%	80%
Vanguard 500 Index	73	10.7%	12.8%	15.8%	93%

Source: Morningstar Principia Pro, data through September 30, 2001.

Here's the bottom line: *if you'd bought Fidelity Magellan and Janus ten years ago, you would be worse off than if you'd simply bought an S&P 500 index fund.* The gap grows considerably if you consider risk, as measured by the standard deviation of each fund. Put another way, an investor wishing to run no more risk than that presented by the Vanguard 500 index fund would have to offset Magellan or Janus with some cash or bonds and that lower-risk asset would bring down total returns.

For investors with taxable accounts, it's really game, set, and match for indexing. Vanguard's tax efficiency—Morningstar's measure of how much total return is left after taxes—is about 15 percentage points higher than that of Magellan and Janus. In other words, you would have kept considerably more of your Vanguard earnings after tax than those from the other funds.

Is Bigger Better?

Another possible approach to choosing an above-average fund would simply be to buy the largest funds. There is some logic to this approach, as there are economies of scale in the fund industry. So, we identified the ten largest funds in 1991, and tracked them to see how they did over the following ten years.[9]

While we've certainly seen worse strategies, this one is not a winner. As a group, the ten largest funds trailed the S&P 500 by 0.6 percentage points per year over the next ten years, before considering taxes. None of the funds beat or trailed the index by a whole lot: the best (American Funds Growth Fund of America) led the index by only 1.3 percentage points per year; the worst (Pioneer Value) trailed by only 3.5 percentage points per year.

These results are not surprising, however, given how large funds are run. *Funds get to be big because they were once successful. They do not get to be successful because they are big. Once a fund gets big, beating the market becomes much harder.* First, the person at the fund who is responsible for the success often retires, moves onto another company, or opens a hedge fund, where the pay is better. Second, successful funds inevitably grow larger, as investors flock to them. The influx of assets forces the fund to choose between closing to new investors (as both Magellan and Janus have done) or changing how they invest.

Why? Funds with growing asset bases must choose between continuing to hold the same number of stocks in increasing amounts or buying a larger number of stocks. Each option has drawbacks for funds attempting to beat the market. To the extent the fund holds a significant percentage of a company's stock, it faces liquidity problems in buying or selling the stock. As we'll see in Chapter 6, selling a large block of stock will push the price down. This will lower returns. On the other hand, to the extent that a fund chooses to hold many stocks in smaller amounts, it is less likely to earn superior returns through a few inspired (or lucky) choices.

Another factor actually prompts large fund managers to track their benchmark index closely. With all the assets they need, managers at the largest funds are more concerned than those at smaller funds with retaining assets than with taking large risks to generate inflows. Our earlier chart on fund manager incentives doesn't apply here.

The phenomenon is known in the United States as "closet indexing." In the United Kingdom it's more vividly called "index hugging." Using Morningstar Principia Pro database, we looked at the monthly correlations between each of the ten largest actively managed stock funds and the overall market, as represented by the Wilshire 5000, over a five-year period. A correlation of 100 percent would mean that their performance was identical (up the same amount on the same day); a correlation of -100 percent would mean that their performance was diametrically opposite (always down when the other was up). Any correlation above 70 percent is considered high.

Correlation of largest actively managed stock funds with market

Fund	Correlation to Wilshire 5000
Fidelity Magellan	98%
Amer Funds Investment Co. of America	94%
Amer Funds Washington Mutual	71%
Amer Funds Growth	93%
Fidelity Growth & Income	94%

Correlation of largest actively managed stock funds with market

Fund	Correlation to Wilshire 5000
Fidelity Contrafund	91%
American Century Ultra Inv	95%
Janus	93%
Fidelity Growth Company	79%
Vanguard Windsor II	70%

Source: Morningstar Principia Pro, as of December 31, 2001.

What you see is more hugging than at a family reunion. The folks at Magellan are the most affectionate, with a 98 percent correlation with the broad market. The Investment Company of America and Janus are emoting as well. There are three funds—American Funds Washington Mutual Fund, Fidelity Growth Company, and Vanguard Windsor II— that look a little more standoffish, but they're just hugging a more distant relative. The Washington Mutual and Windsor II funds are large-cap value funds. When their results are compared to the general benchmark for such funds—the Russell 1000 Value Index—the correlations come out 96 percent, and 94 percent, respectively. Similarly, Fidelity Growth Company has a 96% correlation with the S&P 500. So, if you want the returns of these funds without the fees and turnover, just buy a large-cap value index or exchange-traded fund.

As high as the market correlation of each of these funds is, it rises still higher if you own more than one such fund. At that point, you have further diversified your underlying portfolio to the point where you are really holding a high-priced index fund.

Indeed, one recent study concludes that this phenomenon is rampant in the pension fund industry.[10] The average pension fund employs nine active equity managers, generally with complementary styles (a growth manager, a value manager, and so on). Because the styles are complementary, the result of this strategy—known as the multispecialist model—can result in one big high-cost index fund. The study showed that large pension funds using the multispecialist model trailed their benchmarks by 1.2 to 1.3 percent annually, an amount equal to their costs.

Let's Split the Difference—Funds with Great Five-Year Records

If funds with great one-year records are too risky and funds with good ten- to fifteen-year records have grown too large, how about splitting the difference and choosing funds with the very best five-year records? Researchers at Micropal (now a subsidiary of Standard & Poor's) looked at this strategy.* Starting in 1970, for each five-year interval, they tracked how well you would have done by buying the top thirty funds and holding them until 1998. The results ignore transaction costs and loads but, hey, it really doesn't matter.

Period	Initial 5-year performance	Initial 5-year S&P 500 performance	Initial funds v. S&P 500	Fund performance from end of period thru 1998	S&P 500 performance from end of period thru 1998	Subsequent funds v. S&P 500
1970–74	0.8%	-2.4%	3.2%	16.1%	17.0%	-0.9%
1975–79	35.7%	14.8%	20.9%	15.8%	17.7%	-1.9%
1980–84	22.5%	14.8%	7.7%	16.0%	18.8%	-2.8%
1985–89	22.1%	20.4%	1.7%	16.2%	17.8%	-1.6%
1990–94	18.9%	8.7%	10.2%	21.3%	32.2%	-10.9%

During the five-year period that qualified them as a top-thirty fund, we see the funds trouncing the S&P 500, beating the index by an average of 8.7 percentage points per year. Since then, however, each group of top funds trails the S&P 500 by 3.6 percentage points on average. So, do you think that initial top-thirty performance was more the product of persistent stock picking ability or random chance?

* We first learned of the MicroPal study on the website of William Bernstein, who produces an on-line publication called *Efficient Frontier.* We subsequently contacted the research department of Standard & Poor's to obtain a copy of the original study. Unfortunately, despite the helpful efforts of the S&P staff, they were unable to locate an original. So, take the information with that caveat.

Asking the Experts

So if you can't rely on past performance when selecting a mutual fund, why not turn to the experts? They get paid the big bucks, so they must know something we don't, right? Let's see how the experts do when selecting funds.

Morningstar's Five-Star Funds

Morningstar ratings are wildly popular with investors and the media. They come from a respected source of mutual fund information and have an outward simplicity. Morningstar rates mutual funds according to its "star" system. The star system is a computer-generated rating based on a fund's risk-adjusted return over the past ten, five, and three years. Five-star funds are the best, and one-star funds are the worst.*

These ratings have great influence, as highly rated funds routinely use their Morningstar stars prominently in their advertising. The financial media uses them as a quick shorthand to describe funds and their managers. Gary's twin brother Rob, for instance, is a "five-star" manager.

We must confess to having a soft spot for Morningstar. Their database on mutual fund performance has been enormously helpful in writing this book. Since Morningstar has all the data, you might have assumed they are more likely than anyone to pick winning mutual funds. The history, however, suggests otherwise.

- Of those funds receiving a four-star or five-star ranking in one year, between 40 to 60 percent of those funds had fallen to a three-star ranking or below by the next year.
- Tracked as a group over a seven-year period, Morningstar's top-ranked no-load equity funds—the cream of the crop—lagged the market by an average of almost 3 percentage points a year.

---

* The top 10 percent of funds get five stars, the next 22.5 percent get four stars, the middle 35 percent get three stars, the next 22.5 percent get two stars, and the bottom 10 percent get one star.

- The performance of Morningstar's five-star funds is indistinguishable from its four-star funds, and even its three-star funds. That is, any differences are statistically insignificant.
- Morningstar's stinkers—the one-star and two-star funds—do underperform persistently. Thus, Morningstar's system could serve investors as a warning sign for funds to avoid. Unfortunately, however, *75 percent of no-load funds receive a three-star ranking or above.* Furthermore, many of the one-star stinkers are simply those charging appallingly high loads, something investors can determine pretty rapidly themselves.[11]

Morningstar itself has recognized this problem. It cautions investors against using their ratings as buy recommendations. They liken their star ratings to an achievement test, rather than an aptitude test. They say that the ratings, which tell you who delivered good performance in the past, are not prologue to the future. Indeed, a recent study looked at the persistence of the Morningstar ratings from 1997 to 1999 and found that fund grades can shift considerably even over relatively short time periods.

The news gets a little worse. In an analysis of the quality of Morningstar's model for assigning stars (as opposed to its performance), Nobel laureate William Sharpe found it particularly inappropriate for selecting a portfolio of funds. So, if you are going to buy more than one fund, the star system is particularly likely to lead you astray.[12]

There is another interesting downside to investor reliance on the Morningstar star system, which we learned about in a column by Jean Sherman Chatzky. It results in investors thinking even less about how they invest. E*Trade's experience in allowing its customers to see the Morningstar star system on their website illustrates this point. When E*Trade was putting together the portion of its website dedicated to mutual funds, it included a state-of-the-art database with plentiful information on funds. That database included the Morningstar rankings and numerous search engines allowing customers to investigate the past performance, holdings, and risk of each fund. What E*Trade found, however, was that the average investor was spending less than a minute investigating funds and was looking only at the Morningstar rankings. Frustrated that all its research was going to waste, E*Trade took the surprising step of pulling the rankings from its website. The result? The number of investors reading fund prospectuses went from 5 to 50 percent. Average research time went from thirty seconds to five minutes. As a result of this research, E*Trade's sales of load funds fell from 60 percent of all sales to 5 percent.[13]

Funds on the *Forbes* Honor Roll

One of the longest-lived and best-regarded guides to mutual funds is the *Forbes* Honor Roll. *Forbes* has one of the largest circulations of any financial magazine and dedicates considerable resources to its annual review of mutual funds. *Forbes* puts mutual funds to five tests: capital preservation, continuity of management, diversification, accessibility, and long-term performance. Many investors rely on the judgments they read in *Forbes*.

According to research performed by John Bogle at Vanguard, the *Forbes* Honor Roll over the period 1973 to 1990 underperformed the market by 0.27 percent per year, *before* considering the sales loads charged by the funds.

Forbes itself analyzed the performance of its inaugural Honor Roll funds, from August 1973 to 1998.[14] *Forbes* concluded that an investment of $10,000 in the Honor Roll, updated each year to reflect the new list, would have been worth $2.1 million.[15] This represented a compound annual return of 13.6 percent through June 30, 1998. That 13.6 percent, however, fell short of the 14.3 percent earned by the S&P 500 over the same period. The *Forbes* calculation did not include sales loads, which would have dragged down performance even more.

We decided to take a look at the *Forbes* Honor Roll where they left off, beginning in 1998, and this time comparing performance to a real-live index fund.[16] The results? Well, the song remains the same.

Forbes Honor Roll performance 1998–2001

Index	Initial 8/98	Thru 8/99	Thru 8/00	Thru 8/01
Vanguard Total Stock Index Fund	$120,000	$148,385	$166,061	$129,152
Forbes Honor Roll	$120,000	$132,991	$140,998	$121,816

That's a loss of over $7,000 in three years. So much for the *Forbes* Honor Roll as a market-beating strategy.

Value Line's Recommended Funds

Value Line is a company well known for its investment advisory services, which we'll discuss further in Chapter 9. As with Morningstar, you might have assumed that Value Line would have some insights into which mutual funds were picking the right stocks and were poised for superior performance.

Since 1993, Value Line has offered a Mutual Fund Survey providing mutual fund performance data and recommendations. According to Hulbert's Financial Digest, over the five-year period 1997–2001, the Value Line General Equity portfolio returned an average annualized 3.6 percent. Not so good versus the market (13.1 percent for the Wilshire 5000). From its inception in 1993, the portfolio's returns were about half the market. Value Line also recommends four other model portfolios in each survey—International Equity, Partial Equity, Special Equity, and Taxable Income. The best of the bunch earned only 6.5 percent annually from 1997 to 2001.

By the way, when we last checked, Value Line was charging $345 per year for its survey. So, if you're investing $10,000 per year in mutual funds, consider that a 3.45 percent front-end load.

What About Warren Buffett?

As we described this book to friends and acquaintances, a frequently asked question was, "What about Warren Buffett? Doesn't he always beat the market? Doesn't that prove that active management can work?" Here are three answers to that question:

1. Warren Buffett is not a mutual fund manager.
2. Berkshire Hathaway is not a mutual fund.
3. Warren Buffett doesn't always beat the market.

Warren Buffett has made a phenomenal amount of money for investors in Berkshire Hathaway. Then again, Bill Gates has made a phenomenal amount of money for investors in Microsoft. Yet many people take Warren Buffett's success as evidence that active money management and stock pickers can beat the market. They take Bill Gates's success as evidence that a really smart software developer can make investors a lot of money. The question, of course, is whether Warren Buffett's success is more attributable to *stock picking* skills or *business* skills. No one has ever doubted that a good business leader can succeed where others fail. We think that's the proper way to view Warren Buffett.

What is Berkshire Hathaway? Berkshire Hathaway owns two very large insurance companies, GEICO and General Re. It does not own a small percentage of the shares in those companies, as a mutual fund company might. It owns them completely, and manages them. It has 117,000 employees. Whereas a mutual fund cannot invest more than 5 percent of its assets in any one company, these and other companies make up for more than 5 percent of Berkshire Hathaway's total assets. Thus, at the outset, if asked whether Berkshire Hathaway is closer to a successful mutual fund or a successful insurance company, we would have to say the latter.

Warren Buffett recognized what a great opportunity owning an insurance company can present. Insurance companies take in money in the form of premiums and invest the reserves in financial assets. The essence of Berkshire Hathaway is in managing, or assisting in the management of, the companies it owns, controls, or partially controls. The best analogy to Berkshire Hathaway is a merchant bank with a very low cost of funds, courtesy of its insurance company policies. When Salomon Brothers was in need of money, Berkshire Hathaway did not buy some of its publicly traded stock, as a mutual fund might. It bought a significant, controlling stake in the company, helped manage it back to respectability, and then resold it for a profit. When Coca-Cola appeared to be foundering under then-CEO Douglas Ivester, Berkshire Hathaway (as one of its largest shareholders) did not simply vote its shares. Rather, board member Buffett summoned Ivester to a secret meeting and told him it was time to go.

Berkshire Hathaway has another weapon in its arsenal that a mutual fund does not. Mutual funds are restricted in their ability to borrow money and generally use no leverage at all. Berkshire Hathaway, on the other hand, borrows in the capital markets and from its policyholders to invest in the markets or to make an acquisition.

In other words, the success of Berkshire Hathaway is no more proof of stock picking ability than the success of Merrill Lynch, General Electric, or any other well-run financial company in America.

Like those other companies, there are times when Berkshire Hathaway does not outperform the market. While the stock has outperformed the market over time, its 1999 performance trailed the market by over 40 percent. Berkshire Hathaway got off to a rough start in 2002, reporting a 76 percent drop in annual profits. Insurance claims from 9/11 hit its General Re subsidiary hard, resulting in an annual operating loss for the parent company. In his annual letter to shareholders, Buffett said that Berkshire Hathaway "won't come close to replicating our past record," noting how difficult it is for a company of Berkshire's sheer size to find a sufficient number of good acquisitions to boost returns. Consider Berkshire Hathaway a very successful growth stock.

Conclusion

Well, this has been cheery, hasn't it? We hope we've convinced you of the poor performance of average mutual funds and sapped you of any hope of picking an above-average one. Sorry. Unfortunately, the news isn't going to get much better in the next chapter, "The Ankle Weights on Running an Actively Managed Fund." (You probably guessed from the name.) But if you can hold on until Part IV, good news is just around the corner.

Chapter 6

The Ankle Weights on Running an Actively Managed Fund

How come it's a penny for your thoughts, but you have to
put your two cents' worth in? Somebody's making a
penny.—*Steven Wright*

Mutual fund managers are considered the olympians of investing, well-conditioned market analysts with access to all the
best research. Yet we've seen that they seem to lose just about
every race. Now we'll see why: they're running with ankle weights that
would have brought Carl Lewis and Bruce Jenner to their knees. You
may have been surprised at the grim performance we saw in chapter 4,
but by the time we're finished here, you will understand why it was only
to be expected.

Ask most people about their actively managed stock funds and they
may have some vague notion that the fund charges an annual management fee. That fee is a bigger drag on returns than most investors realize. Yet it is only the beginning of the costs that you pay by having a
mutual fund manager do your investing for you.

Some of these costs are disclosed to investors:

- Monthly management, administrative, and distribution fees averaging over 1 percent per year.
- Sales loads, which are commissions charged by over half of all ac-

tively managed mutual funds when you buy or sell shares. When you do pay, the average load is 4.1 percent.[1] With an average holding period of only three years, the average load fund investor is paying an additional 1.4 percent per year.

While investors may not pay particular attention to these costs, they are at least disclosed at the outset of the relationship. There are also very important costs that go undisclosed:

- Trading costs—the approximately 0.5–1 percent of assets that an actively managed fund pays out in brokerage costs and bid/ask spreads each year.[2]
- The opportunity cost of holding idle cash, about 0.5 percent of assets each year during the 1990s bull market, though perhaps less now.
- Excess capital gains taxes incurred as the portfolio is turned over each year. While difficult to estimate, they probably cost active fund investors 1 to 2 percent of assets per year for taxable accounts.

Many investors might not ever think of these last three as "costs" to them. They're hard to measure. They don't show up on any statement. After all, the fund pays the trading costs. Nobody "pays" an opportunity cost, and it's hard to measure exactly how much a fund costs you in capital gains taxes. Yet all these costs stand between you and the market-beating performance you crave.

Disclosed Costs

Paying the Piper

Mutual fund companies make most of their money by charging management fees. These fees can come with different names:

- *Management fees* are paid to cover the advice the mutual fund company is providing.
- *Administrative fees* go to cover the customer service, record keeping, and other back office costs of running a mutual fund.

- *Distribution* or *12(b)-1 fees* cover the costs of marketing and distributing the fund. They are named after the SEC rule regulating them.

From your point of view, though, there's very little reason to make any distinctions. The fund companies use each type of fee to make a profit, and all of them are being deducted from your account each month. We'll just look at the total, which is called the expense ratio.

A review of the 2,216 actively managed stock funds in the Morningstar database shows an average expense ratio of 1.33 percent. This figure assumes that all holders of multiclass funds choose the A shares, which generally have the lowest expense ratio. Look at all classes and the average rises to 1.61 percent.[3] The SEC arrives at a similar figure of 0.9 to 1.4 percent.[4] The industry does not dispute these numbers. In congressional testimony in 1998, the Investment Company Institute (ICI), the trade group for the mutual fund industry, said that the simple average of fees equals approximately 1.52 percent.[5]

So, if you invest in an *actively managed* equity mutual fund, you will probably pay an average annual management fee somewhere around 1.3 to 1.6 percent of the value of your investment. You pay it whether that investment makes money, loses money, or stays the same. In Vegas, whether you win or lose, at least you get free drinks and a great hotel room and the adrenaline rush that comes with the turn of the wheel. Invest with a money manager, however, and *he's* guaranteed free drinks, a big house, and the adrenaline rush that comes with investing *your* money.

Paying Some Guy Who Introduces You to the Piper

In addition to annual management fees, about half of all mutual funds also charge a sales commission. You generally will pay these any time you purchase a fund through a broker, planner, or other intermediary. These commissions are called front-end loads (if paid at purchase) and back-end or deferred loads (if paid at sale). For stock funds charging loads, the average load (front-end plus back-end) is 4.1%.[6] Investors pay about $20 billion in loads per year.[7]

There is absolutely no reason to pay these loads. They are not like brokerage commissions, which are necessary to execute a trade on an exchange. Your mutual fund is charging you to issue you its *own* shares. Loads don't even help to offset other costs. Expense ratios for such load funds are also high, with an average of 1.75 percent. And as a group load funds actually earn lower average returns than no-load funds, *even without taking the load into account.*[8]

So, why are so many investors paying loads? The mutual fund industry increasingly relies on others—brokers, insurance companies, and financial advisers—to sell its products. This trend accelerated when Schwab offered a mutual fund "supermarket." Full-service brokerage firms then began letting their sales forces offer competing funds in addition to their in-house funds. While initially hesitant to promote a competitor's products, the brokers later developed sharing agreements whereby they would get paid for every new sale they made. Most mutual fund families feel they have to pay, lest they lose access to new assets and market share.

Of course, the mutual fund companies don't eat the cost of paying their new sales force. They pass that cost along to you, either through a 12(b)-1 fee or a sales load. Since SEC rules require that 12(b)-1 fees be included in the publicly disclosed annual expense ratio, the fund companies prefer to use sales loads.

The fund industry's rented sales force is working hard. According to the Investment Company Institute, 62 percent of new sales of funds were direct sales to retail investors in 1990. This number had fallen to 38 percent by the end of 2000, as the majority are now sold through intermediaries. More than 1,600 equity funds now charge a front-end load and an additional 1,900 charge a back-end load. (A few even have the gumption to charge both, getting you both coming and going.)

The industry has apparently concluded that investors are more willing to pay needless loads if they have some choice about which load to pay. (Maybe those who can choose their poison are more likely to ingest it.) If you've been looking over mutual funds recently, you'll notice that a lot of them come in different "classes." Each class of a given fund holds exactly the same stocks and bonds. The only difference among classes is the fee structure.

Generally speaking, Class "A" shares carry a heavy front-end load and the lowest annual fee. They are marketed to investors making large purchases. Class "B" shares carry a heavy back-end load that diminishes and eventually disappears if you hold the shares a few years. These shares are marketed to those making smaller purchases and anticipating a long holding period. Class "C" shares carry the highest annual fee but a reduced load. Class C shares are marketed to investors anticipating a short holding period, where heavy sales loads would eat up returns.

The hope of the fund companies and brokers is that you will forget that there are plenty of fund companies like Vanguard and T. Rowe Price that charge no loads *and* lower fees.

The tactic appears to be succeeding all too well, however. Half of all stock funds carry loads. Investors are paying the fees, and intermediaries are selling funds at greater rates than ever before. The financial media have even begun to advise investors on whether "A" shares, "B" shares, or "C" shares make best sense for them. The implicit suggestion is that at least one of these classes makes sense. In fact, paying anyone a fee to sell you a mutual fund makes no sense.

Undisclosed Costs

Trading Costs

In the year 2000, stock mutual funds sold $3.3 trillion in securities and bought $3.5 trillion in securities. Every purchase and every sale cost those funds' shareholders money. We believe that the average actively managed mutual fund loses between 0.5 percent and 1.0 percent of your assets to trading costs annually.

A fund wishing to minimize these transaction costs would trade infrequently. Very few do. Actively managed stock funds turned over about 80 percent of their holdings in 2001.[9] The SEC requires no disclosures of the costs of trading the portfolio. Absent a requirement to report, the funds are simply silent on trading costs in their reports to you. That's bizarre when you think about it. Imagine a regular corporation failing to report its largest controllable costs in its annual or quarterly reports.

Transaction costs come in several forms.

Brokerage commissions are flat fees charged by brokers executing trades on behalf of funds. Commissions for institutional investors are lower than those charged to individuals, but still average about 4 to 5 cents per share.[10]

Bid/ask spreads are the difference in price charged by market makers to buyers and sellers executing trades. Literally, the bid/ask spread is the difference between the price that a market maker *bids* for the stock (that is, offers to pay sellers) and the higher price a market maker *asks* for the stock (offers to charge buyers). The spread compensates the market maker for risk and also includes a profit margin.

Studies show that a good estimate of a bid/ask spread is 1 to 2 percent. In other words, if your fund sells a stock and buys it back immediately, before there has been any change in price, you'll lose 1–2 percent of the value.[11]

Market effects arise from the liquidity constraints on large trades. When a fund owns a substantial block of stock, it cannot sell that position without affecting the price. A large block of stock represents excess supply that tends to drive the price down. Conversely, large purchases tend to push up the price paid for the last blocks of stock. While funds may attempt to camouflage block trades by breaking them into smaller trades, the market tends to notice.

Imagine that your mutual fund asks for a quote on Acme, Inc. stock and sees it listed at $50 bid/$50.50 ask. If the fund wishes to sell 1,000 shares, it can be pretty confident of getting $50 per share for them. But if, as is often the case, the fund wishes to sell 100,000 shares, then there is a very good chance that it will receive less than $50 per share. The largest fund families like Fidelity, American Funds, and Putnam frequently hold blocks of 1 million or even 10 million shares of a company. When their managers decide they want to sell a position, they often sell it all. That leaves their traders fighting the hard law of supply and demand.

This phenomenon, known as the market effect of trading, is a significant cost of doing business for mutual funds. Estimates are that the market impact of trading can be as much as $0.09 per share or 0.4 percent per year—representing nearly twice the cost of commissions.[12] The costs are probably even greater for small-cap funds, where the market effect of a large order is greater.[13]

Idle Cash

Another cost of fund management is an opportunity cost: the lost return on non-stock holdings—cash and bonds. All funds hold cash in order to fund shareholder redemptions. According to the Investment Company Institute, annual redemptions plus redemption exchanges averaged about 33 percent over the past five years.[14] If daily inflows from new investors do not equal or exceed redemptions, the fund would have to sell assets, thereby disrupting their strategy and incurring even more trading costs. They hold cash instead.

The percentage of a fund's assets held in cash (and cash equivalents) is known as its "liquidity ratio." The average liquidity ratio for actively managed equity funds was 6 percent at the beginning of 2002, low by historical standards.[15] Over the past thirty years, the average has been closer to 10 percent.

The effect of cash holdings on returns depends on the performance of the stock market. Obviously, holding a lot of cash just before the 1929 or 1987 crashes would have boosted returns. The same was true in 2000, when the market fell about 10 percent. Over the long term, though, equities have outperformed cash. Over the fifteen years through 2001, the Wilshire 5000 returned 13.0 percent. Over the same period, the average one-month Treasury bill rate—a good proxy for the average rate of return on cash holdings at mutual funds—was 5.5 percent. Thus, the average annual loss to a fund was the difference in rates (7.5 percent) times the percentage of the fund held in cash. Thus, each year, the average mutual fund has trailed the market by over half a percentage point due to its cash holdings. While none of us knows how the market will perform in the future, economists do estimate that the equity premium over the long-term may be in the range of 3 to 4 percent. If that were to come to pass, idle cash balances of 6 percent would lower annual returns by 0.2 to 0.25 percent.

Taxes

In April 2001 and 2002, millions of investors confronted for the first time the true impact taxes have on their returns. Having watched their portfolios decline substantially, they nonetheless received Form 1099s from their funds showing that they owed capital *gains* taxes. That experience, coupled with new disclosures mandated by the SEC, has focused some investors on the tax costs of fund ownership. (Of course, capital gains taxes are not a concern if you're investing in an IRA or other tax-exempt vehicle.)

Mutual fund shareholders incur tax consequences in two ways. First, when they sell shares of a mutual fund at a gain, they pay capital gains taxes on any appreciation in the value of the fund. Exchanges within the same fund family have the same effect. Second, mutual fund shareholders incur taxes because of turnover in the stocks held by the fund. As a mutual fund sells stocks for a gain, it passes those gains through to the fund's shareholders. You can't control these costs; it's "taxation without representation." Indeed, because you may end up paying taxes on gains that were embedded in the funds' holdings even before you bought it, you may also be getting capital gains taxes without actual gains. (That's why investors who bought funds in 1999 or 2000 may have lost money *and* still paid taxes.)

The exact tax treatment of mutual fund distributions can be very complicated.[16] It's fair to say, though, that every time your mutual fund sells a share of stock with a gain it leads to additional taxes for you.

- First, any gains are accelerated into this year rather than to a later year when the stock could have been sold. You therefore lose the earnings on the taxes you pay early.
- Second, the character of your gains often changes. Hold a stock for more than a year, and a lower long-term capital gains rate applies. Hold it for more than five years and an even lower rate applies. Sell a stock in under a year, as actively managed funds often do, and the higher short-term capital gains rate applies. (Short-term capital gains are treated as ordinary income and taxed at that rate.)

- Third, if you hold your fund until your retirement, those gains may be taxed at a lower rate, since your income is likely to be lower. Accelerate them and you pay the higher rate of your working years.

How important are these unwanted capital gains taxes to your return? According to the SEC, estimates are that more than 2.5 percentage points of the average stock fund's return is lost each year to taxes. An academic study puts the figure at 3 percent.[17] In a study commissioned by broker Charles Schwab, Stanford economists Joel Dickson and John Shoven measured the performance of sixty-two equity funds over a thirty-year period. Comparing how much the funds would have earned in a taxable versus a tax-exempt account, they concluded that taxes reduced returns by 57.5 percent—easily more than half.[18] In the year 2000 alone, American households paid $99 billion in capital gains taxes on mutual funds.[19]

These numbers, however, do overstate the tax losses of fund investing to some extent. Even if you buy and hold stocks or index funds, you will have to pay capital gains taxes if you sell the asset. Determining the real tax cost of active fund management therefore depends on some key assumptions. Where would you have invested the money otherwise, and how long would you have held the investment?

One study by three asset management executives at J.P. Morgan compared the annual tax costs of actively managed stock funds to the costs of an S&P 500 index fund over a ten-year period (1984–93).[20] They concluded that the average actively managed fund incurred 2.4 percent of capital gains taxes and 0.7 percent of income taxes each year. For the index fund, the numbers were 0.4 and 1.4 percent, respectively. In total, the annual tax hit was 1.2 percentage points higher per year for the actively managed fund.

You might ask, given the complexity and lack of disclosure in the world of mutual fund taxes, what you can do to lower your taxes and raise your returns. We have three suggestions. First, only buy low-turnover funds. One thing is certain: the lower the trading, the more you get to defer the gains and make sure that when they come you pay lower long-term rates. Second, before buying a fund, ask what the level of unrealized gains in the fund currently is. You may be buying into somebody else's gains and getting a rude surprise come next April. Try to buy funds with less rather than more unrealized gains. Third, look at Morningstar to determine the tax efficiency of the fund. Morningstar tracks the portion of fund returns you actually get to keep after taxes. Some are quite good, over 90 percent. Of course, most of those are index funds.

SEC to the Rescue

Figuring out the impact of taxes on your returns became easier when the SEC mandated expanded disclosure of the after-tax performance of mutual funds.[21] The disclosures took effect at the end of 2001.

These disclosures, however, need not be included in sales and promotional material unless a fund is claiming to be tax efficient. Investors wishing to know a fund's after-tax performance will need to review the prospectus—something they should be doing anyway, but generally are not.

Conclusion

We didn't have to look very far to find the leading culprit in the mutual fund industry's poor performance. They rack up over $70 billion per year in costs for you, their investors. Money managers simply can't consistently keep up with the markets while running with ankle weights. And the active managers have the heaviest weights. Add Uncle Sam to the mix and the picture is complete. In total, expect to pay something in excess of 4 percent of your fund assets to disappear in costs per year for a load fund. If you are good about picking only no-load funds you should still expect costs totaling close to 3 percent per year. Compound these costs over your lifetime and you'll see the serious serious bite they take out of your savings.

Chapter 7

Whose Fund Is It, Anyway?

Let the people think they govern, and they will be
governed.—*William Penn*

The whole idea of a mutual fund is, as the name suggests, *mutuality*. Mutual funds allow investors to share the costs of professional money management. Investors select a board of directors to oversee the fund and hire a money management group (known as an "adviser") to invest the shareholders' money. The adviser works to get the best returns for the lowest risk. If shareholders don't like the adviser's approach or costs, they can hire a new one. At least in theory.

In reality, you and your fellow mutual fund shareholders have very little power over "your" company. The fund is set up by the adviser, not by individual investors. The fund itself has no employees of its own. All of the research, trading, money management, and customer support staff actually work for the fund's adviser. And while shareholders do vote for the fund's directors, the adviser initially selects the directors. Directors work part-time and rely on the adviser's staff for information. Not surprisingly, mutual fund boards fire their advisers with about the same frequency that racehorses fire their jockeys.

You can be forgiven if you've never realized that legally you actually control the mutual fund and that the company managing your assets is actually distinct from—and legally simply a contractor hired by—your mutual fund. It's not a distinction that advisers have any interest in highlighting. The adviser and the fund tend to have very similar names. The adviser for the Janus Fund, for example, is Janus Capital Corporation. American Century Investment Management, Inc., is the adviser for American Century funds. The fact remains, though, that the shareholders of the Janus Fund, through their board, could choose to hire American Century to run their fund if they wished.

An Analogy

The bizarre governance of mutual funds is unknown elsewhere in corporate America. Think for a moment how a regular company works. Suppose you're a shareholder of Sagawa Motors, which makes cars. To make the cars, Sagawa needs to contract out for tires. The price that Sagawa Motors negotiates for its tires is crucial to its profitability, as the auto industry is highly competitive. There are numerous tire makers in the world, and Sagawa is currently contracting with Danieli Tire Company. As a Sagawa shareholder, you would expect management to negotiate fiercely on the tire contract. Such is life in the competitive real world.

Suppose, on the other hand, that Sagawa Motors' directors dismissed all of Sagawa's management and didn't replace them. Instead, Sagawa's directors rely exclusively on the management of Danieli Tire for advice on how to run Sagawa. Over time, Danieli Tire even begins suggesting the directors for Sagawa. Furthermore, you learn that the Sagawa Motors directors have never sought a price on tires from any tire company other than Danieli. Rather, they ask Danieli Tire what it's charging and accept that price without seeking any competitive bids. When the board meets, the only presentations it receives are from Danieli Tire executives.

Would you want to be a shareholder of a company as dysfunctional as that? Well, if you own mutual fund shares, then you already are.

The Role of Fund Directors

The government is aware of the inherent conflicts of interest and potential for abuses that can arise from this structure. In an effort to address this conflict, the main law applying to the mutual fund industry, the Investment Company Act of 1940, establishes specific roles for fund directors. According to the late Supreme Court Justice William Brennan, the Investment Company Act was designed to place unaffiliated fund directors in the role of independent watchdogs, to furnish an "independent check upon the management of investment companies."[1]

This standard, however, has never been interpreted very stringently. Arthur Levitt, former chairman of the SEC and as zealous an advocate for investors as there is, described the modern-day legal duties of a mutual fund board: "Directors don't have to guarantee that a fund pays the lowest rates. But they do have to make sure that fees fall within a reasonable band."[2]

Let's go back to the real world. Imagine a director of procurement telling the chief financial officer, "I don't try to negotiate the lowest rates with our suppliers. I just check to make sure their prices fall within a reasonable band." In every American industry except the mutual fund industry, such a statement would be met with two words: "You're fired."

In 2001, the SEC took various actions in an effort to make fund directors more independent of the fund's adviser. It raised the required percentage of independent directors from 40 to 50 percent. Independent directors, rather than the advisers, must also select and nominate other independent directors. The SEC also imposed more stringent disclosure requirements for those directors.

In truth, though, the problem with mutual fund management is cultural, not regulatory. Even before the SEC acted, the great majority of funds already had a majority of independent directors. And nothing stopped those directors from negotiating the lowest rates for investors, even if they weren't legally required to do so. In practice, though, directors have a difficult time striking a proper balance between working with the adviser and vigorously pursuing investors' interests. Too often the outcome is simply acquiescence to whatever the adviser proposes. Many directors view their role as simply auditing the performance of the adviser and making sure there is no malfeasance or accounting problems, rather than acting as the shareholders' advocates. Short of a widespread shareholder revolt, we don't expect that situation to change.

Why It Matters

How does the strange governance of mutual funds affect you as a shareholder? First, you pay significantly higher fees than you would if you and your fellow shareholders actually ran the company. A study conducted in 2001 by Stewart Brown and John Freeman showed that the largest mutual funds pay twice as much to their advisers as public-employee pension plans pay for the same services.[3] In some cases, mutual fund advisory fees were three to four times higher than those of pension plans.

Brown and Freeman also reviewed the effect of size on relative fees. They found that the larger the pension fund, the greater its ability to negotiate significantly lower fees. As for mutual funds, size conferred far fewer benefits. For instance, the largest 10 percent of pension funds reviewed, with assets averaging $1.5 billion, paid advisory fees of only 0.2 percent. The largest mutual funds, with assets averaging nearly $10 billion each, paid advisory fees fully 2½ times that. Even within the same fund companies, fees can vary greatly for similar services. The researchers noted that Alliance Premier Growth Fund paid an advisory fee of 1 percent to its fund manager in 1999. That was fully six times the fee paid to the same manager by the Florida State public employees' pension plan for basically the same services.[4]

The only explanation the authors could identify was bargaining power. Pension funds negotiate aggressively for lower fees, while mutual fund shareholders can only rely on directors to do so. As in all matters, directors tend to rely on the adviser for information, but when it comes to negotiating fees, the interests of the adviser and the shareholders are diametrically opposed. It is a zero-sum game: every dollar the adviser earns is a dollar you lose. You don't own shares of the adviser, after all.

The second cost of fund governance comes when the financial adviser, with the acquiescence of the funds' directors, benefits itself at shareholder expense. This is done through something Wall Street calls "soft dollars." It's reminiscent of the "soft money" that political parties used to avoid individual contribution limits.

In the mutual fund world, soft dollars take various forms. Most commonly, the fund's adviser will negotiate a deal with a broker executing the firm's trades whereby a portion of every commission will be retained by the broker as payment for research advice or other services normally paid for by the adviser. Such agreements have a name, "commission recapture arrangements."[5] Basically, it means that you as mutual fund shareholder are paying some of the expenses of the adviser.

For the most benign possible view of soft dollars, let's turn to the mutual fund industry's own publication on directors' duties. We'll highlight the key parts:

> Directors also review a fund's use of "soft dollars," a practice by which some money managers, including mutual fund advisers, use brokerage commissions generated by their clients' securities transactions to obtain research and related services from broker-dealers *for the clients' benefit*. Directors review their fund adviser's soft-dollar practices as part of their review of the advisory contract. They do this because *services received from soft-dollar arrangements might otherwise have to be paid for by the adviser*.[6]

What's hard to figure is how these soft dollar payments can be "for the clients' benefits" when they "might otherwise have to be paid for by the adviser." That sounds a lot more like "for the adviser's benefit" to us.

A Happy Exception

So, what's a fund shareholder to do? You can buy an index fund, where it's very difficult for funds to charge high management fees (since there's no stock picking to be done). You could also buy a fund where the adviser does not have a profit incentive in conflict with the interests of its shareholders. Or you could do both at once.

There are two significant fund families that fall in the second category. The Vanguard Group is a mutual fund family where the shareholders effectively own the adviser, which accordingly provides services at cost. Vanguard takes no profits from the funds. In other words, there is no owner's cut going to the fund management company. The management fee need only be large enough to pay salaries and operating expenses, not large enough to generate a significant return on investment for the shareholders of an adviser company.

This structure has multiple benefits for shareholders. Not coincidentally, Vanguard brought index mutual funds to the retail market and offers the lowest cost index funds in the business. Cost consciousness does not stop with their index funds, however: the average expense ratio of a Vanguard *actively managed* stock fund is only 0.36 percent, with no loads or other fees. (Vanguard actually outsources its active fund management, but drives a very hard bargain.)

You may also want to look at funds offered by the Teachers Insurance and Annuity Association College Retirement Equities Fund, better known as TIAA-CREF. As its name suggests, TIAA-CREF is a nonprofit organization dedicated to offering retirement savings products to educators and researchers. Beginning in 1998, though, it also began offering mutual funds to the general public at Vanguard-like prices. Its Equity Index Fund is a no-load fund that tracks the Russell 3000 Index with an expense ratio of 0.26 percent. While the TIAA-CREF funds have not been around long enough for us to gauge their operational efficiency, their history and structure merit a future look.

Think About It

The company managing your mutual fund does not share your interests. It has its own shareholders and profits to consider. It wants to take more risk in order to attract assets in bull markets. It wants to charge high management fees that come directly from your returns. It wants to justify its existence by trading frequently, even if that increases your tax bill. Are you still so surprised that mutual funds trail the market?

Part III

The Great Stock Picking Hoax

Yossarian was as bad at shooting skeet as he was
at gambling. He would never win money gambling
either. Even when he cheated he couldn't win,
because the people he cheated against were
always better at cheating too.
—*Joseph Heller*, Catch-22

I n Part II, we examined how investors try to beat the market through actively managed mutual funds, and why that strategy is ill founded.

Now, we move to the Great Stock Picking Hoax, where investors are led to believe that they can outperform the market by picking stocks directly. A whole new set of experts are ready to advise you—analysts who follow particular stocks, newsletters that predict the future of the market, technical analysts who look at graphs and charts, authors who claim to have identified a set of stocks that are *sure* to beat the market. These characters are paraded before us in a nonstop moving picture on CNBC, CNN-FN, and in the rest of the financial media—featured on the *Stock Picker's Club, Stock Watch,* and countless other shows dedicated to having experts come in and *pick stocks.* They are always picking stocks, night and day, in good markets and bad. If the market is good, they pick stocks that promise extraordinary returns. If the market is bad they pick stocks that promise defensive plays and bottom-feeding bargains. Rain or snow, *they are picking stocks.*

If you call their call-in shows, they do not ask you what your tax situation is, or whether your existing stocks are diversified, or whether you're investing for the short term or the long term, or whether you can bear risk. Such questions only get in the way of picking more stocks. We heard a nineteen year old call into CNBC and ask whether he should hold or sell the one stock he owned. Nobody bothered to ask him why in the world he owned only one stock, or what his investment goals were. Instead they offered opinions on the stock. It's what they do.

Directly or indirectly, the actors on the financial media's stage are beseeching you to ignore tax consequences, diversification, and risk, and instead to spend your money on brokerage commissions and bid/ask spreads by frequently buying and selling their recommended stocks. They count on your natural optimism and drive to overcome your reason and experience.

If you simply buy and hold, of course, then you don't need to read investing magazines, watch financial news networks, subscribe to newsletters, or pay a broker to execute new trades. Whole industries depend on your continuing to trade stocks. The more often the better.

In Part III, we are going to see why active stock trading is simply a hoax for the unwary. We will see that the expert stock pickers have mediocre records and explain why you should expect them to have such records. We also will see that those records do not reflect the costs to you of implementing their strategies, which would turn mediocrity into tragedy.

One Last Note

Of all investing options, we're probably going to spend the least amount of time talking about the one that troubles us the most. To wit, here is our official list of the four dumbest ideas in human history:

1. The Children's Crusade
2. Invading Russia in the fall
3. Deciding that Linda Tripp was really there to listen, as a friend
4. Day trading

(Not necessarily in that order.)

So why aren't we ranting and raving about day trading? One reason.

There are no data on the performance of day trading, aside from anecdotal bragging on the one hand and bankruptcy petitions on the other. We would bet a considerable sum that such data would scare the wits out of you, and that the companies involved will never part with such data because they know the truth all too well. But we can't prove it. So, let's move on.

Chapter 8

Picking Badly

You don't need a weatherman to know which way the wind blows.—*Bob Dylan,* "Subterranean Homesick Blues"

How well do individual investors fare when they pick their own stocks? There is a magnificent study on the subject. Researchers Brad Barber and Terrance Odean persuaded a large discount brokerage firm to share the position statements and trading activity for 78,000 households, which included more than two million trades over the six-year period from 1991 to 1996.[1] What did they learn?

- Individual investors significantly underperform the market. The average earnings of the 78,000 households trailed a comparable index by 1.5 percentage points per year.
- Investors trade a *lot*. The average household turned over more than 75 percent of its common stock portfolio annually. That means that if a household held twelve stocks at the beginning of the year, it had sold eight on average by the end of the year.
- Returns are lowest for those who trade the most. Investors trading frequently trailed the market by a further five percentage points per year, primarily due to transaction costs.

- Investors tend to sell stocks that subsequently outperformed the ones they bought, even before trading costs.

The results actually overstated investor performance. Investors in the study group tended to buy proportionally more small company stocks than large company stocks, and somewhat more value stocks than growth stocks. During the period covered, that value preference boosted their aggregate pre-cost performance almost 1 percentage point above the market average. This boost in performance, therefore, masked the full extent of the transaction costs and poor stock picking ability. In other words, over the long-term, you could expect individual investors to trail the market by about 2.5 percentage points per year.

Barber and Odean had a theory that investors traded too frequently because they were overconfident about their stock picking abilities. To test this theory, they decided to compare the trading of men and women, as psychological studies consistently show men to be more overconfident than women about their abilities in many aspects of life. To do so, they obtained a new set of trading records from the same broker, this time for the seven years ending December 1993.[2]

The results were interesting. As with the other study, both men and women underperformed the market, but men underperformed women by almost 1 percentage point per year. This poor relative performance was directly attributable to higher trading volume, as the men traded nearly 50 percent more frequently than the women. Single men (lacking the moderating influence of a spouse) were the worst. They traded 67 percent more frequently than single women.

In addition to demonstrating that overconfidence likely causes over-trading, the study demonstrated yet again the perverse stock picking skills of individual investors. As in the earlier study, the stocks that both men and women chose to sell earned reliably greater returns than the stocks they chose to buy. Here, the genders were about equal: stocks sold by men outperformed those they bought by an annualized 2.4 percent; stocks sold by women outperformed those sold by an annualized 2.1 percent.

The Barber and Odean studies are unique in the field of individual investing because they were able to obtain access to comprehensive data. While public information on the performance of mutual funds is mandated by the SEC and readily available, no law requires investors to report their individual performance or brokerage firms to report their clients' aggregate performance.

We strongly believe that brokers would be all too happy to release aggregate information about the performance of their clients if the news were good. But don't hold your breath. Instead, look for more wacky ads featuring truck drivers, tennis stars, and talking frogs (wait, that's beer). Anyway, you get the picture.

Trading Costs: The Negative-Sum Game

To fully understand why individual investors fare so poorly, let's take a look at the costs of stock trading.

At the risk of stating the obvious, encouraging frequent stock trading is critical to the brokerage industry's bottom line.

- First, the brokerage industry profits most *when investors frequently buy and sell stocks.*
- Second, the brokerage industry profits when individual investors buy and sell stocks *on margin.* In a margin purchase, an investor borrows a portion of the purchase price of the stock from the broker, secured by the stock purchased.
- Third, the full-service brokerage industry (and private banks and financial advisers) profit enormously if they can find a way to charge you a percentage of your assets for their advisory services. Recently, they have had considerable success luring investors into such arrangements.

In the long term, the brokerage industry benefits from a rising stock market, as a rising market encourages investors to buy stocks. But do not delude yourself into believing that your interests are the same as your broker's interests. The brokerage industry's profits do not depend on whether individual investors *profit* from frequently buying and selling stocks.

When we reviewed transaction costs for mutual funds, we saw that there were three components: brokerage commissions, bid/ask spreads, and market or liquidity effects. For individual investors, the landscape is a bit different. Brokerage commissions are significantly higher, since individual investors do not have as much bargaining power with brokers. Bid/ask spreads are about the same for most trades. Market and liquidity effects are not a factor, since individuals do not trade in large enough blocks to affect pricing.

The greatest difference between trading costs for institutional and individual investors is that institutional investors recognize these costs, and most individual investors do not. You'll never see a bid/ask spread show up on a brokerage statement. While brokerage commissions are disclosed, you've probably never focused on how they add up, or thought about them in percentage terms.

The Barber and Odean study included data on brokerage costs.[3] They found that the average round-trip transaction (a buy and a sell) cost an investor 3 percent in commissions. That 3 percent excluded small trades—those of less than $1,000. When those trades were included, the average cost was 4 percent. On the other hand, the 3 percent average cost weights all trades equally. When commissions on larger trades are given greater weight, the average cost falls to 1.4 percent.

By way of comparison, let's look at what some of the major discount brokerage firms were charging in 2001. Set out below are some sample trades and what they cost.[4]

Brokerage Commissions

Shares	Price	Exchange	Method	Median cost	Round trip %	Schwab %	E*trade %
100	$50	NYSE	Broker	$29.95	1.2%	2.2%	1.2%
400	$50	NYSE	Broker	$30.00	0.3%	0.7%	0.3%
100	$50	NYSE	Internet	$18.00	0.8%	2.2%	6.0%
50	$25	NASDAQ	Internet	$17.50	2.8%	4.8%	3.2%

Source: Robert's Online Commission Pricer, August 8, 2001; Cyberinvest.com.

The percentage costs vary primarily with the amount of the trade and whether the trade is executed over the Internet or through a broker.

Adding It All Up

When combining commission costs with bid/ask spreads we think your best rule of thumb is to assume that every time you get out of one stock and into another through discount brokerage, 1.5 to 3 percent of your money disappears. Thus, you'd better be pretty darn sure that the stock you are buying is going to perform significantly better than the stock you are selling.

Taxes

The one great advantage of buying individual stocks is complete control of the timing of your securities sales. Here, though, is one of the sad facts in personal investing. The average individual investor turns over his own stock portfolio at almost the same rate as an actively managed mutual fund—around 75 percent per year. Investors are thereby accelerating their payment of taxes, paying taxes at higher rates, and forgoing the future earnings they could receive on these excess taxes paid. *They are paying all of the costs of owning stocks and failing to reap the only real benefit.*

A Piece of the Pie

The costs we detailed above assumed a simple transaction: buying stocks through a discount broker, paying a single commission. Many investors, however, pay additional amounts to financial planners (either independent or affiliated with a brokerage firm), and private bankers. They are the personal trainers of finance—except rather than charging an hourly fee to help you work out, they frequently take a percentage of your wealth in exchange for recommending stocks.

Pause for a moment to consider how odd the idea of paying someone a share of your assets is. A plumber is going to charge you the same amount to fix your toilet regardless of what your house is worth. When Jiffy Lube changes your oil and filter, it doesn't vary the fee based on the

Blue Book value of your car. Nordstrom doesn't ask you the overall value of your wardrobe before quoting you a price on a suit. Yet private bankers and financial planners routinely charge you a percentage of your assets for providing a service whose costs to them are basically fixed.

Independent Financial Planners

Independent financial planners have traditionally been to the brokerage world what insurance agents are to the insurance industry. They are independent, usually working on their own or in small companies. They are fixtures in communities across the country.

(More recently, large brokerages have begun adopting the planner model. We'll discuss this phenomenon in Part V, The Empire Strikes Back.)

Financial planning is a growing industry: the Financial Planning Association claims to have nearly thirty thousand members. Planners have certification and continuing education requirements. Most of the planning industry's growth occurred throughout the 1990s, in the midst of the great bull market.

Used and compensated appropriately, a financial planner can provide you helpful advice on asset allocation and other subjects. Even a relatively sophisticated investor may want a second set of eyes to look at his or her financial situation. Professional advice may let you sleep better at night. As with most services, though, the key is how much you pay a planner and what you get for your money.

Financial planners and financial consultants (which, while they have different licensing, are really about the same) are generally compensated in one of three ways, or a combination thereof.

Flat Fee for Service

Here, you pay a planner for his or her time, much as you would a lawyer or an accountant. Rates are generally $100–150 per hour, or a fixed fee for a given service. In return, the planner generally develops a financial plan tailored to your financial position and goals. A good financial plan focuses on asset allocation and issues such as the appropriate amount of insurance to carry. According to the Financial

Planning Association, such plans generally cost from $250 to $4,000. We like this option—albeit a lot more at the lower end.

Asset-Based Fee

Under this method, you pay a financial planner a percent of your assets. The industry standard is 1 percent. Financial planners generally tie this compensation system to the idea of helping you implement your financial plan. This assistance generally includes helping you pick stocks and funds, sending you regular reports on how those assets are performing, and periodically updating your plan.

We don't believe you need this assistance at this price, particularly if you subscribe to passive investing. Monitoring your investments is simplicity itself, as every mutual fund company and brokerage company is legally required to provide you regular performance statements. And of course you can check the performance of your assets daily in the newspaper and minute-by-minute on innumerable Internet sites. While it's a good idea to update your plan, you don't need to do it every year and you don't need to pay a percentage of your assets.

To put this issue into focus, we cannot improve on an article contained in *Financial Advisor,* the trade publication for financial planners. (By way of background, you will recall that the equity premium is the amount by which stocks outperform the risk-free rate, generally symbolized by Treasury bills.) In "Advisors Must Shift to Value-Based Fees," financial planners are advised:

> First, the same 1% fee that appeared fairly reasonable in a 6% to 8% equity premium environment now is going to look very expensive to many clients. Second, and more vexing, while clients do not hire advisors to generate exceptional returns, they do hire advisors to solve their problems. And most current financial plans are based on an assumption of 6% to 8% returns, after fees. Advisors may suddenly find that their clients view their services as both overpriced and incapable of solving their problems.[5]

We will leave it at that. It's a fifteen-yard penalty for piling on, after all.

Commissions

Planners generally will charge you a fee for your plan and then attempt to get continuing payments by executing your trades. Financial planners generally must partner with a registered broker/dealer in order to get trades executed and obtain research and other services for their clients. Scan the magazines that cater to financial planners, and you'll see a strong focus on "payout rates." This is the percentage of commissions or sales loads that the brokerage house will rebate to the planner. Generally, payout rates average 85 to 90 percent. That is to say, your financial planner will get the vast majority of the commissions and sales loads generated by his or her advice.

This compensation scheme, of course, gives the planner a powerful incentive to advise you to trade frequently or to buy a mutual fund with a sales load.

Summing Up

If you decide to hire a financial planner, we'd offer some advice. First, pay by the hour or service. Second, execute trades on your own. Third, ask friends for references, just as you would with a doctor or lawyer. Fourth, find someone who has some accreditation. There are a bunch of titles a planner can earn—Certified Financial Planner, Chartered Financial Consultant, Registered Financial Consultant—all of which require some training, continuing education, and adherence to a code of ethics. Finally, check out any prospective planner at the SEC's website, *www.adviserinfo.sec.gov*. You'll find information about your planner's business and any complaints that have been filed with regulators. It's a wonderful service.

Private Banking

We won't dwell on private banking, as it's a product for which most investors don't qualify. We do wish to assure you, however, that it is not a product you need to covet. Private banking includes every cost you could imagine—percentage of assets fees, high commissions, you name it. Moreover, these costs are often hidden by an "if you have to ask, you can't afford it" attitude. The thought is that a lot of personal attention, a yearly lunch at the bank's ornate dining room, and occasional tickets to a ballgame will make you forget how much you're paying for asset management.

So, here's our message to the rich. If you want ballgame tickets, they're now available on e-Bay for just about any team. If you want companionship, we'd suggest getting a dog or doing some volunteer work. And if you have the courage, send the following letter to the relationship manager at your private bank:

Dear [fill in banker's name]:
I was just curious. Could you tell me the total amount I paid the bank last year (fees, commissions, etc.), and what percentage of my total assets that represents?
  Thanks for your help.
Sincerely,
[Insert your name.]

You really have the right to know. The only danger is that you might be buried in an avalanche of tickets and lunch invitations.

Chapter 9

Time to Call in an Expert

In the game known as Broken Telephone (or Chinese Whispers) a child
whispers a phrase into the ear of a second child, who whispers it into
the ear of a third child, and so on. Distortions accumulate, and when the
last child announces the phrase, it is comically different from the original. The
game works because each child does not merely degrade the phrase,
which would culminate in a mumble, but *reanalyzes* it, making
a best guess about the words the preceding child had in
mind.—*Steven Pinker*, Words and Rules: The Ingredients of Language

We rely on expert advice in almost all aspects of our lives. And
experts abound in the financial world. Wall Street analysts,
economists, and investing gurus stand ready with ample advice on how to trade the market. They produce the research that your
broker provides you or that you buy through an investment newsletter.
In analysts we trust.

So why should Wall Street experts be any less deserving of our trust
than a cardiologist, or any of the other myriad experts on whom we
rely? Why shouldn't we trust these people to pick the best stocks? Primarily, because millions of dollars of expert advice is already reflected
in the marketplace. The price of each stock balances the opinions of all
the analysts who cover the stock and of the pension funds and other institutional investors who choose whether to buy or sell. Investors seeking stock picking advice from a fund manager or broker are essentially
asking one expert to second-guess all the others.

Imagine if your EKG and other lab tests were sent to fifty of the
world's leading cardiologists—the leading lights everywhere from
Johns Hopkins to the Mayo Clinic—and that they reached a consensus

diagnosis. How much additional value do you think you'd get from having your local cardiologist read the same chart? Well, when you ask your broker, "Is Microsoft undervalued?" you're doing just about the same thing.

In the sections that follow, we'll round up all the usual suspects—the most respected experts to whom you as an individual investor are likely to turn. We will see if they are worth what you are paying them.

The Analyst

The best way to tell how much value analysts add is to look at their performance, and how it affects you.

A Look at the Record

A 2001 study reported in the *Journal of Finance* looked at 360,000 analyst recommendations over an eleven-year period (1985–96) to see whether there were any strategies by which individual investors could profit from this information.* The researchers calculated a composite analyst recommendation for every stock (that is, the average of all the ratings by those analysts covering the stock). Stocks were ranked on a scale of 1 to 5 according to their composite recommendation, with a 1 being the equivalent of a strong buy and a 5 being a strong sell. The study then examined the performance of each of the five classes of stocks.[1]

- With respect to the five hundred largest stocks—representing more than 75 percent of the total market—the researchers found no difference in the performance of the various ratings. That is, stocks that the analysts rated a "strong buy" performed the same as stocks they rated a "sell." That result is pretty discouraging for anyone hoping to beat the market relying on analysts.

* Barber, Brad, Reuven Lehavy, Maureen McNichols, and Brett Trueman, "Can Investors Profit from the Prophets? Security Analyst Recommendations and Stock Returns," *Journal of Finance* 56 (April 2001): 531. The study covered 4,340 analysts at 269 brokerage houses. Ratings were recalculated each day.

- With respect to smaller stocks, the researchers found some predictive ability of the analysts, though that ability depended on
how quickly and frequently investors traded on analyst recommendations. Investors who learned of analyst recommendations
immediately and traded every day would have earned above-
market returns of about 4 percentage points per year; those who
learned of recommendations immediately but traded weekly or
monthly would have earned 2 to 2.5 percentage points above market; and investors learning of recommendations on a delayed basis and trading daily would have earned 1 to 2 percentage points
above market. *But all of these returns assumed zero trading costs for
the investor! Any investor trading daily, weekly, or even monthly
would have seen any gains chewed up and spit out.*

If you'd like a more real-world look at analyst performance, the *Wall
Street Journal* employs Zacks Investment Research to track the performance of the stocks recommended by the major brokerage firms.
These recommended lists are the product of the firm's best research and
are offered to firm customers as an inducement to pay the higher costs
of full-service brokerage. Zacks tracks net returns, including capital
gains or losses, dividends, and assumed commissions.

As of September 30, 2001, the twelve brokerage firms with five-year
performance records averaged a total (cumulative) return of 29.6 percent compared to 62.7 percent for the S&P 500 index.[2] In other words,
the returns of the broad market were double those of the average brokerage firm's recommended list. Only two of twelve firms outperformed
the market. Not so good.

Congress held hearings during the summer of 2001, and again in
2002 after the collapse of Enron, on the independence and integrity of
Wall Street analysts. A central concern was that investment banks inflated ratings for companies in order to gain their business. Congress
wanted to see how brokerage ratings of potential clients compared with
those of nonclients. Fortunately, Investars.com, a company formed in
2001 to document the performance of analyst recommendations, came
forward with volumes of data.

Investars.com had come up with a novel way of tracking the performance of analyst ratings. Basically, it creates hypothetical accounts

and invests them as the analysts recommend. It purchases stocks rated buy, holds stock rated hold, and sells short stocks rated sell.[3]

Investars.com looked at cases where an investment bank rated a company that was also one of its investment banking clients. Investors following such recommendations would have lost an average of 53 percent between January 1997 and June 2001.[4] This performance was 49 percentage points worse than the performance of ratings when the analyst's firm had no relationship with the company being rated.

More surprising, however, was how poor the average performance of analysts was in aggregate. Even if investors had scrupulously avoided analysts pushing their firms' IPOs, they *still would have lost money.*[5] Looking at the 4½ years between January 1997 and August 2001, the recommended portfolios of nineteen of the twenty-one largest investment banks (those with more than five hundred analyst ratings) *lost money.* The best of the bunch, Credit-Suisse First Boston, returned 5.6 percent annually, *less than half the returns of the S&P 500* over the same period.[6]

What the Analyst Means to You

Does all this mean that analysts really don't know anything about the stocks they cover? We don't think so. The fact that brokerage firms provide this service and sophisticated investors pay millions for it is a pretty good indication that it's worth something to someone.

Nonetheless, while this research may be worth something to institutional investors, *it's worthless to you,* as an individual investor. In fact, it may be worse than useless. To see why, we need to take a little deeper look at what analysts do and how their work product is disseminated.

Analysts play a limited role in the great majority of market price movements. Companies generally announce their earning reports or similar news after trading hours in order to allow investors to digest the news. If a significant announcement such as an acquisition is planned during the trading day, the exchange sometimes will halt trading on the affected stock. After the announcement, the stock opens, or reopens, at a new price that reflects the news. If the news is good, then all existing shareholders gain equally, and all new shareholders buy at the same, higher price.

That means that analysts are of limited use for many of a company's most significant announcements. For institutional investors, they may assist in interpreting an ambiguous company announcement, or assessing how an acquisition will play out. Such advice, however, will come via telephone calls or e-mails that you as an individual investor will never see.

Still, there are cases when an analyst makes a true contribution in *anticipating* an earnings rise (or decline) before an announcement. Say, for example, that an analyst covering a toy producer, Izzy Toy, contacts toy retailers and determines that there has been a recent surge in demand. One of Izzy Toy's products has just begun flying off the shelves. This information is not yet incorporated in the stock price. It is valuable. It is part of what we have otherwise called stock picking ability.

Assuming Izzy Toy's stock price would go up by $2 per share if this news were completely known by the market, the analyst's discovery is worth $2 per share times the total number of shares (say, 20 million). That's a $40 million idea, from which someone is going to profit.

But not you.

First, you will not hear about this idea until after the institutional investors who have paid good money for it. By then, the price has risen about $2, and you're in the position of rewarding others rather than being rewarded yourself.

Second, even if you hear about the news immediately, you will be one of millions. In recent years, CNBC reporters have developed good sources among analysts, traders, and institutional investors. They are often able to announce an analyst's upgrade or downgrade immediately after the analyst's morning conference calls with clients. So, sometimes you may be in the first group to hear. But even if that happens, it is a very large group. And when that large a group places a buy or sell order, the price moves. Again, none of that $40 million goes to you.

Third, although you may hear news of the upgrade, you will certainly not have ready access to the lengthy report that underlies that recommendation. This fact is crucial. The report will have many key details that go into the analyst's new forecast and recommendation.

Analyst reports can be over a hundred pages long, and large clients read those pages in order to judge the quality of the research. Some analysts are keen and insightful; others are lazy or timid. Even keen and insightful analysts sometimes make mistakes. Institutional investors get to evaluate the quality of a rating by paying to read the reasoning behind it. You don't hear any detail on CNBC.

Think again about those premarket leaks of analyst reports. What institutional investor would leak the news of a report or conference call if he or she was planning to buy or sell on it? Well, none, of course. An institutional investor would leak the news only if he or she had already acted on it or thought it unimportant. That's the hot news you're hearing over your morning coffee.

In other words, you are not getting any of that $40 million.

The Analyst's Many Bosses

We said earlier that analyst information may actually be worse than useless to you, the individual investor. Why? Because analysts' reports are frequently, and understandably, biased. Analysts labor under many pressures that sometimes make it difficult for them to offer their unvarnished opinions.

We believe that analysts face at least four potential conflicts of interest: (1) an interest in recommending stocks they own; (2) an interest in gaining investment banking business for their firms; (3) an interest in preserving good relations with the companies they cover; and (4) an interest in supplying buy recommendations to a fund industry and public eager to buy.

An analyst would have a financial incentive to recommend a stock that he or she owned, and we believe investors should know about an analyst's holdings. That said, we do not believe that this conflict of interest motivates many analyst recommendations. Analysts are professionals, and are well compensated. You don't often hear of them risking their position to make a quick personal profit.

The second conflict of interest is far more important. Frequently, an analyst's compensation or standing within a firm depends on the ability to generate business for his or her firm. That means persuading companies to use his or her firm to underwrite their stock or to advise them with regard to their next merger. Public companies pay millions of dollars for investment banking advice. Why would a company hire a bank whose analyst is telling investors its stock is overvalued?

Corporate America has every incentive to engage in this behavior. Analyst downgrades can raise the cost of a company's financing, limit its ability to grow, and punish the price of its stock. (Not to mention the options that management holds on that stock.) Analysts used to be better protected from this pressure by a so-called Chinese wall between the investment banking and research side of the major brokerages. That wall, however, crumbled significantly under the weight of the dot-com and IPO dollars of the late 1990s. Only two companies, Sanford Bernstein and Prudential, currently pursue research to the exclusion of investment banking, and are relatively immune from this particular pressure.

The third potential conflict is the analyst's need to preserve good relations with companies in order to continue receiving information. In some ways, analysts are a bit like journalists. To capture breaking news, they need to develop sources. Those sources are generally the people in the news. If journalists or analysts want to continue to have access to information in the future, it pays to treat their sources well in their current reporting (be it a research report or a news story). No analyst is immune to this pressure.

The fourth conflict arises from the analysts' clients. Mutual funds and institutional investors are generally "long" the market—that is, they are buying stocks and hoping they go up. With new money to invest, such investors are always looking for new stocks to buy, not stocks to sell. Thus, a good "buy" recommendation from an analyst is worth a lot more to them—and therefore to the analyst—than a "sell" recommendation.

The power of these pressures shows through in the overwhelming number of "outperform" ratings Wall Street puts out. From Investars.com aggregate data, we learn that analysts rate a remarkable 79 percent of companies as likely to outperform the market (a "strong buy," "buy," or "outperform" rating). They rate only about 20 percent of companies as likely to perform about the same as the market (a "market perform" rating). That leaves only 1 percent that will underperform the market (an "underperform," "sell," or "strong sell" rating). Clearly, there are a lot of Lake Wobegon products in the analyst community.

Wall Street and the financial media listen when investors get angry, and so they have reacted to the analyst credibility problem. CNBC interviewers now use their "serious voices" to ask analysts whether they own stock in the company they're recommending and whether their firm does investment banking business for the company. Of course, they proceed with the interview no matter what the answer, and they never ask the more important questions, like "How many sell recommendations have you issued this year? Why the discrepancy?"

For its part, the trade group for the brokerage industry announced in 2001 a series of new "best practices." But all the firms that signed on said they were already in compliance. Here are the key recommendations (along with our annotations):

- "Research departments should not report to investment banking or any other business units that might compromise their independence." In Wall Street firms, analysts rarely reported directly to the investment banking department. The problem was that the investment bankers were, and are, consulted on the analyst's all-important bonus.
- "Analysts should be encouraged to indicate both when a stock should be bought and when it should be sold, and management should support the use of the full ratings spectrum." Well, right now we see 1 percent of companies rated to underperform. Wake us when this gets up to 20 percent.
- "Analysts should not trade against their recommendations and should disclose their holdings in companies they cover." Of course, the problem was never analysts trading *against* their recommendations.
- "Analysts' pay should not be directly linked to investment banking transactions, sales, and trading revenues or asset management fees." Well, that's one mighty important "directly," isn't it?

Call us doubtful.

Fair Disclosure

There is some good news for individual investors. To help promote the integrity of the overall markets, the SEC enacted Regulation FD, for Fair Disclosure, in 2000. Championed by then-chairman Arthur Levitt, Regulation FD requires that companies share any meaningful information with everyone at the same time, rather than parceling it out to favored analysts. Most investors probably already thought that this was the law. For years, though, corporations have courted analysts by giving them special access to internal revenue projections, sales numbers, and other important data. Mostly, this meant special access to the corporation's senior management, but in many cases the corporation's financial staffs regularly reviewed the details of analysts' forecast models—right down to the formulas built into individual analysts' spreadsheets. The analysts were able to use this access to deliver reports and news to their clients. The implicit quid pro quo was that analysts generally would be slow to downgrade the stock and would *never* issue a recommendation below a hold.

Most of the praise for Regulation FD has centered on how it democratizes access to information on Wall Street. It has accelerated the trend of allowing individual investors to listen in on the conference calls that companies have with analysts after an earnings announcement. We believe, however, that there may be an even greater benefit to Regulation FD. Regulation FD should be retitled the "Hardworking Analyst Protection Act." Companies have less ability to barter information for favorable ratings or reports. Regulation FD is therefore good news for those analysts who crunch their numbers and do their homework. It is bad news for less diligent analysts and for companies looking to influence their recommendations. Let's hear it for Regulation FD.

Opposition to Regulation FD has generally come from the companies and analysts who benefited the most from the old system. The primary line of attack on FD has been that it would increase volatility, as the market would be more surprised by earnings reports that previously had been leaked to favored analysts. (It's also a nice argument for why the SEC should allow insider trading.) In any event, an academic study has shown that volatility around earnings announcements is actually down a bit since FD went into effect.[7] That said, efforts to repeal FD and put analysts back behind the iron curtain of access may continue.

Investment Newsletters and Investor Services

Many individual investors seeking expert stock picking advice are not satisfied with hearing secondhand what Wall Street analysts are recommending. These investors seek advice from other sources, hoping to get more complete and up-to-date information. Here are some of the most popular sources of such information.

Investment Newsletters

Hundreds of investment newsletters are now available to the investing public. Generally priced between $50 and $500 per year (making our book look like a bargain), these newsletters provide forecasts about where the market is headed and recommend portfolios of stocks to outperform the market.

Hulbert's Financial Digest is the one newsletter we like. Rather than picking stocks, it reviews the performance of other newsletters—specifically, those that pick mutual funds and stocks. Efficient-market theorists will note with approval that Hulbert's data show more than 84 percent of newsletters underperform the market over five years. Over ten years, that number rises to 90 percent.

The *Hulbert's Financial Digest* also reports the risk-adjusted return of the stocks chosen by these newsletters, with the risk-adjusted performance of the Wilshire 5000 index used as a benchmark of one hundred. Pretty simple. *The average newsletter returned less than half of the risk-adjusted Wilshire and S&P 500, with a risk adjusted return of only 49 percent that of the Wilshire.*[8]

Also, don't forget our old friend survivorship bias. In this context, it means that the reported average performance of newsletters is biased upward, as it does not include those newsletters that have folded. Therefore, the true average performance is likely to be worse than reported.

Louis Rukeyser

We have lampooned the stock picking ability of frantic traders televised from the floor of the New York Stock Exchange or tense analysts given forty-five seconds on CNBC. Nothing contrasted more nicely with that atmosphere than *Wall Street Week in Review,* hosted by the venerable Louis Rukeyser and presented by PBS. Never hurried, always interested in hearing the "why" and not just the "who," Mr. Rukeyser was academic in comparison to his more harried peers. Thus, if you were looking for someone who was likely to present thoughtful stock picks, Mr. Rukeyser and his esteemed guests seemed to be a good place to start. While Mr. Rukeyser was let go by PBS in early 2002, he triumphantly hooked up with CNBC shortly thereafter, and promised to continue offering viewers his unique style even with the change in venue.

So, back in the good old days at PBS, how good a resource were Mr. Rukeyser and his guests, and what can we expect for the future? Mr. Rukeyser publishes two newsletters. The first includes his own predictions about the best one hundred mutual funds to buy in seventeen different investment categories—the "Rukeyser 100." The second, *Louis Rukeyser's Wall Street,* is more akin to his TV show and features "buy" recommendations of analysts interviewed for each issue. You can get both newsletters for $69 a year.

Individual Investor

Individual Investor has been one of the magazines of choice for investors. *Individual Investor* has offered since 1990 a *Special Situations Report* recommending one stock each month. The track record, however, is not so good. According to *Hulbert's Financial Digest,* as of through 2001, annual returns were -4.1 percent for 5 years and 1.2 percent for ten years. Ouch! We won't even bother contrasting those results with the relevant indexes.

Thus, we thought it rather shameless when we saw *Individual Investor's* website advertising in May 2001 that "Our gain from 1991 through 1993 was an outstanding 220 percent, according to Hulbert, America's most prestigious investment newsletter rating organization. This consistent performance earned *Individual Investor's Special Situations Report* a ranking among the top three of 112 newsletters monitored during the rating period." Clearly, *Individual Investor* is going after that very small Rip Van Winkle segment of the investing public that has been asleep for the past nine years and is too incurious to ask what has happened since 1993. Next thing you know they will be selling rare Salvador Dali prints on their website.

Value Line

Value Line, founded in 1931, is the best-known investor service. Before the Internet let investors learn the most recent price/earnings ratios or earnings with the click of a mouse, investors across America (including Gary's father) awaited the arrival of their Value Line service before making stock investing decisions. Public libraries still carry Value Line's publication, *Value Line Investment Survey,* which currently provides subscribers detailed reports on more than seventeen hundred companies. Subscribers receive a detailed one-page report on the fundamentals of each company and on more than ninety industries, updated weekly. Subscribers can now access Value Line on-line.

The *Value Line Investment Survey* mines data to find the best stocks, which are then ranked according to timeliness, safety, and technical indicators. The timeliness ranking represents Value Line's prediction of which stocks will outperform the market in the near future. Value Line is not shy about advertising its past successes in its on-line advertisement. Its website proclaims:

> The results of *Value Line's Timeliness Ranking System* have been nothing less than remarkable—exactly what a savvy investor would expect from one of the most trusted and time-proven information providers in the industry. Just consider: a stock portfolio of #1 Ranked stocks for *Timeliness* from *The Value Line Investment Survey,* beginning in 1965 and updated at the beginning of each year through December 2000, would have shown a gain of 15,915% through December 29, 2000. That compares with a gain of 1,083% in the Dow Jones Industrial Average over the same period. Value Line #1 Ranked stocks outperformed the Dow by over 14 to 1. This gain would have beaten the NYSE Composite by 12 to 1 for the same time span.[9]

So let's take a critical look at Value Line's claims.

First, use your common sense. If buying Value Line's service really got you fourteen times the return of the Dow, wouldn't everyone be subscribing? Wouldn't there be lots of articles about Value Line millionaires? Wouldn't Warren Buffett have retired years ago due to feelings of extreme inadequacy?

Okay, let's proceed, with suitable skepticism.

First, let's give Value Line some credit. Over the past twenty years, the *Value Line Investment Survey*'s average annual return of 17.3 percent leads both the S&P 500 and the Wilshire 5000 by a healthy margin. Risk-adjusted performance is equally good. Indeed, this superior performance is significant enough that it even has its own name, "the Value Line enigma." There is also a whole body of academic analysis, including articles by a Nobel Prize winner, attempting to explain it. We will explain what all those academics have come up with in a moment.

Let us first explain, though, why the answer doesn't matter to you. *Here is our number-one rule for evaluating any investing scheme: any assessment of an investment scheme must include the costs of implementing it.* None of Value Line's advertisements do so. That fact is extremely significant because the returns that Value Line touts assume that investors (1) buy a large number of stocks and (2) trade them frequently in order to implement each new recommendation from the survey. In the real world, the costs of following this investment scheme drag down returns.

The best way to examine how you'd do buying Value Line's recommended stocks is to look at the performance of mutual funds that Value Line itself operates. Four of those funds state in their prospectus that they use Value Line's timeliness ranking system as their means of stock selection. Here's the record through 2001:

Performance of Value Line Mutual Funds versus Market

Fund Name	5-Year Return	10-Year Return	15-Year Return	Turnover Ratio
Value Line	6.5%	9.0%	12.0%	17%
Value Line Income	12.1%	10.7%	11.1%	41%
Value Line Leveraged Gr Inv	11.8%	12.3%	13.5%	28%
Value Line Spec Situations	16.3%	12.5%	11.2%	78%
Average	**11.7%**	**11.1%**	**11.9%**	**41%**
S&P 500	**10.7%**	**12.9%**	**13.7%**	
Wilshire 5000	**9.7%**	**12.3%**	**13.0%**	

Source: Morningstar Principia Pro.

As you see, Value Line hasn't made its system work for investors over the long term. When Value Line has to pay to implement its own recommendations, it trails both the S&P 500 and the broader market over ten and fifteen years. And these returns are all prior to those pesky capital gains taxes one would have to pay, given the funds' average 41 percent turnover ratio.

The academic studies of the Value Line enigma vary somewhat in their conclusions. They tend to agree that most of Value Line's superior precost performance is attributable to its ability to capture, by rebalancing its recommended portfolio weekly, the momentum effect in stocks and something called "post-earnings announcement drift." One study concluded that these two factors explained all of Value Line's superior performance, and thus that its system did not demonstrate stock picking ability. Later, more comprehensive studies, though, seem to indicate that Value Line's precost returns still exceed the market, even controlling for these factors.[10] *What almost all the studies agree on, however, is that individual investors cannot profit from Value Line's recommendations because the transaction costs of weekly or even monthly portfolio rebalancing are too high.* The academics reach in theory the same result reached by the Value Line mutual funds in fact.

Investment Clubs

Another way that many Americans have tried to beat the market is through investment clubs. These clubs generally consist of friends and acquaintances shopping ideas and giving each other support. While the participants obviously aren't experts, the hope is that collective research will yield the best possible stock picks—expertise by committee.

Investment clubs have their own association, the National Association of Investors Corporations (NAIC), with its own magazine, *Better Investing*. The NAIC claims membership of over 35,000 investment clubs, with 600,000 investors nationwide. These numbers don't surprise us; since we've started writing this book, numerous friends and acquaintances have told us that they are part of this world.

While investment clubs have a lot of benefits—encouraging savings, fostering friendship—increased stock picking ability, unfortunately, is not among them. The only academic study that managed to gather aggregate data on investment clubs concluded that they perform worse than individuals in selecting stocks.[11]

More specifically, 166 randomly selected investment clubs underperformed the Wilshire 5000 by almost 4 percentage points per year, after costs. Like individual investors, they trade too much, and the stocks they sell tend to outperform the stocks they buy. Because they execute smaller trades on average than individuals, their transaction costs are proportionately higher. According to the NAIC, its average member invests $45 per month in an investment club portfolio, and around $350 per month in a personal portfolio. These are relatively small amounts, for which a $10 to $30 brokerage commission would be a large percentage.

Mutual Fund Managers

There is one other group of experts that frequently offers its services to individual investors hoping to pick stocks: mutual fund managers and other institutional managers (from pension funds, for example). They are frequent guests on CNBC and CNN and are often quoted in the financial print media. Their goal in appearing on these shows, of course, is to promote the reputations of their employers, their funds, and themselves.

They also are talking up their current holdings. Put it this way: *no mutual fund or pension fund manager has ever or will ever appear on CNBC to discuss a stock he or she's going to buy tomorrow.* Managers talk about the stocks that they've already bought, in the hopes that you will follow suit. Perhaps the SEC should require any appearance by such a person on the public airwaves to be followed by a Surgeon General–type warning: "This expert appears to advance his own interests, not yours. Listen for entertainment value only."

Conclusion

Wall Street is the repository of vast knowledge and expertise on finance. Investment banks provide valuable services to corporations, governments, and other institutions looking to engage in mergers and acquisitions, raise debt, manage risk, or just about any other financial endeavor. The focus of this chapter, though, has been on what services of value Wall Street offers to individual investors, in particular individual investors trying to pick stocks. The answer is: very few. Reaching that conclusion is not to say that Wall Street firms are not very good at their business; it is to say that making money for individual investors is not really their business.

Chapter 10

The Darts*

When I entered the garage for my first darts lesson Keith
turned suddenly and gripped my shoulders and stared me
in the eye as he spoke. Some kind of darts huddle. "I've
forgotten more than you'll ever know about darts," says this
darting poet and dreamer. . . . He then went on to tell me
everything he knew about the game. It took fifteen
seconds. There's nothing to know.—*Martin Amis,*
London Fields

N

othing better symbolizes the battle between active and passive
investment than the *Wall Street Journal*'s investment dartboard
contest. The *Journal* began the contest in 1988 in response to a
comment by Burton Malkiel, one of the leading proponents of the
efficient-market theory. Malkiel had remarked that "a blindfolded
monkey throwing darts at a newspaper's financial pages could select a
portfolio that would do just as well as one carefully selected by experts."

Taking up that challenge, the *Journal* constructed a contest where,
each month, four experts (usually analysts or fund managers) each select one stock, and *Journal* staff select four stocks by throwing darts at
a printout of the *Journal*'s stock tables. Results are later compared, and
the two best-performing experts (the *Journal* calls them Pros) are in-
vited back for another contest, joined by two newcomers. (The *Journal*
announced in April 2002 that it was winding down the contest, declar-
ing that fourteen years was long enough for any newspaper feature.)

---

* We wish to thank Nataliya Mylenko for the invaluable research assistance she provided on this chapter.

According to regular tallies by the *Journal,* the Pros did well, winning 61 percent of the 140 contests since 1990. This did not go unnoticed on Wall Street, where a certain amount of chest thumping attends any mention of the contest. Some of the winning Pros have trumpeted their success in print and on-line advertisements. The dartboard contest, it is said, validates professional money management.

Given the prominence of the contests, we thought it would be worthwhile to take a closer look. Therefore we decided to rerun the contests with a bit more rigor. Our results are good news for the forces of chance, passive investing, and America's dart manufacturers. As for professional money management—well, not so much.

Digging Deeper

We calculated the returns of each pick not just at the six-month mark when the *Journal* contests end, but also after longer holding periods of twelve months and twenty-four months. These longer periods better reflect the actual holding period of most investors.[1] Our results are comprehensive, including every stock picked from the beginning of the contest until the contest ending on February 21, 2002.*

The Envelope Please

Here are the results.

Contests won: Darts Versus Professionals

Winner	6 months	12 months	24 months
Pros	55%	50%	45%
Darts	45%	50%	55%

* When reporting results, the *Journal* generally ignores the first fifteen contests from 1988–89, since in 1990 it changed the length of the contest from one month to six months. But we tracked the performance of those first contests as well. As it turns out, the Darts were winning eight of those first fifteen contests at the six-month mark. Twenty-four-month returns are compounded, not annualized.

Average Performance of Darts Versus Professionals

Average Return

	6 months	12 months	24 months
Pros	6.7%	11.6%	24.6%
Darts	3.6%	11.5%	25.3%

The results are no advertisement for professional money management. At the six-month mark—the traditional end of the contest—the Pros lead the Darts only modestly in contests won, albeit more clearly in average returns. But it's no landslide. At twelve months, the contest is basically a dead heat. At twenty-four months, the Darts lead contests won and also lead fractionally on returns. In general, though, most of the differences are statistically insignificant—that is, as likely to have been produced by chance as anything else.

You may consider this news rather unsettling, particularly if you're paying for active fund management or investment research. What's more, these results actually *overstate* the performance of the Pros relative to the Darts. By a fairer measure, the Darts are even or ahead for all periods. Why? Because the *Journal*'s contest contains significant biases, all of which skew the results in favor of the Pros: (1) it confers a publicity benefit on the Pros' picks; (2) it fails to consider risk; and (3) it fails to include dividends. Furthermore, it fails to include the costs of trading. When these (very relevant) factors are taken into account, the Pros never lead at any point.

Publicity Bias

Early on, questions were raised about whether the results were biased by a publicity effect. In other words, were the Pros benefiting from a self-fulfilling prophecy—that is, a rise in their picks' stock prices attributable solely to the fact that they had been chosen? (Stocks chosen by a dart would not receive a corresponding boost.) Malkiel identified this bias in an interview for the very first contest, and subsequent academic studies confirmed it.[2] To its credit, the *Journal* commissioned its own study, concurred, and in June 1990 lengthened the contest from one month to six months, so as to diminish the publicity effect.

Our results clearly show that even at six months, the *Journal*'s contest is biased by a publicity effect. We measured performance from the closing price on the date that the picks were announced in the *Journal*. The *Journal* uses the closing price on the day *before* the contest. We think our methodology is more appropriate, for two reasons. First, the purpose of the contest is to measure stock picking ability. The first-day jump is more a testament to the *Journal*'s wide and devoted subscription base than to the quality of the stocks picked by the Pros. Second, the contest purports to compare how well a hypothetical investor would have performed following recommendations from the Darts versus recommendations from the Pros. But no investor, hypothetical or not, has the option of reading that day's *Journal* and buying the Pros' picks at *yesterday's* prices. The publicity effect generally means that the chosen stocks open higher, and investors would have to buy them at that price. (Given that the *Journal* acknowledged a first-day publicity effect of 3.5 percent back in 1990, moving the start date back would have probably also been a prudent move.)

The resulting difference in six-month returns is large. On average, the first-day price change alone increases the Pros' performance by 2.6 percentage points over the life of the contest. As a result, while the *Journal* reports the Pros winning 61 percent of the 140 six-month contests ending between June 1990 and February 2002, our results show the Pros winning 56 percent (and only 55 percent since the beginning of the contest in 1988).[3]

The twelve-month and twenty-four-month results appear to confirm that even at six months, some publicity benefit for the Pros remains. With any lingering publicity effect gone at twenty-four months and the Pros picks left to their merits, they succumb to the forces of chance and the Darts pull even, and even a bit ahead.

Risk Bias

The quality of an asset's returns depends on the risk an investor runs to obtain those returns. Thus, any judgment about the relative performance of the Pros and the Darts in the *Journal*'s dartboard contest must weigh the relative risks of the stocks chosen by each group. In fact, the Pros pick riskier stocks. When one examines risk-adjusted returns, the Pros' advantage at the six-month mark disappears. The draw at the twelve-month mark becomes a win for the Darts. And by twenty-four months, it's time to be taking your Darts out for a big steak dinner to celebrate.

To measure the relative risks of professional and dart-based stock picking advice, we asked for help from RiskMetrics, a company that does state-of-the-art risk assessment. Its clients include nearly every major commercial and investment bank in the world.

Rather than using standard deviation as a measure for risk, Risk-Metrics uses what it calls RiskGrades. Calculating a RiskGrade is more complex than computing a standard deviation, but the resulting number is easier to understand. A RiskGrade of 100 implies a level of risk equal to holding a diversified, global *portfolio* of stocks. A RiskGrade of 0 is assigned to the holding of cash. Most *individual* stocks carry RiskGrades significantly higher than 100, since alone they do not receive the benefits of diversification. Just as a quick yardstick, as we went to press, the S&P 500 carried a RiskGrade of 105, Home Depot 255, Microsoft 211, and a Treasury note around 50.

The folks at RiskMetrics tracked the daily volatility of the *Journal's* Darts and Pros for the five years ending September 2001. They then calculated a RiskGrade for each stock and an average RiskGrade for the Pros and for the Darts. Finally, they adjusted the returns of each to account for risk and produced a risk-adjusted return for each period. One potential bias in the RiskMetrics data comes from corporate events. RiskMetrics was unable to conduct the analysis for companies that disappeared during the five-year review period. The remaining sample, though, included more than two thirds of the entire set of picks during this five-year period. With that caveat, here's what they found.

	6-month results		12-month results		24-month results	
	Avg. Risk-Grade	*Risk-adjusted return*	*Avg. Risk-Grade*	*Risk-adjusted return*	*Avg. Risk-Grade*	*Risk-adjusted return*
Pros	315	2.1%	335	-1.5%	321	0.2%
Darts	285	2.4%	297	3.6%	287	3.9%

For all periods, the Pros ran more risk than the Darts. When a risk-adjusted return was calculated, the returns for the Darts were higher for all periods—significantly higher over the twelve- and twenty-four-month periods.

Dividend Bias

Investing is about total return. The returns reported by the *Journal* are not total returns, however, because they ignore dividends. In setting up the contest, the *Journal* may have wished to ignore dividends, since they complicate the contest. The *Journal* may also have reasonably assumed that they'd end up being a wash between the Pros and Darts. We checked, though, and such an assumption is incorrect. Ignoring dividends biases the results in favor of the Pros.

A close look shows that the Pros have been tending to pick higher growth, lower dividend stocks than the market as a whole, and the Darts in particular. (We believe this result comes from the Pros choosing more growth stocks and avoiding utilities and other high dividend stocks, either because they know growth stocks best or believe they're more likely to generate attention-getting returns.) For contests between January 1992 through March 2001, the Darts' annual dividend yield was about half a percentage point higher than the Pros'—1.3 percent for the Darts and 0.8 percent for the Pros.

Cost Bias

Another drawback of the *Journal*'s dartboard contest is obvious and unavoidable, yet worth stressing. The contest implicitly equates the transaction costs of passive investment and active money management. In reality, most money managers trade very frequently, incurring transaction costs, whereas adherents of passive investing tend to buy and hold low-cost index funds or, increasingly, exchange-traded index funds.

The challenge of active money management is to pick stocks that will outperform the market by a wide enough margin to recoup fees, transaction costs, and taxes. Over time, almost all money managers fail at that challenge. The *Journal*'s dartboard contest, though, assumes that all of those costs are irrelevant.

The Sad Truth

The Pros selected by the *Journal* represent an all-star team for professional money management. Not only are they among the best of their breed, but they need only pick one stock that will beat the market. Surely, you might think that every money manager must know of at least one stock that's going to outperform the market! Efficient-market theory would say no, and efficient-market theory has won this contest hands-down. Once the publicity effect is washed away, the Pros just look like the market. When risk and dividends are factored in, they look worse.

And that's just the results for relatively small portfolios of dart-selected stocks. Those who believe in passive investing, however, don't really pick four stocks at a time. They tend to buy index funds, which benefit from diversification. Looking at the contest with that measure, the Pros sink further underground. Measured at the twelve-month mark, the average returns of the Darts were 11.5 percent over the life of the contest, about the same as the Pros. The returns of the broad market, however, were higher, at 12.1 percent. Furthermore, when one looks not at the overall average for the Darts and the Pros but instead at each four-stock portfolio chosen in each contest, the Wilshire 5000 outperforms both the Darts and Pros 59 percent of the time. In other words, the Pros are lucky to have faced only four dart-picked stocks in each contest, rather than the whole big, bad diversified market.

We miss the *Journal*'s investment dartboard contest, albeit in the same way we miss *Hill Street Blues* and *Seinfeld.* It was great entertainment, but never much help in deciding what stocks to buy.

Chapter 11

The Myth of Technical Analysis

The various modes of worship which prevailed in the
Roman world were all considered by the people as equally
true; by the philosopher, as equally false; and by the
magistrate, as equally useful.—*Edward Gibbon*, Decline
and Fall of the Roman Empire

Technical analysts make an enticing pitch to investors: you can
construct winning strategies *without knowing anything at all
about the companies whose stocks you're buying.* They say that you
can beat the market through a combination of mathematics, psychology, and history. By studying how stock prices have behaved during
similar periods in the past, you can predict how stocks will behave in
the future.

As sold to individual investors, technical analysis of stocks is a myth.
Individual investors cannot construct winning strategies based on technical analysis. The myth is perpetuated by brokerage firms, who employ
technical analysts because they spur investors to trade more frequently,
and by the financial media, which give technical analysts a prominence
all out of proportion to their true role on Wall Street because they make
good copy.

Puncturing the myth of technical analysis is difficult, though, because technical analysts are often hard to pin down. They are not obligated to report how their predictions perform. They also tend to speak
in the language of Nostradamus, vague and allowing of multiple inter-

pretations. How, for example, does one assess the accuracy of the statement, "If it breaks through the resistance level at 9800, the Dow could go 500 points higher over the next six to twelve months"? Suppose it "breaks through" and goes 300 points higher. Is that a win? Suppose it goes 500 points higher in five months, but then falls 1,000 points in the next three months. Is that a win? You can bet that in both cases the technical analyst will claim success.

If technical analysis really worked for stocks, you'd think it would probably work for sports. There, the importance of psychology is undisputed. But you don't hear hosts on *Sports Center* saying, "The Mets are twenty-five games below .500, approaching their fifty-two-week low of twenty-six games. We're expecting them to rebound at this resistance level, beating the Reds on Friday." Or, "The Red Sox have had a mediocre season, but we don't expect there to be a turnaround until you see capitulation, a five-game losing streak where everyone will realize that the only place to go is up." We think the reason you don't see technical analysis in sports is that *people in sports actually keep score,* and they know it doesn't work.

Because technical analysis is offered in such a way that no one can keep score, it's difficult for us to construct a rigorous case against it. But we'll do the best we can with what we have.

The Germ of Truth

In referring to the "myth" of technical analysis, we have chosen the word carefully. Myths generally have some basis in fact. Myths then build on those facts until the story takes on a life of its own. We believe that technical analysis, especially technical analysis for individual investors, is a classic myth.

First, let's start with the germ of truth. When Gary was starting out at Goldman Sachs in the 1980s, the head of the equity trading floor was Robert Rubin (later head of President Clinton's White House economic team, Secretary of the Treasury, and a senior Citigroup official). He was already something of a legend as a trader. One reason he was (and is) so highly regarded was his receptiveness to new ideas. Consistent with his open-mindedness, he decided to break with tradition and hire an academic, a Ph.D. economist, to assist in trading. His colleagues thought this idea a bit odd, but waited to see how it turned out. The person he selected was Fisher Black, now best known for the Black-Scholes model on option pricing that later won the Nobel Prize for Economics for Myron Scholes. (Unfortunately, Black did not live long enough to join in the award.)

At Goldman Sachs, Black was inexperienced and uninterested when it came to analyzing the fundamentals of individual stocks. Instead, he began to use quantitative analysis of past market prices to try to predict future market movements. He made a lot of money doing so, and became a partner at Goldman. Thus, Fisher Black's Goldman experience is a clear case where technical analysis of stocks yielded market-beating performance.

Technical analysis continues to yield some opportunities, albeit more so in currency markets than equity markets. In recent years, with the speed and capacity of modern computers, technical analysts have been able to "data mine." Data sets can be correlated instantly, and patterns noted. In the pre–computer age, researchers had to construct a theory and then (laboriously) run data to see whether it held true. Today's researchers can reverse the process, using data to generate a theory.

Data mining, used correctly, can be a good thing. Data mining can cure diseases and predict the weather. In the financial world, most data mining focuses on the concept of reversion to the mean. Reversion to the mean is the notion that much of the universe is orderly and that its elements will continue to relate in the future in the same way that they have in the past. In financial markets, data miners look for past relationships among various elements of the market (sector prices, stock prices, volatilities, you name it). They then attempt to make money by presuming that those past relationships will continue to reassert themselves in the future. For example, data mining might recognize a strong correlation between two stocks or a stock and a futures contract, thereby allowing an arbitrageur to profit when the prices diverge and subsequently converge.

At its best, technical analysis uses sophisticated mathematical models to identify past relationships among financial assets, and then tests the predictive ability of that relationship in various ways. A good technical analyst will run a theory against a variety of data sets (different time periods, market environments, etc.). A good technical analyst will talk with market participants and academics to better understand the identified relationships and see if there is any logical foundation for their existence. Last, a good technical analyst will test a theory before committing real money to it.

So, here is the germ of truth. In the hands of very bright and diligent people, technical analysis can occasionally identify profitable investment opportunities.

The Germ of Truth Spreads and Infects

Now, here are four additional caveats that you must bear in mind in deciding whether to employ technical analysis as an individual investor.

1. Technical analysis in the hands of very bright and diligent people also can produce disaster.
2. When a technical analysis does identify a profitable opportunity, that opportunity is exploited and disappears quickly. If CNBC had existed in the 1980s, we absolutely guarantee you that neither Fisher Black nor Bob Rubin would have been discussing their trading strategies on television.
3. Even if an individual investor was among the first to hear of an opportunity, trading costs for individual investors—costs not shared by Goldman Sachs and other Wall Street traders—make implementing even a good idea too expensive.
4. Legitimate technical analysis produced through rigorous data mining is very difficult for the individual investor to distinguish from completely spurious analysis produced through cynical data mining.

As we examine each of these four points, they should help you develop a heartier skepticism about technical analysis.

Caveat 1: "Oops, where did I put that $4 billion?"

There is a very nice illustration for our first caveat. The largest financial firm ever devoted solely to technical analysis of markets was Long Term Capital Management. Its roster of all-star executives included many great economists. Long Term Capital Management, as you may recall, failed to the tune of around $4 billion in losses for its investors.

One of the principals of Long Term Capital Management was the very same Myron Scholes who was awarded the Nobel Prize for his work with Fisher Black. The fact that a Nobel laureate in economics could fail by relying on technical analysis should make you hesitate to do so yourself or to listen to some guy you've never heard of who's pushing a technical analysis scheme in a newsletter or on TV.

Caveat 2: Going, Gone

All investing schemes based on technical analysis are basically an attempt at arbitrage. Briefly, arbitrage is an attempt to identify imperfections in the market and profit from them. Such imperfections are thus "arbitraged away." A simple example of arbitrage would be if the dollar was trading higher against the yen in the U.S. currency market than in the Japanese market. An observant arbitrageur would thus buy yen for dollars in the United States and simultaneously sell those yen for dollars in Japan. Even if the difference were fractional, a sufficient volume of trading would yield a profit. A more nuanced example might be a wider than usual spread between the spot (cash) market for pork bellies and the futures price of pork bellies on an exchange. While there is more risk here than in the currency example, it may nonetheless be an opportunity worth seizing.

One constant of arbitrage, however, is that opportunities rarely exist for long. Once identified by traders, such opportunities disappear quickly. In the commodities example above, arbitrageurs would continue buying dollars against yen until the price discrepancy disappeared. The same would be true of the spot and futures prices for pork bellies. Think of an arbitrage opportunity as a small dollop of fish food in a crowded fish tank. The food is immediately gobbled up by the first fish or two to notice it, and none remains for the rest. Go back a few minutes later, and there's no food floating there.

This basic truth has great resonance for technical analysis. Technicians would have you believe that whenever a stock is at its fifty-two-week low, you should buy (or sell—we can never remember) because stocks at their fifty-two-week lows are generally a buy, even though everyone knows that they're a buy and would presumably have bought the stock at its fifty-one-week low. Similarly, you should buy the highest yielding Dow stocks because they're always a bargain, notwithstanding the fact that everyone has been told they're a bargain for twenty years.

We think it is fair for you to assume that anytime a technical analyst makes public a method for picking stocks, sectors, or the market as a whole, the method has already run its course. At this point, the analyst is either trying to stimulate brokerage business for his firm, sell a book, or convince individual investors to buy stocks the analyst already owns.

Caveat 3: The Cost of Implementation

We aren't going to beat a dead horse here, as we trust that you remember our number-one rule for evaluating any investment scheme: you must include the cost of implementing it. Suffice it to say that *technical analysis leads to a very high turnover.* Even the best technical analysis at the best Wall Street firms—the analysis you'll never see—yields only tiny arbitrage opportunities. Those firms can seize on such opportunities by trading at very low cost and in very large volumes. You can do neither. If you are trading your own stocks and paying a round-trip cost of 1.5 to 3 percent on your trades, we simply cannot imagine any arbitrage opportunity that could overcome that expense. *At those costs, technical analysis is a dead option to you.*

Caveat 4: "Honey, Tiger made a birdie putt—buy some more Intel!"

Many historical patterns have no particular logic behind them, and thus are unlikely to be repeated in the future. In 2001, the *New York Post* reported that when Tiger Woods played in a golf tournament on the previous Sunday, the Dow had risen for thirteen consecutive Mondays. The

Post tracked the streak as it continued up to twenty-one consecutive winning Mondays. Although this correlation was clearly only the product of random chance, the *Post* couldn't resist quoting an analyst as saying, "We dismiss out of hand the relationship between good things psychologically and stock-market increases, but they are hard to ignore."[1]

Tiger Woods is an easy case, because the connection is so clearly illogical. What makes spurious data mining—also called data snooping—hard to spot in the financial world is that you will probably find most relationships somewhat logical. You will not be told how many sample correlations were run in order to produce the one that is now being presented to you as a market beater. Keep this in mind as we look at two prominent investing schemes that have been sold to American investors.

Case Study 1: This Dog Won't Hunt

You may have heard of the Dogs of the Dow, or the Dow Ten. The simple theory is that investors should buy at the beginning of each year the ten stocks that have the highest dividend yield out of thirty stocks in the Dow Jones Industrial Average. The strategy was first touted in 1988 by analyst John Slatter in the *Wall Street Journal,* and it has been wildly popular. Slatter claimed at the time that the Dow Ten portfolio had outperformed the broader Dow Jones Industrial Average by 7.6 percentage points. That got a lot of people's attention. So, too, did a follow-up bestseller in 1991 by Michael O'Higgins and John Downs called *Beating the Dow.* Other books touting the strategy included Damon Petty's *The Dividend Investor* (1992) and *The Motley Fool Investment Guide* (1996).

Estimates are that as of 2000, more than *$20 billion* was committed to the "Dow Dog" strategy through direct purchases and unit investment trusts that invest solely according to the strategy. Merrill Lynch's Strategy Power Ten Strategy UIT, which buys the Dow Dogs, claims more than $10 billion in assets.*

---

* There are no Dow Dogs mutual funds, since mutual funds cannot hold more than 5 percent of their assets in any one stock, something a Dow Dogs strategy would require by definition.

The only logic offered to support the Dow Dogs theory is that value stocks will outperform growth stocks. The Dow Dogs would be considered value stocks. That said, value stocks have over time outperformed only marginally and certainly not anywhere close to the returns claimed for the Dow Dogs. We would expect the Dow Dogs to perform about the same as the other twenty stocks in the Dow, less some benefits of diversification. So, we were skeptical.

So what does a look at the claims and performance of the Dow Dogs show? We must say that, as skeptical as we were going in, the results have left us amazed. Recently, Mark Hirschey of the University of Kansas did a little detective work on the Dogs and their promoters.[2]

Hirschey found that the claims of how well the Dow Dogs had performed in the past—the major argument for investing in them in the future—were simply wrong. Although determining the beginning- and end-of-year prices of ten Dow stocks would appear to be a childishly simple task, the promoters claimed wildly different, albeit universally incorrect, returns for the Dogs. One or more of the promoters has tracked how the Dogs have done every year from 1961 to the present. There are fourteen years where all of them reported results, 1973–87. Remarkably, every year, the Dow proponents fail to agree on what the results of the strategy would have been. So you can visualize the enormity of the problem, and with Mr. Hirschey's kind permission, here are the results of his detective work for the first five years of the Dogs, as well as their fourteen-year average.

Reported Returns of the Dow Dogs Investing Strategy

	Year	Slatter	O'Higgins & Downs	Knowles & Petty	Merrill Lynch	Motley Fool
	1973	-2.9%	3.9%	3.9%	-4.1%	3.9%
	1974	58.9%	-1.3%	1.0%	-2.4%	1.0%
	1975	35.6%	55.9%	53.2%	55.7%	51.0%
	1976	1.1%	34.8%	33.2%	33.3%	33.2%
	1977	3.3%	93.0%	-1.0%	-2.9%	1.2%
Average	1973–1987	19.4%	27.4%	17.7%	16.6%	17.9%

Thus, whether the Dow Dogs were the result of data mining or of an ersatz value strategy, they were from the outset the product of bad data. This is the low science behind a theory into which Americans have sunk $20 billion of their savings. That doesn't necessarily make the Dogs a bad investing strategy. But it's almost like wondering if you're adopted, and having your parents disagree on your birth date. It doesn't exactly inspire confidence.

So, how have the Dogs actually performed? According to Hirschey's study, over the period 1961 to 1998, the Dow Dogs beat the DJIA in twenty-one years and lost in seventeen. Looking at five-year periods, the Dogs won three and lost four. Looking at ten-year periods, the Dogs won two and lost one. Overall, the Dogs do slightly better than the DJIA, but this advantage is explained by the fact that the Dogs have higher risk as measured by their volatility. Furthermore, implementing a Dogs strategy requires higher transaction costs and tax liability.[3]

To sum up, if you buy the Dow Dogs, you're not going to beat the market, and you're going to pay a lot of commissions and taxes—which is about what efficient market theory suggested eight chapters ago. By the way, just in case you think we're beating a dead dog here, you should know that CNBC rang in 2002 by introducing viewers to the Dow Dogs.

Case Study 2: The Foolish Four

There is a more recent version of the Dow Dogs that has also attracted sizable amounts of investor money, called the Foolish Four. The Foolish Four is a product of the folks at the Motley Fool, one of America's most popular on-line financial sites. Derived from the Dogs of the Dow, the Foolish Four strategy advocates purchasing, on January 1, a four-stock portfolio chosen from the five lowest-priced stocks of the ten Dow stocks with the highest dividend yield. The very lowest-priced stock is dropped, and 40 percent is invested in the second-lowest priced stock, with 20 percent invested in each of the three remaining stocks.

The relevant question is whether the Foolish Four is a strategy grounded in logic, and thus likely to be successful going forward, or a product of data snooping, and thus the moral equivalent of Tiger Woods. A recent article by economists Grant McQueen and Steve Thorley in the *Financial Analysts Journal* points out a few reasons to doubt the Foolish Four:[4]

- Switching from five to four stocks by dropping one stock while simultaneously putting a double weighting on the one remaining stock *most similar* to the discarded one does not appear to make any logical sense. It has the feel of a strategy built to fit the data.
- Basing the strategy in part on the *price* of a stock is nonsensical. A stock split would halve the price, even though its value remained constant.
- Finally, when the data was rerun with stocks bought in July instead of January, the past returns of the portfolio were cut by one third. If the core idea behind the Foolish Four—basically, that value stocks outperform the market—were valid, then the Four should outperform in July as well as January.

By the way, the Motley Fool subsequently launched its Foolish Eight, whereby for $50 you can receive a list of eight small growth stocks each month. Personally, we'd rather watch Tiger Woods.

Summing Up: Caveat Monica

These stories generate what we call the "Monica Seles Rule of Investing." In March 2001, the *New York Times* did a profile of the tennis player and her investing habits.[5] Readers learned that although she generally relied on an investment adviser, she invested some of the money on her own and was a big fan of the Dogs of the Dow investing strategy. So, here is the Monica Seles Rule of Investing: if an arbitrage opportunity has been identified for a period of time sufficiently long enough for a professional athlete to be touting it, then the arbitrage opportunity no longer exists. There is also a corollary for the individual investor: if you are identifying arbitrage opportunities by the same method as Monica Seles—watching television and reading magazines and newspapers—then any arbitrage opportunity that you learn about is already bankrupt.

We don't mean to pick on Monica Seles. She's a wonderful tennis player who appears to be a good and thoughtful person. She should not be embarrassed in the slightest at having fallen into the Dogs of the Dow trap. Numerous other investors have done so as well. Her financial adviser, on the other hand, should be embarrassed. It is his responsibility to sit Ms. Seles down and say, "I know you read about this investing strategy somewhere, but it's really nonsense. The chances of your discovering an untapped arbitrage opportunity in the stock market are about the same as some guy in a bar in Atlantic City getting an inside tip that you've got a strained hamstring and that he should bet on Lindsay Davenport in your upcoming match."

Chapter 12

Bad Timing

"Very simple was my explanation and plausible enough—as most wrong theories are!"—*Time Traveler in H. G. Wells,* The Time Machine

Beyond fundamental or technical analysis, investors also try to beat the market with another strategy: market timing.

"Market timing" includes: (1) increasing or reducing stock holdings based on a prediction of whether current market prices are collectively too high or too low, and (2) shifting assets from one sector of the stock market to another based on a prediction of which sectors will outperform or underperform.

Discussions of market timing dominate the airwaves. Examples of the first type of forecasting include:

- "Has the market hit bottom?"
- "Is this a dead cat bounce?"
- "Our chief economist is raising her model equity allocation from 70 to 80 percent."
- "It's time to take some money off the table."

Examples of the second strategy include:

- "Technology is due for a rebound."
- "We believe retailing is a good defensive play at this point."
- "I believe that the chip sector is going to lead this market up."
- "The financial services sector is currently undervalued."

All of these statements assume that investors are poised and ready to decide daily whether to move in or out of the market, or some sector of the market. Each of these questions and statements can be heard or read in the financial media *every day*. Every day, you are being told that it's time to get in or time to get out (or both). In other words, every day you're being told that you should be paying all the costs of trading in order to capitalize on the latest forecasted market movement.

The Record

In fact, individual investors have demonstrated no ability to time the market. Rather, they've demonstrated a penchant for mistiming the market. Numerous studies confirm that individual investors tend to buy high and sell low. The brokerage study by Odean and Barber described earlier found that when investors sold one stock and bought another, the stock they sold outperformed the stock they bought by 3.4 percentage points on average over the next year.

Individual investors frequently attempt to time the market by buying or selling equity mutual funds rather than stocks. Here again, they fall short. Researchers at Leuthold Weeden Capital Management compared the performance of the market after a month of mutual fund net inflows (investors getting into the market) and a month of net outflows (investors getting out of the market). The S&P 500 returned 19.6 percent in the year after net outflows and 13.9 percent after net inflows.[1]

Professionals don't seem to do any better than individual investors when it comes to market timing. A 2001 study looked at the market timing ability of Fidelity sector funds.[2] Presumably, sector mutual fund managers will know whether that sector is poised to rise or fall. In fact, the study found that Fidelity's managers had persistent *negative* timing ability. Their decisions to increase or decrease cash holdings generally hurt performance.[3] The study also explored whether fund managers adjusting their risk profiles did so in a way that anticipated moves in the market. They found nothing positive here either.

A similar study looked at how well 570 mutual funds timed the market over the ten-year period of 1987–96.[4] Depending on how statistical significance is measured, researchers found only between 1 and 5 percent of the total with positive market timing ability. That's not much to write home about.

One fertile source of information about the performance of market timers is the investment newsletter industry. Newsletters recommend to subscribers appropriate weightings of stocks, bonds, or cash. They regularly adjust those weightings based on market timing.

Unfortunately, they do a rather poor job of it. Over the course of twelve years of market timing calls by these newsletters, 31,038 total market timing recommendations in all, only about 15 percent of the newsletters did better than a passive buy-and-hold strategy.[5] Weighing each newsletter's returns equally, researchers John Graham and Harvey Campbell calculated that between 1983 and 1995, the average newsletter returned 12 percent whereas a portfolio of S&P 500 futures and cash with identical risk would have returned 16.8 percent.

More recent experience is no different. At the end of 2001, the *Wall Street Journal* looked back on what the leading stock strategists at the major brokerage firms had predicted for the market in 2001.[6] With the S&P 500 starting the year at 1,320, forecasts for where it would end the year ranged from 1,300 to 1,715, averaging 1,515. In fact, the S&P 500 closed the year at 1,148, down 13 percent. Lest you think that the failure of analysts to anticipate the market's drop was attributable to the unpredictable events of September 11, the S&P closed at 1,093 on September 10.

Market timing depends on short memories, though. So, you will now routinely hear these same strategists explain how of course the market was overvalued and ripe for a correction going into 2001, how the economy was weakening, and how stock prices were at unsustainable multiples of earnings. Of course, in retrospect, that's easy to say. *But without the benefit of hindsight, the average brokerage strategist predicted the market would go up* 15 percent. Don't ever forget that fact.

Given the dismal record of market timers, you might wonder why the newsletters keep cranking out the market predictions, and why the investment banks continue to issue calls on market timing. We believe the answer is quite simple: money. Running a newsletter is a nice source of income, and there's nothing like an investment bank's call for investors to get into (or out of) stocks to generate brokerage commissions.

Indeed, one former broker reports that when the investment firms make an asset allocation change, they do not track whether the call turned out to be right. Rather, they track the increased revenue commission revenue generated by the call.[7] Doesn't that say it all?

Conclusion

Watching the parade of market timers across the airwaves, we can only think of the late Jeanne Dixon, the psychic who became famous for predicting the assassination of John F. Kennedy and remained famous for thirty years even though she never made another accurate prediction of consequence. She is proof that, whether it is market timing or fortune-telling, all you need to remain famous is one good call. (Perhaps not even that: it turns out that Jeanne Dixon never really predicted John F. Kennedy's assassination. She did predict that the winner of the 1960 election would be assassinated, but she also predicted that JFK would lose that election.)

Chapter 13

Why We Draw to Inside Straights and Invest Poorly

A scorpion sees a turtle about to swim across a lake. The
scorpion says, "Please give me a ride to the other side." The
turtle responds, "Absolutely not—you'll sting me and I'll drown." The
scorpion promises, "Not to worry. I won't climb on your shell
until you're in the water, and that way, if I sting you, I'll
drown too." The turtle agrees. Halfway across the lake, the
scorpion stings the turtle. The turtle cries out, "Why
did you do that? You're going to die too." The scorpion
replies, "I guess it's just my nature."

Individual investors often make poor choices when it comes to
building their own wealth. Human psychology plays a big part in
explaining why.

Overconfidence

Overconfidence is one of the central obstacles to escaping the trap of
active fund management and stock picking. You probably believe that
your investments are doing a lot better than they really are. You probably also believe that other people's investments are doing a lot better
than they are.

This tendency is hardly unique to investing. Studies show that people overrate their abilities in all walks of life. Interestingly, the only
professions where psychologists thus far have found that workers real-
istically assess their own skill are meteorology and horse handicapping.[1]
According to Daniel Kahneman, professor of psychology at Princeton
University, these professions are "well calibrated" because: (1) they face

similar problems every day; (2) they make explicit probabilistic predictions; and (3) they obtain swift and precise feedback on outcomes. Wall Street traders probably frequently satisfy these criteria as well. Individual investors almost never satisfy them.

Surveys of investment clubs conducted by the National Association of Investors Corporation (NAIC) showed 60 percent of clubs self-reporting above-market performance.[2] Such a number is not credible on its face, and is contradicted by the earlier study we noted showing investment clubs trailing the market badly. Yet people stand ready to report and believe such figures because they have fallen prey to their overconfidence. They do not receive the clear feedback of a meteorologist ("You idiot! It's raining!") or a handicapper ("You fool! Every fifteen-to-one shot has won its race today!")

Because investors are overconfident, they tend to trade too much, seeking to take advantage of their imagined abilities.

Optimism

People are naturally optimistic. For example, one wonderful Kahneman observation was that most college undergraduates, asked to assess the chances of developing cancer or having a heart attack before the age of fifty, rated their own chances as lower than their roommates'.

Generally, optimism is good. Optimism keeps us going when we hit hard times. It keeps us motivated. Unfortunately, it also leads us to keep making the same mistakes because we believe that things will quickly turn around. As Kahneman puts it, "The combination of overconfidence and optimism is a potent brew, which causes people to overestimate their knowledge, underestimate risks and exaggerate their ability to control events."[3]

Because investors are generally optimistic, they tend to believe that a strategy that has brought them losses in the past may yet bring them gains.

Avoidance of Losses

You may have assumed that investors are rational profit maximizers. Kahneman and another pioneer in the field of behavioral finance, Amos Tversky, have shown that they are not. According to their "prospect theory," investors are much more distressed by losses than pleased by gains. The theory is confirmed by empirical research finding that a loss of $1 is approximately twice as painful to investors as a gain of $1 is pleasant.[4]

This asymmetry alters investor behavior. Applying prospect theory specifically to the world of investing, two other psychologists, Hersh Shefrin and Meir Statman, discovered what they called the "disposition effect." In order to avoid recognizing that they have made a bad investment, investors will tend to hold losers. In order to realize the psychic gains of making a good investment, they will sell winners.[5] Of course, this behavior is a very poor tax strategy.

The disposition effect received solid support in research by Terrance Odean when he studied six years of trading records for ten thousand accounts at a large discount brokerage house. Sure enough, investors realized their gains more readily than their losses. Only in December of each year, with tax consequences uppermost in their mind, did investors reverse this trend. The other eleven months, they traded in a way that maximized their tax liability.[6]

Such is the pain of recognizing a loss. This phenomenon should not be news to anyone who has looked at the chat board for a depressed Internet stock. There you see people who bought a stock at $120, bought more at $60, still more at $4, and at $1.60 are still telling anyone who will listen that it's coming back.

Because investors dislike recognizing losses, they tend to sell winning stocks rather than losing stocks, thereby deferring the need to recognize losses.

I'm Beginning to See a Pattern in These Random Numbers!

Most superior performance from mutual funds is random and thus transitory. Only a few exceed the broader market over the longer term, and then only by small amounts. *Nonetheless, investors continue to pour money into "hot" funds with great short-term performance, expecting that performance to continue. Why?*

The tendency to see patterns even among random events is a natural human trait. How many times have we heard that "deaths always come in threes"?

The world of sports presents wonderful examples of this tendency. Any fan of baseball or basketball is familiar with the concept of the streak hitter or streak shooter or, conversely, the slumping hitter or shooter. Announcers tell us that a basketball team has called timeout to make sure they're getting the ball to the "hot" hand. Slumping hitters readjust their swings (and, in extreme cases, diet and marriages) in an attempt to "get out" of their slumps.

Believe it or not, an Indiana University professor, S. Christian Albright, actually examined the pattern of batting for all regular players in Major League baseball for a four-year period, charting whether each at-bat for each player was a success (hit, walk, sacrifice) or failure (out).[7] He then compared the pattern with what one would expect to see if the outcomes were completely random, like coin flipping. To isolate streaks and eliminate possible biases, he (somewhat amazingly) controlled for factors such as whether the game was home or away, whether it was night or day, whether it was played on turf or grass, whether the opposing pitcher was right handed or left handed, and also factored in the opposing pitcher's earned run average. In other words, the question was whether streaks were independent of the tendency, for example, of right-handed batters to hit better against lefties than righties (and thus to perform better than average if they happen to face several lefties in a row).

The results showed that there were no more streaks than one would expect from randomness. A career and season-long .300 hitter on a 0 for 17 streak is a .300 hitter at his next at-bat. A career and season-long

.300 hitter on a 5 for 5 streak is a .300 hitter at his next at-bat. Thus, all those hitters adjusting their swings after going 0 for 17 are like someone switching coins after flipping a string of "tails"—worse actually, since they may be screwing up a good swing (or marriage).

The study does not mean that batters lack skill or that skill is random. Rather, it means that given each batter's own skill level, one cannot predict future events based on recent past events.

Lest you think such results are confined to baseball, other researchers charted each shot taken by the members of the NBA's Philadelphia 76ers over an entire season.[8] Again, the pattern of makes and misses was indistinguishable from what one would expect from random chance. There were consecutive makes and misses, to be sure, but with no more predictability than one would expect to see with coin tosses.

So, what is the relevance to investing? If a mutual fund or a particular stock outperforms the market for the past year, most people are disinclined to view that result as a random variation from average performance. People don't want to believe that simple random chance is causing some of the thousands of mutual funds and stocks to beat the market averages, just as they don't want to believe that an average baseball player's twenty-game hitting streak is fully consistent with, and merely a random departure from, his average ability. Instead, in each case, people want to believe that things have changed. They want to believe that the average hitter has now become an above-average hitter or that the average mutual fund manager will now be able to beat the market every year.

The tendency to see patterns becomes dangerous when it is combined with overconfidence. Not only do investors tend to see patterns where none exist, they tend to believe that they are the only ones who can see them! How else, really, could millions of people watch CNBC and read *Money* magazine and all believe they were getting an edge over other investors?

Because investors see patterns where none exist, they are attracted to "hot" funds and stocks. Thus, investors tend to make risky investments and trade excessively.

Obstacles to Learning

Having seen that we all have weaknesses that tend to make us poor investors, why don't we notice the problem and change our behavior? Why don't we ever learn? We believe there are three main reasons.

1. Investors are not self-critical when it comes to their choices. While they are anxious about their financial choices, this anxiety does not breed self-examination. Furthermore, because investors want a zone of privacy around their finances, they are reluctant to discuss ideas with friends and family.

2. The financial services industry spends billions in advertising to keep investors excited about the prospect of better returns around the corner.

3. And most important, as Terrance Odean has put it, "Equity markets are a noisy place to learn." To learn from one's experience, one must first understand it. Yet an investor who earned consistently high returns in a fifteen-year bull market probably would not have noticed if those returns trailed the even-higher returns of the overall market. Also, many of the costs of investing are practically invisible—you never have to write a check to anyone for fees or commissions. And while investors may feel the volatility of their investments, they probably have neither the time nor the background to calculate whether their investments are more volatile than the market as a whole.

This information should better prepare you on each of these fronts. Though still human, you should be better able to view investing dispassionately and analytically.

A Final Thought

In the spring of 2001, *Money* magazine interviewed Daniel Kahneman, the cofounder of prospect theory. Asked how he invested his money, he said that he favors index funds. "I don't try to be clever at all."[9] What a truly wonderful summary of everything we believe about investing.

Part IV

Passive Investing for (Less) Fun and (More) Profit

Two men are camping, asleep in their tents, when they hear a loud crashing sound. One of them peeks outside the tent and says, "Oh, God, it's a bear!" The other begins lacing up the running shoes he's brought along. The first asks him, "What are you doing? You can't outrun the bear. They can run twenty miles an hour and climb trees!" The second man responds, "I don't have to outrun the bear; I just have to outrun you."

I t's the first day of classes at Harvard Law School in 1984, and Dean James Vorenberg is delivering opening remarks to the first-year class. He begins with the joke about the bear. An uncomfortable silence follows, as the story is cold comfort indeed for nervous law students seeking reassurance that they are about to commence an enjoyable, collaborative experience. As inappropriate as the bear story may have been for Greg and his fellow students, it is also among the best investing advice we have ever heard.

Why?

Just as you cannot win and should not enter a footrace with a bear, you cannot win and should not enter a performance race with the stock market. Rather, you should buy the market as a whole and stop trying to outrun it through active fund management or stock picking. Just take satisfaction in outrunning all of your peers, who still have the ankle weights of active management slowing them down.

Passive investment means investing broadly in the stocks that make up the market, based solely on those stocks' proportion of the market. *Passive investing means accepting the valuation that the market has as-*

signed each stock and not trying to profit from speculation on which of those values may prove wrong.

Over time, passive investing—an idea—has become largely synonymous with index investing—an application of that idea—and index mutual funds—a product. While this book is called *The Great Mutual Fund Trap*, we consider index funds a very different animal from actively managed funds. (Sadly, *The Great Actively Managed Mutual Fund Trap* doesn't really roll off the tongue.) Increasingly, passive investing is also synonymous with a relatively new product, exchange-traded index funds, which share some of the best attributes of index funds and stock ownership. Recent developments in the brokerage industry also may allow some investors with time and money to assemble a passive portfolio directly (though we'd be cautious).

We will take a look at index mutual funds in Chapter 14, turn to exchange-traded funds in Chapter 15, and a new breed of brokers we call discount portfolio companies in Chapter 16. You will see not only the reasons to choose those products as the vehicle for passive investment, but also how to choose among them. Finally, in Chapter 17, we'll discuss the best way to shed your active investments as you move to passive investing.

Chapter 14

Index Funds

No one has ever said anything witty or charming about
index funds.—*Gregory Baer and Gary Gensler*

I ndex funds are the one type of mutual fund that we like. You won't
hear much about them from the financial industry or the financial
media, though. For the financial industry, they are a low margin
product. Since mutual funds are in business to make money for their
own shareholders, not the shareholders in their funds, we can certainly
understand why they are not pushing index funds. (Vanguard, with its
unusual ownership structure, is a happy exception.) For the financial
media, nothing makes worse copy than an index fund. Index fund managers won't pick hot stocks or identify winning investment strategies.
There's no news in their world.

What that means is that your journey as an index fund investor must
be largely self-directed. Lacking daily prompting from your television
or your mailbox, you'll need to educate yourself. So let's proceed to
learn how to earn more money with less risk.

Index Funds in a Nutshell

Index funds basically buy and hold stocks that make up a market index. Investing through index funds comes down to a two-step process. First, choose an appropriate index. Second, choose a fund that tracks that index at the lowest cost. With index funds, the equation should always be: market returns - cost = your returns. Isn't that nice and simple?

Choosing an Index

Stock indexes have been around for a long time. Charles Dow and Edward Davis Jones began the Dow Jones Index in 1884. Two years later, they christened the Dow Jones Industrial Average and began publishing it in the *Wall Street Journal*. Indexes like the Dow were used to gauge the performance of the market as a whole, and later came to serve as a benchmark for evaluating the performance of money managers. In the 1970s, large institutional investors began to see the virtues of simply investing in a portfolio tracking a given index, rather than paying managers to try to beat the index. Individual investors only began to follow suit years later.

Recently, some financial firms have sought to expand the use of indexing by publishing indexes focused on narrower segments of the U.S. and world markets. The result has been a proliferation of new indexes, covering every business sector and investing style you could imagine.

Which index to choose, then? Here are our criteria:

1. *The index should track the broad market.* In order to gain all of the risk-reduction benefits of a diversified portfolio, you need to own many stocks from all segments of the market. While buying that many stocks on your own would be prohibitively expensive, you lose nothing by choosing an index fund that tracks a very broad index.

2. *The index should be value neutral.* A value-neutral index takes no point of view about the future direction of the market or any of its numerous sectors. Such an index—generally referred to as a total-

market index—invests in all types of stocks in all sectors of the economy.

3. *The index should be market-capitalization weighted.* Market weighting simply means that an index holds an amount of each stock that is proportional to that stock's share of the total market capitalization of the index.

A market-weighted index reduces transaction costs for the index funds tracking it. These funds do not have to buy or sell shares due to price movements, as holdings automatically rebalance. Good news: most major indexes are market-weighted.

4. *The index must be investable.* By "investable," we mean that the stocks in the index must be available in sufficient quantity for an index fund to purchase them at reasonable bid/ask spreads. In the U.S. market, investability is not a significant concern. For international indexes, though, investability can be a bigger issue.

5. *Ideally, the index should be float adjusted.* Market-weighted indexes must define the market capitalization of each stock and the index as a whole. A common way is simply to include all outstanding shares of each company at its current market price. A better way is to exclude shares held by insiders and count only those shares that can be bought and sold in the market. This is known as float adjustment. It saves money for funds tracking the index, as they don't have to buy as many shares of companies that are largely privately held.*

And the Verdict Is In . . .

Most indexes fail to meet all five criteria. The Dow Jones Industrial Average, for example, does not track a broad number of stocks, is not value neutral, is not market-capitalization weighted, and is not float adjusted.

---

* Suppose that the Wile E. Coyote family holds 90 percent of Acme company after a successful IPO. If an index is not float adjusted, all of Acme's shares will be counted in determining Acme's proportion of the index. All of the index funds will therefore have to buy Acme shares in that proportion, even though only 10 percent are available to the public. If the index is float adjusted, they need buy only the proportional share of 10 percent of Acme, excluding the Coyote family shares.

Sector indexes do not track the broad market, are not value neutral, and most are not float adjusted.

Here is a brief description of the major indexes that do meet all or most of the criteria set forth above. All are investable.

Indexes	Coverage of market	Value neutral?	Cap weighted	Float adjusted
Wilshire 5000	99%	Yes	Yes	No
Russell 3000	98%	Yes	Yes	Yes
Russell 1000	92%	Yes	Yes	Yes
S&P 500	77%	Not really	Yes	No

Wilshire 5000

The broadest representation of the market is the Wilshire 5000 Total Market Index. Founded by Wilshire Associates in 1974, the index attempts to measure the performance of all U.S.-headquartered companies whose stocks have readily available price data. Stocks are selected for the index based on minimum daily trading volume and level of institutional holdings. The index includes common stocks, real estate investment trusts, and even limited partnerships. Stocks that represent interests in foreign-based companies are excluded.

Although the index tracked about 5,000 stocks when first created, it now includes over 6,500. These stocks make up 99 percent of the U.S. equity market. The Wilshire 5000, however, is not float adjusted.

Russell 3000 and 1000

The Russell 3000 Index measures the performance of the three thousand largest U.S. companies based on total market capitalization. It is one of many indexes published by the Frank Russell Company. Those three thousand stocks represent 98 percent of the U.S. equity market, so the coverage (and performance) is basically similar to the Wilshire 5000.[1] The performance of the Russell 3000 and Wilshire 5000 did diverge unusually over the period 1999–2001, but the reason was not the composition of the indexes. Rather, because the Russell 3000 is float adjusted and the Wilshire 5000 is not, the Russell 3000 held proportionally fewer shares of technology companies (whose founders tended to retain a lot of shares); Microsoft, for example, consistently represented a higher percentage of the Wilshire 5000 than the Russell 3000. Furthermore, Wilshire adds recent IPOs to its index sooner than Russell, which added to its higher technology weighting. As a result, the Russell 3000 trailed the Wilshire 5000 in 1999 and 2000 but then led in 2001 as technology shares sank. Absent another single-sector and IPO boom, though, you can expect the two indexes to perform about the same.

The Russell 3000 Index has a sibling, the Russell 1000 Index, which simply tracks the one thousand largest stocks in the Russell 3000. It covers 92 percent of the U.S. equity market. Think of the Russell 1000 as about the same as the Russell 3000 but with a slight leaning toward large capitalization stocks.

S&P 500

The S&P 500 Index is published by Standard & Poor's, which is also well known for its ratings of corporate debt. The S&P 500 Index is the most popular choice for index funds. It is easy for index fund managers to track, as it holds large-cap liquid stocks. It is also heavily marketed by Standard & Poor's, which has licensed it for numerous uses. The index attracts about $1 trillion in indexed investment. It is also the benchmark against which most diversified mutual funds are measured.[2]

That said, the S&P 500 Index is a large-cap, managed index. Contrary to popular belief, the five hundred stocks in the S&P 500 Index are not the five hundred largest stocks in the U.S. markets. Rather, a seven-member committee at Standard & Poor's selects the stocks. In the year 2000, S&P made a record eighteen changes to the index that were discretionary—that is, not forced by merger or liquidation of a member. Jason Zweig of *Money* magazine has noted that the S&P committee has also tended to choose growth stocks for the index.[3]

The S&P 500 Index has performed better than the overall market over the past ten to fifteen years. Over the ten years ending in 2001, the S&P 500 returned 12.9 percent annually, better than the Wilshire 5000's 12.3 percent. We would not expect the S&P 500 Index to continue to outperform the broader market over the long term, however.

From 1975 to 2001, the performance of the Wilshire 5000 and S&P 500 was about the same, with the Wilshire 5000 having slightly less volatility. Since 1975, the Wilshire 5000 has outperformed in fifteen years, and the S&P 500 outperformed in twelve. The S&P 500 had a five-year winning streak from 1994 to 1998, but that streak was exceeded by the Wilshire 5000's six-year streak from 1976 to 1981.

Nonetheless, we feel that the S&P 500 is roughly on par with the other broader indexes. We admit to a modest preference for the Russell 3000 or Wilshire 5000, or even the broader S&P 1500. That said, we wouldn't really object if you decide to track the S&P 500. Its behavior is sufficiently close to a broad-market index that the quality of the overlying fund can make the difference. As we'll see in a moment, there are some excellent funds that track the S&P 500 Index at very low cost.

How to Choose an Index Fund

Once you have decided on an index, you need to decide which fund tracking that index is best for you. All index funds are not alike, so the decision is an important one.

Index funds for individual investors are a relatively recent development. The first index fund for retail investors, tracking the S&P 500 Index, was introduced by Vanguard in 1976, and it was the only such fund in existence for the next eight years.[4] As recently as 1990, there were only about a dozen stock index funds open to retail investors.

Vanguard continues to dominate the field of index funds for retail investors. Vanguard operates seven of the ten largest index funds. Two other companies, Barclays Global Investors and State Street, dominate indexing for pension funds and other institutional investors. They also act as "subadvisers" for other index funds, and thus may be the real managers of the index fund offered by your bank or broker.

Expenses and Turnover

Set out below are the expenses of the largest retail stock index funds. We have broken them into two groups: the five largest broad-market index funds (the ones we like) and the five largest specialized funds (the ones we don't).[5]

Expenses and Turnover of Large Index Funds

Broad-market index funds	Expense Ratio	Turn-over	Benchmark Index
Vanguard 500 Index	0.18%	9%	S&P 500
Vanguard Total Stock Index	0.20%	7%	Wilshire 5000
Fidelity Spartan 500 Index	0.19%	5%	S&P 500
Schwab 1000 Investor	0.47%	9%	Schwab 1000
T. Rowe Price Equity Index 500	0.35%	9%	S&P 500
Sector-index funds			
Vanguard Growth Index	0.22%	33%	S&P 500/Barra Growth
Vanguard Small-Cap Index	0.27%	49%	Russell 2000 S&P 500/Barra
Vanguard Value Index	0.22%	37%	Value
Vanguard Extended Market Index	0.25%	33%	Wilshire 4500
Vanguard Mid-Cap Index	0.25%	51%	S&P Mid-Cap 400 Index

Source: Morningstar Principia Pro, data through December 31, 2001.

At the outset, we should emphasize that any of these index funds, including the specialized ones, are a bargain compared with their actively managed counterparts. None of these funds charges a sales load. Their turnover is about one tenth that of actively managed funds. With the exception of one Schwab fund, the management fees are universally very low, about a sixth of those charged by the average actively managed fund.

You do see, however, two major advantages of true passive management over specialized funds: the best broad-market index funds have slightly lower fees and significantly lower turnover than the size and style sector funds. While none of the business sector funds was large enough to make the chart, those funds have even higher fees than their size and style cousins. The average expense ratio for a business sector index fund is around 0.7 percent.

Don't make the mistake, however, of thinking all index funds of the same type are the same. Here is a sampling of S&P 500 Index funds. We'll ignore loads, so as to isolate the difference that fees and operational efficiency can make.

Fund	5-year returns	3-year returns
Vanguard 500 Index	10.7%	-1.1%
T. Rowe Price Equity Index 500	10.4%	-1.3%
Schwab S&P 500 Index Investor	10.3%	-1.3%
Wachovia Equity Index Y Shares*	10.2%	-1.5%
Munder Index 500 K Shares*	10.0%	-1.7%
Wells Fargo Equity Index A	9.9%	-1.7%
S&P 500 Index	**10.7%**	**-1.0%**

Source: Morningstar Principia Pro, data as of December 31, 2001.

* For funds with multiple classes, we chose the lowest load alternative, to allow better comparison to the other no-load funds.

In addition to the variation in returns, you may be surprised to notice that the Vanguard 500 index fund has actually equaled the performance of the S&P 500 Index over the past five years. You may wonder how in the world an index fund, with its fees and expenses, can stay even with the index it tracks. The answer requires a detailed understanding of how index funds actually operate and the efficiencies they can achieve. While we find that subject interesting, you may not, so we present it in an appendix.

Consider the Tax Man

Index funds have significantly lower turnover ratios than actively managed funds. This leads to lower taxes for investors. Morningstar ranks the tax efficiency of funds as a ratio of after-tax to pretax returns (with 100 percent meaning no returns were lost to capital gains or income taxes). As so measured, the five largest broad market index funds averaged 94 percent and 93 percent tax efficiency over the past five and ten years.

As you would expect, the specialized indexed funds are less tax efficient, with the Vanguard Extended Market index fund, a small-cap index fund, registering only 81 percent tax efficiency over ten years.

Just to flash back to active fund management, the average ten-year tax efficiency for the ten largest actively managed domestic stock funds is 83 percent.[6] The Janus Fund, for example, has tax efficiency of 80 percent. In other words, if the net asset value of your holdings in both the Schwab 1000 Investor index fund and the Janus Fund rose $1,000 next year, you would lose only $40 of that $1,000 to taxes with the Schwab index funds and $200 with the Janus Fund. That is a very significant difference.

How to Invest in Index Funds

Here's how we advise you invest in index funds.

1. Select an index, preferably a total market index with at least as much coverage of the market as the S&P 500.
2. Identify funds that track that index.
3. Choose a fund with low fees and no load, and which minimizes trading costs and remains continually invested in stocks. The easiest way to identify such a fund is to compare its annual returns to the returns of the underlying index over at least a five-year period. A fund that tracks its index closely probably fits the bill.

We believe the case for Vanguard is very strong. Both its Total Stock Index fund and 500 Index funds have low costs and solid track records. Fidelity customers who have grown disillusioned with active management, but nonetheless appreciate Fidelity's excellent customer service and other resources, also have an excellent index fund to choose.

Chapter 15

Exchange-Traded Funds

An invasion of armies can be resisted, but not an idea
whose time has come.—*Victor Hugo*

The exchange-traded mutual fund is a wonderful new vehicle for passive investment, particularly if you have a lump sum to invest in a taxable account. ETFs, as they are often called, are a genuine innovation in finance, presenting opportunities for both individual and institutional investors. For larger investments, they combine the best of stock ownership with the best of index fund ownership.

As a result, exchange-traded funds have become one of the hottest products in the mutual fund industry, with assets under management doubling every year for the six years ending 2000, and growing to over $82 billion by the end of 2001. Such growth continued even through recent bear markets. That said, ETFs are still a nascent product, representing about 2 percent of total industry assets.

Think of an ETF as an index fund in stock clothing. Like a stock, an ETF trades on an exchange. Because ETFs are exchange-traded, they can be bought and sold at any moment of the day. Like a mutual fund, however, an ETF represents the net asset value of a basket of other stocks, and its value rises and falls with the value of that basket of stocks, not the value of the company that sponsors the ETF.[1]

While ETFs have not been around long enough to establish a long-term track record, there is every reason to believe that their returns will mirror their indexes in the same way as traditional index funds. Their investment strategies generally are the same as those of index mutual funds, and they are managed by some of the biggest firms in indexing, Barclays, State Street, and Vanguard. The one broad-market ETF with a five-year track record, State Street's S&P 500, SPDR, trails its S&P 500 benchmark by only four basis points (0.04 percent) per year over that period.

Fees for ETFs are extremely low. None of the seventy-plus ETFs that track the U.S. market has an expense ratio higher than 0.6 percent. The ETFs tracking the broad market have fees even lower than the already low fees of their corresponding index funds. The expense ratio of Barclays's iShares S&P 500 Index ETF, for example, is only nine basis points (0.09 percent) per year.

For taxable accounts, ETFs feature even lower turnover than index funds. This means better control over realization of capital gains and lower taxes for you.

Exchange-traded funds do have one cost that traditional index funds do not: the brokerage commission and bid/ask spread paid to acquire the shares. These trading costs will offset some of the cost advantages that ETFs hold over index funds. How much they offset depends on how often you trade and in what amounts. For investors who like to invest small amounts on a regular basis, brokerage commissions will make index funds a better choice than ETFs. On the other hand, if you have a lump sum to invest in a taxable account, we believe that ETFs can be a superior choice.

Generally speaking, if you have more than $5,000 to $10,000 to invest in a taxable account, you should be giving ETFs a very good look.

Who They Are, How They Work

A general description of ETFs and the major players in the ETF market is set forth below. You may wish to gather further details about individual ETFs by visiting the ETF center at Morningstar.com, the ETF section of the American Stock Exchange's website, www.amex.com, or the indexfunds.com website—all of which provide excellent, up-to-date information.

Who They Are

You may recognize some of the major names in exchange-traded funds.

- The biggest player in ETFs has been State Street Global Advisors, which offered the first ETF in 1993. State Street's products are offered under the name of StreetTracks. Its most popular offering is its Standard & Poor's Depository Receipt, SPDR (pronounced "spider," which invests in the S&P 500). The ticker symbol is SPY.
- Barclays Global Investors moved into the ETF arena in 1996, and now offers more than seventy-five ETFs in conjunction with Dow Jones, the Frank Russell Company (of the Russell stock indexes), and Standard & Poor's. Its product is called iShares. Investors can invest passively through an iShares Russell 3000 index fund (ticker symbol IWV), iShares Dow Jones U.S. Total Market index fund (IYY), or iShares S&P 500 index fund (IVV). Barclays also offers iShares targeted to particular business sectors (e.g., chemicals, telecommunications) and large- and small-cap sectors (e.g., Russell 1000 Growth, S&P SmallCap 600). It also launched the first broad international index ETF in 2001, trading under the ticker symbol EFA.
- The Vanguard Group entered the ETF market in 2001 with its product, VIPERs (short for Vanguard Index Participation Equity Receipts). Vanguard's plan is for VIPERs to hold the same stocks as some of Vanguard's traditional funds, though as of 2002 its only offering is the Total Stock Market Index Fund, ticker VTI. (One unique feature: Vanguard will allow holders of its Total Stock Market index fund to exchange into the comparable ETF.) Interestingly, Vanguard lost a court battle with McGraw Hill, owner of Standard & Poor's, which had refused to let Vanguard offer ETFs based on the S&P 500 (having already made a deal with Barclays).
- Merrill Lynch has a product akin to ETFs, known as HOLDRS (short for holding company depository receipts). HOLDRS generally focus on particular industry segments. The first HOLDRS represented the various spin-offs of a Brazilian telecommunica-

tions company, Telebras. Then came HOLDRS focused on the Internet, biotech, and telecommunications industries. Later, however, Merrill Lynch launched a slightly broader market HOLDRS, its Market 2000+, which contains fifty of the largest stocks from around the world.

- The second largest ETF is now the Nasdaq 100 Index Tracking Stock, best known by its ticker symbol, QQQ (also known as Qs or Qubes), managed by the Bank of New York. Qubes allow investors to own the tech-heavy one-hundred largest stocks on the Nasdaq. It is the equivalent of a large-cap technology sector index fund.
- DIAMONDS Trust Series I, DIAMONDS, initiated in 1998, tracks the performance of the Dow Jones Industrial Average and is managed by State Street. The ticker is DIA.

How They Work

The basic difference between traditional mutual funds and exchange-traded funds is how they are traded and valued. With a traditional mutual fund, the fund creates and distributes new shares whenever you or another individual investor signs up. The assets of the fund increase by the amount of your purchase, and the fund invests those assets. Conversely, should you decide to leave the fund, the assets will have to shrink (however marginally) in order to pay back your money.

Index fund shares are valued at the end of each day by the fund's sponsor. The sponsor calculates the net asset value (NAV) by adding up the value of the underlying stocks and dividing by the number of outstanding shares. That's the price you pay or receive when buying or selling an index fund.

With an ETF, on the other hand, shares are created or redeemed by large institutions. There is no cash involved; the transaction is an in-kind trade of ETF shares for the underlying stocks. The ETF sponsor holds the stocks and issues ETF shares to the institutional investor, which can then trade them. Individual investors then buy and sell ETF shares in the market along with institutional investors. The important fact to recognize is that trading by individual investors does not affect the asset size of the ETF, as such trades occur on the exchange and simply transfer ownership of the ETF shares to another party. We'll see in a moment why this is important.

ETFs are valued through real-time exchange trading. Because institutional investors can swap shares of the ETF for the underlying stocks at any time, ETF shares trade extremely closely to their underlying NAV the vast majority of the time. For example, if for some reason the price of an S&P 500 ETF should fall below the collective value of its underlying shares, institutional investors can buy the ETF shares and trade them in for the underlying shares, making a profit. This buying pressure will drive the price of the ETF shares back up to fair value. In effect, the market performs through arbitrage the function that the sponsor of a traditional mutual fund performs at the end of the day.

What we loosely call exchange-traded funds actually come in three different legal structures: open-end mutual funds, unit investment trusts, and a grantor trust. Barclays and State Street (for sector ETFs) use the open-end structure, which is basically the same structure used by traditional mutual funds. SPYDR, QQQ, and DIAMONDS are all unit investment trusts. The grantor trust is unique to Merrill Lynch's HOLDRS.

The open-end structure has one significant advantage over UIT form: it allows automatic reinvestment of dividends. Your money can be immediately reinvested in ETFs, rather than lying in a money market account until you have time to reinvest it. While the boost to earnings is relatively small, we think this feature should lead you to give the Barclays iShares broad market funds a first look.*

The grantor trust is an intriguing structure, as it represents a true buy-and-hold strategy. The portfolio is not rebalanced if companies are acquired or bankrupted, or if one company's stock comes to represent a substantial percentage of the HOLDRS. There are accordingly no management fees to pay, only the original brokerage commission and a small annual custody fee. That said, HOLDRS have not been diversi-

---

* There are a few other, less important differences among the different forms. Open-end funds can lower costs by use of sampling and derivatives, while those tools are forbidden to UITs. UITs avoid the cost of maintaining a board of directors, but that cost is minimal.

fied, so watch out. For more information, check out www.holdrs.com or www.amex.com.[2]

Buying an ETF

Once you've identified an ETF you like, purchasing it is extremely easy. You buy it just like any other stock, using a broker (preferably a low-cost, on-line discount broker). You pay about the same commission and bid/ask spread you would for any other stock.

The Benefits of ETFs as a Vehicle for Passive Investment

ETFs are a good vehicle for passive investment for five primary reasons:

- they can offer the same total market diversification as index mutual funds
- they are more tax efficient than index mutual funds because of their structure
- they remain fully invested in stocks because they operate with no cash holdings
- their fees tend to be slightly lower than index funds because they have fewer administrative costs
- their trading costs are marginally lower than index funds because of their low turnover

The first advantage is relatively simple. Issues of organization aside, exchange-traded index funds hold the same assets as traditional index mutual funds. Vanguard, for example, offers its Total Stock Market Index through both ETF and open-end share classes. So, all the passive investing advantages of traditional funds apply to ETFs as well.

The second advantage, tax efficiency, derives from how ETFs are structured. Because ETFs trade on an exchange, every sale is matched with a purchase and therefore the assets of the fund do not change. So, unlike a traditional mutual fund, an ETF is not forced to sell stock and create capital gains when shareholders decide to leave the fund.[3]

ETFs are not immune to tax issues. They must deal with turnover in the underlying index, just like an index fund. In doing so, they have a major advantage. When *institutional* customers redeem ETF shares, the ETF sponsor must return to them a basket of all the stocks contained in the index. The ETF, though, generally returns the shares of each company's stocks with the lowest tax basis.[4] Then when a stock is dropped from the index, the ETF is left with only the highest-basis shares of that stock in its inventory. The ETF thus incurs less capital gain from disposing of a profitable stock than an identical index fund would.

As a result, the broad market ETFs we recommend are extremely tax efficient. Between 1993 and 2000, for example, the SPDR ETF paid out only one nine-cent long-term capital gain distribution and no short-term distributions.

The third advantage of ETFs is that they remain fully invested in stocks. Because they need not be ready to fund individual redemptions, ETFs hold zero cash balances, while index funds hold around 2 percent. Even the modest 2 percent cash holdings of the standard index fund can lower returns by six to eight basis points (0.06 to 0.08 percent) per year over the long run.[5] When it comes to the drag of idle cash, ETFs are the equivalent of stealth fighters.

The fourth benefit, lower fees, derives primarily from the fact that ETFs need not pay for shareholder accounting. Whereas traditional mutual funds must track who buys and sells their shares, ETFs are traded on an exchange. Responsibility for determining who owns its shares falls to the brokerage industry. Estimates are that transferring this function saves ETFs at least five basis points of costs per year.[6] The final benefit of ETFs is lower trading costs, resulting from their lower turnover and the absence of retail redemptions.

The expense ratios for the largest broad market ETFs confirm that they are cheaper to operate than their traditional mutual fund cousins.

ETF	Assets $MM	Expense Ratio
SPDRs	$27,521	0.17%
iShares S&P 500 Index	$2,601	0.09%
iShares Russell 3000 Index	$616	0.20%
iShares Russell 1000 Index	$444	0.15%
Vanguard Total Stock Market VIPERs	$153	0.13%
iShares Dow Jones U.S. Total Market Index	$81	0.20%

Source: Morningstar Principia Pro, data through September 30, 2001.

The Barclays iShares version of the S&P 500 Index has the lowest fees of any retail fund: nine basis points, or 0.09 percent per year. The ETF version of Vanguard's Total Stock Market fund has fees of 0.13 percent compared to 0.20 percent for the fund version.

ETFs Aren't for Everyone

While ETFs can be a wonderful tool for investors investing a lump sum and facing taxation, they are a poor alternative to index funds for investors who are saving a little bit each month. Buying or selling ETFs means paying a brokerage commission and bid/ask spread. You pay no similar cost with a no-load index fund. For someone putting away a few hundred dollars a month, these costs disqualify ETFs as a sensible investment.

For this reason, we believe that even the most enthusiastic ETF investor will want to hold an index fund as well, in order to invest smaller amounts from time to time.

Furthermore, the significant tax benefits of ETFs are irrelevant if you're investing through an IRA or other tax-exempt account. Here again, a no-load index fund is probably going to be a better investment, even if you're investing pretty large amounts.

Where ETFs Fall Short

You may wonder whether ETFs, with their reduced fees and costs, can make sector investing work for you. The answer is no.

Sector ETFs are numerous and growing rapidly. The second most popular ETF, QQQ, is basically an industry fund focused on technology. The next three largest industry ETFs are the Technology Select SPDR, the Financial Select Sector SPDR, and the Consumer Staples Select SPDR. Barclays offers the largest number of industry ETFs through its iShares program, over twenty in all.

ETFs also offer investors the chance to invest by style and size. Through 2001, the third largest ETF was the MidCap SPDR.

Thus far, the biggest buyers of sector ETFs have been institutional investors, who wish to have exposure to a particular part of the market without picking individual stocks. The financial industry, though, is also peddling them to individual investors. Their pitch is that with one trade, you can bet on a particular sector rather than a particular stock.

The industry also markets the idea of building a portfolio of sector ETFs. A diversified portfolio of sector ETFs, however, will be much the same as owning a single broad-market ETF. The only differences are higher costs and risks. The average business-sector ETF, for example, has an expense ratio of 0.5 percent, and turnover rates of 20 percent—both higher than diversified index funds or ETFs. But the industry is hoping that you'll overlook this relatively small difference in costs in exchange for the opportunity to "overweight" a particular sector and try to beat the market.

The industry makes one plausible case for sector ETFs for a small group of better-off investors. Given their jobs or current stock holdings, some investors may already have significant exposure to a particular business sector. Suppose that you work in the technology industry and own a large number of technology stocks with large gains, or have options for your own company's stock. Convinced of the value of passive investment, you may wish to buy a broad-market ETF. Doing so, however, effectively means investing over 20 percent of that new money in technology stocks, where you already own stocks and where you earn your income. To manage that risk, ideally, you would buy a broad-market fund that covers all sectors *except* technology. Since no such fund exists, you may wish to buy a half dozen sector funds covering other industries, and then sit tight with a more or less diversified portfolio. The goal of such a strategy, it is important to note, is to *reduce risk, not pick winning sectors.*

For investors in that position, using sector ETFs may make sense. But for the great majority of investors, a single diversified ETF will be cheaper and easier than a series of sector ETFs.

Wrapping Up

Exchange-traded funds are a wonderful new tool for lump-sum passive investment. If you have more than $5,000 to $10,000 to invest in a taxable account, then we believe that ETFs offer the closest thing to cost-free taxable investing than has ever been available to an individual investor. Buy $10,000 of the iShares S&P 500 Index fund, and at the end of ten years you will have paid a grand total of $90 in management fees, plus a one-time $10 to $30 brokerage commission. As Greg's dad used to say, you can't beat that with a stick.

We strongly suggest, though, that you only use ETFs as part of a passive investment strategy. ETFs have made sector investing a more inviting prospect, as you can choose sectors without having to employ and pay an active fund manager. With management fees cut by about two thirds, sector investing may start to look enticing. Keep in mind, though, that sector ETFs still have higher management fees than diversified ETFs. They have higher turnover and less tax efficiency. They are generally much smaller than diversified funds, trade less frequently, and carry wider bid/ask spreads. Most important, they are still more risky than a diversified fund—as investors who bought the QQQs before the great Nasdaq swoon of 2000 will well remember.

Resist temptation, and ETFs can be a wonderful addition to your passive investment tool kit.

Chapter 16

If You Feel You Must . . . How to Buy Stocks the Right Way

> Discipline is the soul of an army. It makes small numbers
> formidable; procures success to the weak, and esteem to
> all.—*George Washington, Letter of Instructions to the Captains
> of the Virginia Regiments, 1759*

As we left the Great Stock Picking Hoax in Part III, we saw that individuals have fared badly trading stocks. So, what is the answer for the individual investor looking to buy individual stocks?

The simple, easy answer—and for just about all investors, the only answer—is to *stop looking to buy individual stocks.* Passive investment is simply a better strategy than active investment, and index funds and ETFs are terrific vehicles through which to execute that strategy.

What if for one reason or another, though, you have decided to hold stocks directly? There may be valid reasons for such a decision. For example, you may have a large inheritance to invest, where the costs of trading represent a small proportion of the total amount. In such cases, owning individual stocks may represent a low-cost way of implementing a buy-and-hold passive strategy, and of retaining total control over your tax liabilities. Then again, to our chagrin, you may just be bound and determined to own stocks.

The question then remains: if you are absolutely committed to direct stock ownership, is there a viable structure through which you can retain most of the benefits of passive investment and also capture some of the benefits of direct ownership?

The only way that you can approach the same long-term, risk-adjusted returns as an index fund or ETF is by replicating their low-cost, low-risk attributes. That means: (1) a buy-and-hold strategy; (2) portfolio diversification; and (3) low costs. The problem, however, is that two of these goals—diversification and low costs—are in fundamental conflict when you buy individual stocks. We'll see if there's a way for some investors to reconcile this conflict.

One caveat before we begin. Done right, buying stocks isn't going to be a lot of fun. You're not going to be a cowboy or cowgirl. You're not going to be able to buy yourself an island. You're going to choose stocks in such a way that the chances of doing exceptionally well are as small as doing exceptionally poorly. You are going to aim to match the performance of the aggregate market at very low cost. It's going to be a lot like a good steady job. It can certainly have its satisfactions, but it is not the same as winning the lottery.

Filling the Basket

By investing in an index fund or ETF you obtain portfolio diversification the easy way. You and your fellow shareholders share the cost of buying numerous stocks in their proportion of the overall market. By holding stocks directly, though, you must shoulder the cost of diversification alone.

The question is, can an individual investor cheat a little—that is, obtain diversification by buying stocks that represent only a tiny portion of the overall market?

How Big a Basket

Modern portfolio theory and the capital asset pricing model teach us that firm-specific risk can be reduced through diversification. (Systematic, or market, risk is unavoidable.) Research suggests that a portfolio of at least thirty stocks, and possibly as many as fifty stocks, is necessary to be adequately diversified.[1] From 1963 to 1985, a randomly selected portfolio of twenty stocks reduced firm-specific risk by about 90 percent. Between 1986 and 1997, however, it would have required a portfolio of fifty stocks to reduce firm-specific risk by 90 percent.[2]

Why are more stocks necessary now than before? Simply because over recent years, the volatility of individual stocks has increased. Investors are seeing greater price swings among the stocks they hold today than they had seen before. And that means more firm-specific risk.

Filling Your Basket of Stocks with Different Types of Eggs

Not every combination of stocks will achieve sufficient diversification. If you pick fifty retailing stocks, you're not going to achieve the full benefits of diversification. So, if you're going to rely on only thirty to fifty stocks, you're going to need to take a few steps to ensure that their performance will vary randomly.

The most effective way to ensure the benefits of diversification is to purchase stocks across the various business sectors of the economy. What are these industries and what are their relationships to the overall market? While different market analysts define sectors differently, a look at Morningstar's sectors is illustrative.

*Morningstar Sectors**	*Percentage of Russell 3000*
Consumer durables	2%
Consumer staples	6%
Energy	6%
Financials	17%
Health	14%
Industrial cyclicals	11%
Retail	5%
Services	12%
Technology	24%
Utilities	3%

* Morningstar Principia Pro, sector weightings as of December 31, 2001.

If you're looking to build a diversified portfolio, buying stocks from each of these sectors, roughly in their percentage of the overall market, is a good way to start. For instance, let's assume that you were going to assemble a portfolio of thirty-three stocks. Basically, that means you are going to allocate 3 percent of your portfolio to each stock. Thus, you could buy two energy stocks, three financials stocks, eight technology stocks, and so on.

Selecting the Eggs

That said, you still have to pick the stocks. And you have to do it yourself. Paying a full-service broker for investment advice raises your transaction costs so high that it pushes an already suspect investing strategy right over the cliff.

Doing so may not be as difficult as it first appears once you accept the fact that a diversified basket of thirty to fifty stocks isn't going to beat, or trail, the market by very much.

Really, you could just randomly select a few stocks from each sector. But trusting to true random chance may make you a little nervous. Alternatively, FOLIOfn, one of the new discount portfolio companies, offers a preselected market portfolio, designed to track the overall market. Its computers try to pick the most average stocks rather than the best stocks, so the portfolio is passive.

If you wish to console yourself that your picks are the product of the best minds on Wall Street, you could determine the highest rated stocks in all the categories you wish to buy. FOLIOfn allows you to do this effortlessly. Who knows? Maybe poor analyst performance will become a thing of the past, and you'll have a chance of slightly outperforming the market.

If you still have a nagging belief that mutual fund managers know something you don't, you could buy the same stocks they're buying. Funds are only required to disclose their portfolios semiannually, but they release their top ten holdings quarterly. If you go to a website like quote.com (run by Lipper Analytical Services), you can easily see who owns what. Go about fifteen days after the end of a quarter, and you'll have the freshest information.

We are not suggesting to you that these strategies will "beat the market." We are not describing can't-miss schemes or arbitrage opportunities. We are simply trying to describe methods of choosing particular stocks to fill up a diversified basket if you are inclined to hold stocks directly. Even a random walk has to start in some direction.

Buying the Basket

Having seen how to go about selecting and managing a diversified portfolio of stocks, we now face the question of how to *buy* one. Here we face the conflict between diversification and cost. If you have $1,000 or even $25,000 to invest in the stock market at a given time, traditional brokerages offer no structure through which to directly buy thirty to fifty stocks at low cost. Buying a single share, or ten shares, of so many stocks will result in trading costs that are very high as a percentage of your investment. Your chances of outperforming an index fund or ETF over the long term are practically nil.

The Old-Fashioned Way: Direct Purchases Through a Broker

Until the late 1990s, the only way to purchase a portfolio of stocks directly was through a broker. While discount brokers have certainly lowered the cost of buying stocks, they still have not been able to beat indexing. Some quick math shows why.

Even with a discount broker's low commissions of, say, $30 per trade, that's still $900 to $1,500 in brokerage commissions to purchase thirty to fifty stocks. Even ignoring bid/ask spreads, and assuming (generously) you were to hold each stock for ten years, you would need to invest at least $65,000 to $107,000 *at a time* in order to break even with the annual costs (0.2 percent per year) of an index fund. If your alternative is investing in an ETF (with fees as low as 0.09 percent), the threshold at which direct purchases make sense doubles.[3] Adding something in for the bid/ask spreads, we think it is more realistic to think of a breakeven investment amount for a disciplined buy-and-hold investor in the range of $200,000 to $250,000 for *each purchase*. That's obviously not going to work for most investors.

A New and Better Way: Discount Portfolio Companies

A new breed of brokerage company allows individual investors to purchase a portfolio of thirty or more stocks at markedly lower costs than discount brokerage. They do so in one of two ways: first, by allowing practically unlimited trading for a preset monthly fee, or second, by charging only a small commission per trade, sometimes as low as $3. Thus, investors can directly accumulate a diversified portfolio at a fraction of the traditional brokerage costs. We call these companies "discount portfolio companies."

How do these companies manage to charge so much less than their brokerage peers? Their low pricing is universally attributable to one particular design feature: allowing trading only within select trading windows during the day. Instead of taking each order, one at a time, and immediately executing it on the relevant stock exchange, the discount portfolio company stores up many orders and then matches them electronically. Computer software allows these companies to match, say, your sale order for one hundred shares of Cisco with your neighbor's buy order for one hundred shares of Cisco. Then, the companies—all of which are SEC-registered broker-dealers—can engage in what is known as "self-clearing."[4]

In essence, these companies allow you to give up execution speed in return for lower costs. With traditional brokerage, your trade is executed within minutes or even seconds, and you incur your share of the costs of a system that made that possible. If you intend to buy a stock and hold it for a few years, however, you shouldn't care whether your trade is executed in three minutes or three hours. Now for the first time, you have the chance to choose three hours and pay less.[5]

Portrait of the Major Discount Portfolio Companies

We will now introduce you to the major discount portfolio companies. This area is experiencing rapid change. New companies and products will be arriving. Some existing companies may go out of business. Prices will change monthly. No book, or even magazine article, will be sufficiently timely to tell you for sure which discount portfolio companies are best at the moment you're reviewing them. Thus, the goal here is to acquaint you with some of the companies offering discount port-folios, the types of features they offer, and how they charge for their services.

FOLIOfn

We like FOLIOfn because the company's products are specifically designed to allow you to buy or assemble a diversified portfolio of stocks (hence the name). FOLIOfn offers investors the ability to invest in a large number of stocks for a fixed monthly charge. Additional investments can be made daily, weekly, or monthly at no additional charge. The cost is $30 per month for up to 150 stocks (three folios of up to fifty stocks each), or $295 if you sign up for a full year.

FOLIOfn's website is superb. It runs quickly and its methodology and costs are explained clearly. It's compatible with most financial planning and tax software. Most important, investors can set up hypothetical folios and run them for three months in order to get a feel for how the site works. A minimum of personal information is demanded in order to set up a hypothetical portfolio.

The process for selecting stocks is excellent. The best option is probably to purchase one of the major market folios chosen by FOLIOfn to track the performance of a given index. Basically, this option uses modern portfolio theory to duplicate an index using thirty to fifty stocks.

One indication that FOLIOfn was on to something was when the mutual fund industry petitioned the SEC to classify FOLIOfn as an unregulated mutual fund company, providing investment advice to clients. Such a finding would have forced it to immediately stop the practice. FOLIOfn responded, rather sensibly we think, that providing a basket of the largest stocks, or randomly selected stocks, is not investment advice. The fact that FOLIOfn was founded by former SEC commissioner Steven Wallman, who presumably had a pretty good grip on the law, was also a bad sign for the petition. The SEC subsequently denied the request.

Lest you think it's all milk and honey, there are a few potential downsides of FOLIOfn. You may be tempted by a lot of fun and cute folios that are not diversified. You can buy the Dogs of the Dow Folio (ugh . . .) or the Stockcar Champs Folio, representing the primary sponsors of the winning NASCAR Winston Cup drivers for the previous year. We're guessing that NASCAR stocks are weighted toward the automobile and tobacco industries.

Keep in mind that FOLIOfn also is promoting itself as a good option for frequent traders, a group you should not wish to join. Last, we note that FOLIOfn has begun selling itself through financial advisers and broker Quick and Reilly, as well as directly to the public. Remember that financial advisers generally take 1 percent of your money each and every year before using FOLIOfn to build a portfolio for you. Save the annual 1 percent of your money by using FOLIOfn or another discount portfolio company on your own. The couple of extra hours will be well worth your effort.

BUYandHOLD

The first thing we liked about BUYandHOLD was its name and its logo, a very appropriate acorn. Fortunately, the company's products are true to its name and oak-building promises. As with the other discount portfolio companies, BUYandHOLD is able to offer extremely low brokerage commissions by allowing trading during three trading windows per day.

BUYandHOLD can be described as a specialized type of discount broker. It allows unlimited investing for a low set fee ($14.95/month at the beginning of 2002) but does not offer preselected portfolios for passive investment. BUYandHOLD also offers its E-ZVest automatic stock purchase program, which allows for direct deposit of your paycheck into preselected stocks. For those wishing to impose a savings discipline on themselves, E-ZVest may be a good idea. Alternatively, an investor can pay $7 per month for two trades or E-ZVests, with a charge of $3 for additional trades.

BUYandHOLD touts itself as "the financial services firm that pioneered dollar-based stock investing." Dollar-based stock investing can be good when it correlates with allowing the purchase of a small number of shares for a low price. But someone could easily design a dollar-based system with high costs. Thankfully, BUYandHOLD is not such a system.

One weakness of BUYandHOLD is in the research area. Investors needing guidance on portfolio diversification and stock selection will find precious little available on the BUYandHOLD website. There is nothing equivalent to FOLIOfn's preselected folios.

ShareBuilder

ShareBuilder is a lot like BUYandHOLD except for being more costly in a sneaky sort of way. Sharebuilder uses the same window trading idea, executing trades just once a week. Sharebuilder's website proclaims prominently that it allows you to buy all the stocks you like for $12 per month or, alternatively, to pay $4 per transaction (prices as of the beginning of 2002). What ShareBuilder does not proclaim so prominently is that it charges $15.95 per trade when you *sell* your stocks. Sort of like the Eagles' Hotel California—you can check out any time you like, but you can never leave. While this pricing structure certainly gives you an incentive to buy and hold, we prefer the lower prices and greater candor of FOLIOfn and BUYandHOLD.

E*Trade

E*Trade offers a product that sounds a lot like FOLIOfn. E*Trade utilizes window trading, executing trades twice a day. Rather than folios, E*Trade refers to baskets. Unfortunately, E*Trade charges significantly more. Rather than charging a flat fee, E*Trade charges an annual fee based on the size of your assets. The fee ranges from 0.75 percent of assets (for accounts of $100,000 or more) to 1.25 percent (for accounts of less than $50,000). While that fee buys you unlimited trading, it's very difficult to imagine a scenario where these fees work out cheaper than the competition.

Furthermore, while E*Trade offers "off the shelf baskets" akin to FOLIOfn's preselected folios, those baskets are very narrow. With names like Dow 30, Nasdaq 25, and S&P 20, none of them purports to track the broader market. The baskets also generally include fewer stocks than the folios at FOLIOfn.

Fidelity

We'll have a look at Fidelity's faux portfolio product in Part V, The Empire Strikes Back. We don't believe it merits inclusion here.

Managing the Risks

Portfolio investing brings with it additional risks that need to be managed. Thankfully, technology has made that task a bit easier.

There once was a time when only the most sophisticated institutional investors could readily measure the risk of their portfolios. Fortunately, technology now offers a way to help individual investors build and measure the risk of a diversified portfolio.

The best service available to individuals is provided free of charge on the Internet by a company called RiskMetrics, which you'll recall helped us defend the honor of the Darts in Chapter 10.

First, a little history. In the 1980s and 1990s, as commercial and investment banks grew globally, they became concerned about how to measure their trading risk. With traders all over the world, it did not make sense to measure risk trading desk by trading desk. Firms wanted one consolidated analysis.

Modern computers and some very thoughtful mathematicians and finance Ph.D.s made that possible through what are known as value at risk (VAR) models. A firm's trading positions worldwide were fed into its VAR model, which summarized the source and extent of the firm's trading risks. These models generally measure risk based upon the past volatility and correlation of the firm's various holdings.

The VAR model of the old J.P. Morgan was considered one of the best. Morgan made its model public in the early 1990s, and according to RiskMetrics this model has since been adopted as a core component of the risk-management process by more than five thousand institutions around the world. J.P. Morgan spun off this part of its business as RiskMetrics in 1998. RiskMetrics derives its revenues from these five thousand institutions as well as from offering courses, workshops, and training.

RiskMetrics also makes its model available to the public through its product, RiskGrades, at riskgrades.com. You can now enter a portfolio—stocks, mutual funds, bonds, and cash—into your home computer and have access to a sophisticated model that can tell you the risk of each asset as well as of *the portfolio as a whole*. In other words, riskgrades.com will allow you to evaluate each of your eggs individually or your basket as a whole. You'll be able to see how much benefit you're obtaining from diversification.

You will also be able to see what percentage of your aggregate risk is presented by each stock. Many investors rebalance their portfolios when one stock becomes a large percentage of their holdings. That may or may not be appropriate. To know, one must consider how risky that stock is, and how its performance correlates with the rest of the portfolio. In using RiskGrade, for example, we've noticed that Coca-Cola tends to correlate negatively with technology stocks. When one is up, the other generally is down. Someone who held a lot of Coke stock and various technology stocks might be tempted to reduce a large concentration of Coke. In fact, doing so might actually increase risk.

So, why not enter your portfolio (including stocks, mutual funds, and cash) and have a good look at the risks you're running with your current investment strategy?

A Simple Check

For all of the computer wizardry available to assist in portfolio diversification, we offer a final, simple check on whether you've assembled a diversified portfolio. If you obtain a regular summary of how your stocks have performed, is there one stock you always look to first? It's probably a pretty good bet that you own too much of that stock. That doesn't necessarily mean that you should sell it immediately, as the stock may offset some other risk or carry a large unrealized capital gain. But it is time to measure the risk and think about a plan for reducing the holding.

Special Risks of Discount Portfolio Companies

Given that the discount portfolio companies we've discussed are new and far from established, one question you may have is, "What happens if the portfolio company fails, and how likely is that to happen?" The closing of NetFolio, a FOLIOfn rival, in 2001 sharpens the question.

First, you needn't worry about losing your securities. Each is a registered broker-dealer and is regulated by the SEC. As such they are required to comply with various customer protection rules and regulations, such as properly segregating your securities. The Securities Investor Protection Corporation (SIPC) works to protect and return customers' cash and securities held at troubled brokerage firms. Although your portfolio securities will generally be held in "street name"—that is, with the discount portfolio company listed as the shareholder of record with the issuer—the securities they hold belong to you.

The risk you run is that if your discount portfolio company fails, you'll end up transferring your stocks to a company that will charge you a lot more to sell them than you did to buy them. And since discount portfolio companies allow you to buy a lot of stocks—that's the point, after all—selling them could be expensive. So, keep that in mind before you take the plunge.

Comparing Discount Portfolios to ETFs and Index Funds

For a limited number of investors, discount portfolio companies may offer a new way to passively invest. While we would recommend that most investors use index funds or ETFs to implement a passive investing strategy, some investors may have significant enough assets for investment to consider using a discount portfolio company.

The question will ultimately be, How much does one need to make discount portfolio companies worthwhile? Even with a significant amount to invest, you will certainly have less work to do if you simply choose an index fund or ETF. With regard to costs, it's best to look at the prepackaged portfolios at FOLIOfn. Its annual fees are $295. For comparison purposes, the Vanguard 500 index fund charges management fees of 0.18 percent per year. Broad market ETFs charge 0.09–0.17 percent. So depending upon which passive investing alternative you select, the point at which annual FOLIOfn fees become cheaper than those of an index fund or ETF is $165,000 to $300,000. These are significant amounts for most investors.

The Best of All Worlds

We can think of one way that discount portfolio companies could be of use to a broad range of investors: as a low-cost way of investing in exchange-traded funds. One of the only drawbacks of ETFs is that brokerage fees could erode returns if you're seeking to invest a small sum every month rather than a large sum every year or two. Now, there may be an alternative.

Using BUYandHOLD, for example, you could pay $7 per month ($84 per year) and buy two ETFs per month. With FOLIOfn, you could pay $14.95 and buy ETFs as frequently as you like for the month.

Conclusion

We're not sure what the future will hold for discount portfolio companies. That said, we get excited any time we see innovation in retail brokerage. For those determined to own stocks directly, they offer the best means to do so. Others should keep an eye on developments in this area. In the meantime, keep adding to that index fund or ETF.

Chapter 17

Breaking Up Is Hard to Do—
Moving from Active to
Passive Investing

*Freedom's just another word for nothin' left to lose.—Kris
Kristofferson, "Me and Bobby McGee"*

Your conversion from the active to the passive investment bandwagon is easy to manage if you have new money to invest. If you have small amounts, then you should use an index fund. If you have larger amounts and your investment returns are taxable, then you should consider an exchange-traded index fund. But now comes the hard part: what to do with all the money you've *already* invested actively? Here, moving to passive investment may end up costing you a little bit.

That cost comes primarily in the form of taxes. If you're fortunate, then the actively managed equity mutual funds and individual stocks that you hold have appreciated in value since you bought them. Selling them and reinvesting passively means realizing that gain and having to pay taxes earlier than you might otherwise have paid them. You're going to want to do a little thinking before you take that step, though we suspect that in most cases you'll find the end result well worth the cost.

If your stocks or actively managed funds are within a tax-deferred investment account—a 401(k), 403 (b), or IRA—or if they have not appreciated in price, then you have no tax worries and should sell them immediately and begin investing passively.

If you have unrealized taxable capital gains in your funds or stocks, then matters get a little more complicated. There are two fairly easy steps you can take. First, you should immediately begin reinvesting any dividends or distributions from your existing investments in an index fund. Simply tell your actively managed fund or dividend reinvestment (DRIP) program that you'd like to begin receiving cash distributions. Then reinvest them. Second, if you have capital losses in other stocks, then you can sell those stocks along with stocks with corresponding gains, thereby negating any tax effects.

If you have unrealized gains that are not offset by losses, however, then you face a choice. You probably should not sell any stock that you have held for less than a year, if it has significant gains. After one year, the lower, long-term capital gains rate applies, and you will save on your taxes by waiting for it to kick in. As for long-term gains, your course of action should depend on the amount of unrealized gain, the volatility and risk of your portfolio, and the current level of your management fees and costs. Basically, the less you have in unrealized gains, the more reason to make a change. The less diversified and more volatile your stocks are, then the more reason there is to sell quickly. The higher your current cost structure, the more reason to sell as well.

If you currently hold actively managed mutual funds, there is actually some good news. Given how they've been treating you all these years, they'll be easier to leave ("no love lost"). That active fund you've held dear has been churning its portfolio so much that you have been paying capital gains taxes all along. Plus, any dividends have been reinvested at a higher basis. The tax cost basis in your current active fund holdings may therefore be higher (better) than you believe. The result is poetic justice: *because your actively managed mutual fund has been increasing your tax load all these years, you now have far less to lose by moving to an index fund or ETF.*

If you hold individual stocks, the news may be similar. If you or your full-service broker has been trading frequently, then you've been paying taxes on your gains all along.

So, now the big question. When should you sell appreciated investments in order to reinvest passively, and when should you hold off for a while? The answer to that question will vary according to the shape of your portfolio and your current tax situation. You may wish to consult a tax professional, but here are a few thoughts.

You should begin by estimating the total unrealized gains in each of your holdings. If you need help, call your mutual fund company or broker and ask them for your current tax cost basis. Subtract your basis from the fund's current NAV to arrive at your unrealized gains. Then, calculate what these gains would represent as a percent of the current value of each investment. If the ratio is relatively small, say less than 25 percent, then we believe you should sell the holdings and move on to passive investment. At 20 percent long-term capital gains tax rates, and a 25 percent embedded gain, your tax bill will be just 5 percent of the value of your investment. Since active fund management and regular stock trading chews up at least 2 percentage points of your money each year, you will probably make all of that back within two to three years.

Assuming you have significant gains, you should consider how risky your current holdings are. If they are concentrated in just a few stocks or sectors, you should probably sell, even if you're above the 25 percent threshold. For example, if you own only two stocks and a technology fund, then we believe that the importance of diversification demands that you sell them regardless of how much gain you have in them. The more volatile those stocks, the greater the need to sell. On the other hand, if you have 90 percent of your stock assets in an index fund and 10 percent in three stocks, the diversification gains of selling are not great. So, if you have substantial unrealized gains, you may wish to defer the capital gains taxes.

Beyond taxes, there may be some brokerage commissions or a back-end load to pay. Commissions shouldn't be enough to deter you from your escape. Back-end loads, however, can be significant. If you're close to the date when the load disappears, you may want to wait for it to pass before you sell.

The above guidance is based on logic and arithmetic. But you may have other, nonfinancial reasons for continuing to hold a stock. You may have some relationship with the company or management and feel a need to own shares to show support or continue an affiliation. You may even feel compelled to continue holding stocks that have been in the family a long time or were inherited. While we can't specifically assess these situations, our general view is that people are usually more understanding than you might first think.

You may also wish to consider the cautionary tale presented by Enron's employees. As Enron went from high flier to bankruptcy in 2001, its employees' savings went right along with it. Not only did employees depend on Enron for their salary and own a lot of the stock, but over half of the company's 401(k) plan was invested in the company's stock. By the end of the year, Enron was hiring grief counselors to discuss 401(k) options with its employees, many of them near retirement. No such grief counseling was necessary for CEO Ken Lay, however, since he had exercised tens of millions of dollars in options and sold a significant amount of his shares.

ETFs for a Peaceful Thanksgiving Dinner

When it comes to making the move to passive investing, ETFs offer one interpersonal advantage over index funds. If you are one of the many Americans whose stockbroker is also your cousin, or even your client's secretary's brother, then you may feel uncomfortable closing your account (that is, firing your broker) and sending your money off to an index fund. Here's the beauty of ETFs: you get to keep your broker and even issue a few buy-and-sell orders. You needn't mention your conversion to passive investing, or the fact that these will be your final trades. Just keep smiling and start quietly sending any small amounts you have to invest off to a new index fund. You'll still be able to tell your parents or your client that you've kept your brokerage account open, and with any luck your broker won't figure out what you're up to for a year or two.

Conclusion

While passive investment is never going to be sexy, in almost all circumstances it is the right way to invest in stocks. Even if you currently hold stocks with embedded gains, it is usually best to sell them and move on in the investing world. Stay with those old active funds and full-service brokers, and they will keep doing you wrong. If you move fast, ETFs are still sufficiently new that you can feel like an adventurous pioneer and impress your friends by explaining how they work. Then of course there's also the fact that you're going to be wealthier. . . .

Part V

The **Empire** Strikes **Back**

You can fool some of the people all of the time.
Those are the people you have to
concentrate on.
—*George W. Bush*

T he U.S. financial industry is the strongest in the world. Our banks, brokers, and mutual fund companies are highly competitive and innovative. They also are very profitable. They plan to stay that way.

Wall Street firms make a lot of money from individual investors. Frequent trading means commission volume; active fund management means high, predictable fees whether markets rise or fall. Every trade, every new customer paying a fund or full-service broker a percentage of assets, rings the cash register on Wall Street.

That said, the industry faces numerous challenges. Innovative products like exchange-traded funds offer investors better choices and Wall Street lower margins. Technology threatens to disrupt established business models, as the emergence of discount portfolio companies demonstrates. Investor education also represents a threat. As investors become increasingly aware of the mediocre record of Wall Street advice and the disastrous results of frequent trading, their appetite for buying and selling stocks may diminish.

Like any vibrant business, the financial industry fights to promote and protect its most profitable product lines. How? We've explored the industry's use of media, both through paid advertising and free appearances. Now we'll look at some other ways that mutual funds and brokerage firms have recently responded to these threats. In Chapter 18, we will explore some of the new products and pricing structures the industry has developed to promote and protect its active investing lines of business. In Chapter 19, we will explore how proposals to establish private accounts for Social Security recipients could allow the financial industry to reap billions of dollars of fees annually at the expense of our nation's retirees.

Let us be clear, these activities are part of the strength of American capitalism. Management owes shareholders a duty to maximize returns. Protecting high margin businesses and charging what the market will bear is a fundamental part of business. So, too, is taking old products and marketing them as new products, as anyone who's ever bought "new and improved" laundry detergent knows.

We have this gnawing impression, though, that while investors recognize that soap companies have a profit motive, many may believe that they are in partnership with their brokers, financial planners, and fund companies. Whereas most consumers recognize that every extra dollar you pay for detergent is one dollar less for you, many somehow feel that dollars they pay for financial products are an investment. *Please remember: the investment is the money you keep, not the money they take.*

Chapter 18

New and Improved!

The lamb . . . began to follow the wolf in sheep's
clothing.—*Aesop,* The Wolf in Sheep's Clothing

N ew financial products are a key part of Wall Street's success. As
financial products are intangible, they can be shaped and re-
shaped quickly. So, too, can the fees charged for those products.
There is no need for FDA approval or a test track.

In designing new products and pricing, Wall Street appears to follow
an old maxim from litigation. If you have a "bad fact" in your case, you
don't run from it, you embrace it. If your murder defendant is a crazed
maniac, well then by golly he's much too crazy to have been able to plan
the crime.

So, Wall Street responds to concerns about stock picking ability by
telling investors they should really be choosing sectors instead. They respond to outrage over the poor tax consequences of mutual funds by
creating new "tax-managed" funds. And they respond to discount portfolio companies by creating products that look similar but preserve all
of the same old costs. It's actually kind of fun to watch—so long as you
don't invest in these products. Let's look at a few prominent examples.

Wrap Accounts

Wall Street listened when investors sought investment advice or grew concerned with its fee structure. Wrap accounts are part of its answer.

A "wrap" account bundles (wraps) various financial services into a single package at a single price calculated as a percentage of assets under management. Wrap accounts, first introduced by E.F. Hutton in 1975, have had a renaissance, as brokerage firms have lowered minimum balances and marketed them aggressively.

A wrap account provides investment advice and a large number of transactions for an asset fee of between 1 and 3 percent of assets. Merrill Lynch, for example, offers an account that charges the higher of 1 percent of assets or a $1,500 fee per year. In return, you are provided access to research reports from the firm's analysts and the ability to trade frequently at no additional cost.

A special breed of wrap accounts has focused on mutual funds. Merrill Lynch, for example, offers its clients more than two thousand mutual funds. Investors can have a broker select funds for them, or participate in the selection themselves. Fee arrangements vary significantly between and even within firms, but the broker charges a wrap fee *on top of the fees charged by the mutual funds selected.*

Why the renaissance?
First, many investors have been concerned about how to pick mutual funds or stocks. Brokers also were facing increased pressure from independent financial advisers who provide investment advice and financial planning. Wrap accounts mimic this structure.

Second, full-service brokerage companies wanted a way to fight back against discount brokers and their low-cost alternative. One method was to emphasize the importance of investment advice. Another method was to appeal to frequent traders who were tired of paying brokerage commissions. Wrap accounts serve both goals by including investment advice and virtually unlimited trading within the bundle of services offered.

Finally, full-service brokerage companies had an image problem with investors—namely, a self-interest in advising investors to trade frequently. Brokers' compensation generally depends to some extent on the activity of their accounts. Investors quite rightly wondered whether they should listen to someone with such a clear conflict of interest. Wrap accounts helped address that image problem. By eliminating commissions per trade, firms claim that they have aligned the interests of the broker with those of the investor.

So what's wrong with wrap accounts?
First, such accounts are extremely expensive. Paying out 1 to 3 percent of your assets each year should make you queasy. While mutual fund wrap fees are a bit lower than the average, they are paid *in addition to the management fees of the funds you purchase.* When stocks were rising 15 percent per year, these asset-based fees were camouflaged. When returns are stagnant, you're more likely to notice because at the end of the year *you're poorer.* Enough said.

Second, wrap accounts don't really align the interests of the broker and the investor. Aligning those interests would mean paying the broker a percentage of your risk-adjusted profits or losses. With wrap accounts, the brokerage firm profits regardless of how you do and regardless of the risks you take.

Third, conflicts of interest pop up with mutual fund wrap accounts. You might wonder how a brokerage firm decides which of the thousands of mutual funds to include on the shelves of its supermarket. Here's the answer: the fund companies pay for the shelf space. Not only do they pay to be included, they also pay for the right to have special access to the firm's brokers (salesmen). For example, they pay to make presentations at brokerage sales conferences. After the conference, there may be some drinking and golf, and some souvenirs handed out. In other words, the fund supermarket in which you're shopping doesn't necessarily have the best food. Rather it has the food of companies that have paid it money and bought a round of golf for the local manager.

Let's wrap up with this thought. Assume you sign up for a mutual fund wrap account with a 1 percent fee. The broker puts you in a no-load (if you're lucky) mutual fund with a further 1 percent management fee, cheap by industry standards. The market goes up 8 percent this year—pretty good by long-term standards. *You are paying out a quarter of your earnings in fees even before trading costs and taxes. Think about that really, really hard.*

Funds of Funds

As the number of mutual funds has grown well into the thousands and evidence of poor performance has mounted, individuals have grown confused about how to go about selecting a good fund. The mutual fund industry has offered up a self-serving alternative. Through a "fund of funds," you can pay one fund manager to select other fund managers. In other words, these mutual funds invest in other funds rather than stocks. Who better to select winning mutual funds than the mutual fund industry itself? Hence the name, "fund of funds."

The advantage of this service to the mutual fund industry is immediately clear: additional fees. You pay the first manager to pick the second manager and the second manager to pick the stocks. From the industry's point of view, it's nirvana.

From your point of view, welcome to the netherworld. The effect of paying two fees is predictably disastrous. The fund managers aren't any more adept at picking funds than they are stocks, and the costs are oppressive. Those focused on stocks have an average expense ratio of 0.7 percent, front-end loads of 1.0 percent, and back-end loads of 0.8 percent, all *on top of the fees of the underlying funds.* Over the ten years 1992–2001, these funds lagged the S&P 500 Index *by 3.8 percentage points per year.*[1]

Basket Trading—Without the Basket or the Trading

You would have expected Wall Street to answer the challenge of discount portfolio companies. Visiting Fidelity's website in early 2002, you'd see a description of its offering that looks almost exactly like FOLIOfn's. The site proclaims, "Now you can track, trade, and manage up to fifty stocks as one entity with Fidelity's new Basket Trading. Use it to build personalized portfolios and gain more control over your investments."

The first signs of trouble come when you read this cryptic announcement a few pages later: "Commissions will be charged according to the commission schedule applicable to the account. Each purchase or sale of a security position in a basket is treated as an individual transaction and will be subject to separate transaction commissions." What does that mean, exactly? Read on and you'll see in the User Agreement exactly what that means:

- If you place an order, for example, to buy $10,000 worth of stock and spread it among thirty stocks, then Fidelity charges you a brokerage commission of $14.95 *for each stock*. There is no bulk discount, as at FOLIOfn. Nor is there even cheap trading, as at BUYandHOLD and ShareBuilder. For your $10,000 basket trade, you'll pay $448.50 in brokerage commissions, or about 4.5 percent of your investment.[2]
- As with FOLIOfn, you are free to add to your basket—*but, again, at full commission for each stock you buy*. Whereas the marginal cost is zero at FOLIOfn, you're right back to the old commission schedule at Fidelity.
- Fidelity's basket trading is missing a central innovation of all the new discount portfolio companies: "window trading" only once or twice a day, allowing offsetting trades to be matched. With Fidelity, you buy all the bells and whistles every time you trade.

Accordingly, the whole notion that you can buy a "basket" of stocks is a complete fiction. Buying stocks with Fidelity's "Basket Trading" is simply buying them through traditional discount brokerage with a new name.

Fidelity may one day offer a new version of its basket trading. By all means have a look. But if past experience is any guide, keep your hand on your wallet.

Tax-Managed Funds

Numerous articles and TV reports have highlighted the tax consequences of mutual fund investing. This culminated in the SEC's new
after-tax disclosure requirement. That said, nothing hit home for investors like paying capital gains taxes in April 2001 and 2002, even
when their mutual funds had gone down the prior year.

Faced with this bad fact regarding taxes, the mutual fund industry
has not sat quietly. They've given the tax issue a big hug. They now offer "tax-managed funds." (Those investors who haven't paid attention
are still sold the same old funds with the same high turnover ratios.)
According to Morningstar records, there were 50 tax-managed stock
funds in 2002, compared to only nine such funds five years earlier.[3] Just
about all the major fund families now offer such a fund.

So, what exactly is a tax-efficient fund? Such funds attempt to limit
the capital gains incurred by shareholders. The easiest way is to lose
money, incurring capital losses. (A lot of funds have been inadvertently
using this strategy lately.) The best way to limit capital gains taxes is by
reducing turnover. Unfortunately, so-called tax-efficient funds still have
average turnover of 45 percent.[4] These funds attempt to better manage
their purchases and sales to lower capital gains. Mutual funds usually
acquire stock of a given company at different times and prices. When
tax-efficient funds sell securities, they are diligent about selling the
highest priced shares in order to minimize the realized gain. They also
attempt to pair sales of stocks with capital losses with sales of those
with capital gains.

Our advice? Don't let tax efficiency lure you away from passive investment. To quote our favorite psychologist, don't try to be clever.

Donor-Advised Funds

In order to benefit from investors' charitable instincts, the mutual fund
industry has worked out a way for you to establish your own private
foundation of sorts. You can take charitable tax deductions while defer-

ring your charitable contributions and pay the fund industry a lot of money.

We admit to considerable ambivalence about these products. On the one hand, they may stimulate greater charitable giving, and Vanguard's program appears to be a genuinely charitable structure that would be a good choice for some investors. On the other hand, we can't help gnashing our teeth about the potential cost of most of these products.

The Tax Man Giveth

These new products are the mutual fund industry's attempt to replicate for the general public what bank trust departments and the wealthy have been doing for generations through family foundations. (Think of the Ford Foundation.) The logic of a private foundation is this: you have a substantial amount of money you'd like to give to charity, but only over time. Although you may segregate that money in your mind as your "charity money," the tax code does not recognize mental donations.

A family foundation allows a donor to earmark money for charity in a way the IRS accepts. Then the foundation invests the money and accumulates earnings tax-free. The only conditions for receiving this favorable tax treatment are that the funds eventually be donated to charity, and that at least 5 percent of the assets be donated each year. In effect, a donor can create a parallel, tax-free investment track.

More recently, the tax laws have allowed the formation of so-called donor-advised funds. Rather than paying substantial costs for a lawyer, bank, or broker to establish a personal foundation, investors can share those costs. By law, an individual donor to these funds does not have the explicit legal right to decide which charities will receive donations but only to advise the board of trustees where to donate the money. Hence, the term "donor-advised fund." In fact, though, if you request that a portion of your assets be donated to a given charity, that request will be honored. The board's authority to overrule you is simply a legal fiction necessary to obtain favorable tax treatment.

The Mutual Fund Industry Taketh

Donor-advised funds were pioneered by the nation's community foundations, but they have become a business opportunity for the mutual fund industry. By sponsoring donor-advised funds, they get to invest clients' money in their own mutual funds and charge an administrative fee to cover all expenses, and then some.

Fidelity was the first fund company to establish a donor-advised fund, in 1992. Its Charitable Gift Trust has over $2 billion in assets. Vanguard, Charles Schwab, and Eaton Vance have all followed suit.

Beyond the annual fees, some of your hard-earned money may end up in the hands of a middleman rather than your favorite charity's. According to the *Wall Street Journal,* both Eaton Vance and Fidelity pay a fee to compensate brokers or advisers who steer business to their funds. In an advertisement directed to financial advisers, the American Gift Fund promised to pay advisers an up-front fee of 1 percent and an ongoing stream of 0.75 percent of assets a year. The ad summed it all up nicely: "Generosity has never been so profitable."

From the industry's point of view, the beauty of donor-advised funds is that no one internalizes these fees. The individual donor receives the same tax deduction for the original contribution regardless of how the donated funds perform. A $10,000 donation is a $10,000 donation for tax purposes regardless of whether the annual management fee is 0.2 percent or 2.0 percent or even if there is an up-front load. Charities, as well, are always happy to receive any money and unlikely to grouse about how much more there might have been if it had been invested better.

The mutual fund companies also excel at making the donor feel important and noble. Sign up for information about one of the major funds, and you will receive personal phone calls from helpful people and beautiful brochures on heavy bond paper that feels wonderful to the touch.

Pros and Cons

We believe that there are some valid reasons to use a donor-advised fund, but we suggest caution.

It is easy to convince yourself that by investing some charity money tax-free for a period of years, you will end up writing a bigger check to your favorite charities. This reasoning ignores the fact that if you give the money to the charity now, the charity itself has the same ability to invest your donation tax-free. Moreover, the charity might "invest" the money in a program that earns a different type of return—say educating at-risk kids or building low-income housing. *If "I'll be able to give more later" is your only rationale for using a donor-advised fund—then we'd advise against it.*

Still, you may reasonably wish to invest more money into a donor-advised fund than you would otherwise donate to charity in a given year. For example, if you receive an inheritance or an unusually large bonus, you might earmark some of this money not just for current-year charitable giving, but also for future years. You get the tax deduction immediately, and the donor-advised fund allows your gift to earn tax-free returns until you're ready to disburse.

A donor-advised fund may be particularly appropriate when you hold securities with significant unrealized capital gains. Alternatively, you could donate the stock to your favorite charity, allowing it to sell the stock without having to pay taxes. Many smaller charities, however, do not accept securities as donations. Also, if you're making a lot of relatively small donations, you may feel a little silly giving each charity three shares of stock.

Which Donor-Advised Fund?

If you should decide to use a donor-advised fund, Vanguard has by far the lowest costs. Its administrative fee is only 0.45 percent, compared to 1 percent for most of the rest. The other fund companies are either half as efficient as Vanguard or they are using their administrative fees as a source of profit. With Vanguard, your donation also benefits from being invested in their index funds, which carry the lowest fees in the business.

You may alternatively wish to consider using a donor-advised fund sponsored by a community foundation. (You can find one for your community by using the search engine at the Council on Foundations website, www.communityfoundationlocator.org.) Here, any profit from the administrative fee will help support the foundation, and you can get more involved in your local community. On the downside, many community foundations invest your donation in actively managed funds. We urge you to ask the folks at your community foundation how your money will be invested, and why they think your charitable fund will grow more with them than it would with an index fund. (We'll admit to a hidden agenda here: we're hoping to spur a little more interest in transparency and indexing in America's community foundations.)

ETFs: The Next Generation

ETFs are now a product geared toward passive investment. There is some risk, however, that with further product innovation, the fund companies will be able to actively manage the underlying portfolio of ETFs. Currently, there are legal and practical impediments to development of such a product. One of the biggest impediments is the natural desire of active fund managers to keep their holdings secret. That's currently thwarted by rules requiring that the holdings of an ETF be disclosed daily. In November 2001, however, the SEC issued what it calls a "concept release" seeking input on how these problems could be fixed.

If and when actively managed ETFs do appear, please don't buy them. They will combine the high management fees of active funds with the brokerage commissions of individual stock picking. You don't want to own such a product.

Conclusion

Managing your money and executing your trades are profitable businesses for Wall Street. Putting your money in an index fund or ETF makes those businesses a whole lot less profitable. That's why you can expect to be tempted by new products from Wall Street offering novel pricing structures and promising to cure all the ills of the old products. Just smile, don't forget to ask how much they cost, and go back to spending time with your family.

Chapter 19

The Great Social Security Heist

Nearly all men can stand adversity, but if you want to test a
man's character, give him power.—*Abraham Lincoln*

Try to imagine a business opportunity of such incredible propor-
tions that it would nearly double the reach of the U.S. mutual
fund industry, radically increase the revenue of brokerage firms,
and give a significant boost to the insurance industry. Welcome to the
Great Social Security Heist.

The nation's Social Security system is facing serious challenges. As
the baby boomers reach retirement age, the ratio of working people to
retirees is shrinking. That's a big problem going forward for our "pay-
as-you-go" Social Security system, where today's workers fund today's
retirees. Unfortunately, the most plausible approaches for righting the
system—decreasing benefits, increasing payroll taxes, raising the retirement age, running deficits—are all extremely unpopular. Hence, the
search for a talisman, a magical way to solve all of Social Security's
problems without having to make any painful political choices.

Many lawmakers have fixed on investing a portion of Social Security
payroll taxes in the markets as the easiest pain-free solution. President
George W. Bush campaigned for office on a partial privatization proposal and has pursued it since his election. A robust debate about par-

tial privatization has begun, focusing on big-picture issues like the appropriate role for Social Security and the wisdom of moving from a government-run to a private sector–led system.

Unfortunately, we believe that the debate has largely overlooked a major, albeit less glamorous, problem with partial privatization: how individual accounts would be administered and what *net* returns they could be expected to deliver.

Partial privatization would mean one of the greatest transfers of wealth in our nation's history. Billions of dollars would be taken from America's retirees each year and given to the mutual fund, brokerage, and insurance industries in the form of fees and transaction costs. While such accounts might earn a higher gross rate of return than the government securities currently held in the Social Security trust fund, those higher returns would be overwhelmed by costs and higher risk. Sadly, those most likely to do the worst under privatization are the very people that Social Security is intended to help the most: the working poor, the widow or widower, the disabled, and the very old. For them, the costs of a partially privatized system would represent a significant portion of their retirement money.

What Social Security Does, and What All the Fuss Is About

Throughout its history, Social Security has offered an inflation-indexed lifetime annuity—that is, regular inflation-indexed payments from retirement to death—in return for payment of payroll taxes during your working years. It has also provided important protection to workers and their families against the loss of income from disability or the death of a wage earner. The full faith and credit of the U.S. government has unconditionally backed up these payments. Social Security has generally succeeded in ameliorating extreme poverty among America's retirees.

So, what's the problem? Unlike most private pension programs, the Social Security system funds the bulk of its payments from current receipts. There is a specific Social Security trust fund that holds a significant number of U.S. Treasury securities. The earnings on these securities help fund only a small portion of the payments to current retirees, though, so ongoing tax collections are necessary to meet the bulk of current and future obligations. That is why many people call it a "pay-as-you-go" system.

In the future, the fundamental challenge for Social Security will be the pending retirement of the baby boom generation coupled with increasing life expectancies. Currently, there are about 3.3 working adults for every retiree in America. By 2030 there will be only two for every retiree. By the year 2016, when the first baby boomers will be reaching seventy, Social Security tax receipts will no longer fully cover outgoing payments. That's the arithmetic challenge of an aging population.

How the Free Lunch Looks on the Menu

The solution proposed by the pain-free reformers of Social Security is to establish individual accounts for each working person in the United States. Workers would use a portion of their payroll taxes to buy stocks and bonds. The hope is that these mutual funds will perform well enough to allow benefits to continue at current levels without political leaders having to make painful choices.

With privatization, beneficiaries would trade in part of the government's guarantee of future income for a current asset held in their own names. In some ways, it would be similar to your employer switching from a defined-benefit pension plan to a 401(k) plan. Under most plans, you could choose from among a variety of mutual funds, just as you might in a company-sponsored 401(k).

We are talking about big dollars here. During the campaign, President Bush proposed diverting 2 percentage points of each worker's wages to such an account. (That's about one sixth of the total 12.4 percent payroll tax currently paid to fund Social Security.) That would mean over $80 billion in the first year alone. More than a trillion dollars would be taken from Social Security and invested in individual accounts within ten years.[1]

We are also talking about some very significant problems here as well. One of the largest is how the nation will continue to fund retirement payments while one sixth of Social Security revenues is being funneled off into individual accounts. Another is whether the government might have to bail out such accounts in the event of a major market decline, and, if it doesn't, what happens to that generation's retirement security? Privatizers also generally ignore the important *insurance* benefits that Social Security provides in case of death or disability—equaling one fifth of Social Security payments, and including three million children as current recipients. Individual accounts carry no insurance component.

Finally, it is doubtful that privatization would do anything to boost savings. Most economists agree that the best way to prepare for the retirement of the baby boom generation is to boost our future economy by increasing national savings. As a family is well served by saving for retirement, so too is a nation. Private accounts won't necessarily boost savings. They may even lead to lower national savings if Americans believe that individual accounts will make retirement better than ever, requiring them to save less on their own. So, privatization looks like one big exercise in rearranging the nation's investing deck chairs.

President Bush's Social Security Commission may have debated these difficult issues, but the charter for the commission directed the members to conclude that individual accounts were the correct answer. According to one of its six guiding principles, "Modernization must include individually controlled, voluntary personal retirement accounts, which will augment Social Security."[2] While the commission's final report presented a series of options for reform, all included individual accounts. (They did note, though, that such reform would be considerably more costly than candidate Bush had promised.) Thus, if Social Security reform legislation is enacted during this presidency, you can expect to face the equivalent of a 401(k) plan as part of Social Security, come hell or high water.

We'll leave it to others to discuss the big picture issues of funding, insurance, bailouts, and national savings. We'll focus on a narrower, but very important issue: how individual accounts would actually work.

The Bush Plan

If the Bush plan goes into effect, workers will end up being able to invest one sixth of their payroll taxes themselves. The past experience with 401(k) plans and the plans of the privatizers suggests that mutual funds will be the vehicle chosen for investment, with workers able to select from a menu of government-approved funds. After some time, diversified actively managed stock funds—that is, funds akin to Fidelity Magellan or the Janus Fund—will be the most popular items on the menu. Other selections will most likely include actively managed bond funds, actively managed funds that mix stocks and bonds, and a few index funds. In the 401(k) world, the majority of assets are invested in actively managed stock funds.

Relative to the average mutual fund account, Social Security accounts are likely to be small. Half of all workers would be putting only $400 into an account each year. Higher income workers would be putting around $1,000 away each year. Social Security accounts would therefore be smaller than the average mutual fund account of $25,000.[3]

Despite the small size of individual Social Security accounts, the total volume would probably overwhelm the existing mutual fund industry. With over 155 million workers in America, the number of new accounts would dwarf the 88 million mutual fund accounts in existence in early 2001. Due to their unique nature, Social Security accounts could not be merged into any existing account. If you already have a mutual fund account or 401(k), you would still have to open a new investment account for your Social Security money. New funds would have to be created and tens of thousands, perhaps hundreds of thousands, of new staff would have to be hired.

So What Do We Get?

So, here's the big question: how would such funds perform for Social Security beneficiaries?

The Top Line: How Much Would Mutual Funds Earn Before Costs?

Here is a fundamental truth that is easy to overlook in the privatization debate. If you invest a trillion dollars in the stock market, then the gross— that is, before any costs—return on that money will be the same as that of the stock market as a whole. (The same is true with the bond market.)

Why? Experience and logic show that the aggregate performance of stocks held by all actively managed funds tends to track that of the market as a whole prior to any costs. That's because such funds end up holding pretty much all the stocks in the market. As a single investor in one mutual fund, you might end up beating or trailing the market by a considerable amount in a given year. The chance of 155 million investors *as a group* investing hundreds of billions of dollars in a variety of funds and beating the market (even before costs) is nil. It simply can't be done.

Even assuming that aggregate returns from equity investments in Social Security accounts would simply track the stock market, privatizers would probably claim that this result is preferable to the current system. After all, they say, individual accounts invested in equities would still capture the equity risk premium—the traditional spread between stock and bond returns. But these claims ignore macroeconomics and risk.

Macroeconomics.   On a macroeconomic level, the idea that individual accounts can capture the equity risk premium and improve the retirement of the baby boomers makes little sense. A dollar invested in the market adds to wealth only if you would have otherwise spent it. The same holds true even for $1 trillion. If the government simply borrows more money so that you can set up individual accounts, it creates no wealth at all: no additional savings, no additional investment, and no additional jobs.

What about the equity premium and capturing the extra rate of return? It is true that over long periods of time, stocks generally outperform bonds. This is particularly true when compared to the government bonds in which Social Security funds are invested. Over the past 130 years, the difference has been around 5.5 percent per year. Many economists believe that in the future the gap will return to earlier levels of between 3 and 4 percent. That equity premium, however, doesn't just appear. If private accounts earn an extra 4 percent, then somebody, somewhere in the economy must be paying or giving up an extra 4 percent. It could come from the corporations who issue stock, the people who sell stock to these new accounts, or other investors, but it has got to come from somewhere. In the end, it's probably going to end up coming from those same retirees, maybe not while they're wearing their retiree hat, but while wearing their taxpayer hat or shareholder hat or consumer hat or bond owner hat. *The government cannot create $40 billion in wealth each year by simply shifting money from one asset class to another.*

Another macroeconomic consideration is the challenge of transitioning from a pay-as-you-go system to a prefunded retirement system. As the current system has only modest assets set aside in relation to its future obligations, this transition would present enormous economic and political challenges. Even if done successfully, it would be likely to take up to fifty to seventy-five years to fully transition the current social security system.

Risk. Higher returns are necessary for equity holders because they bear greater risk than do bondholders. In other words, over time, fully adjusting for risk, returns on stocks and bonds should be the same. Privatizers are asking Social Security beneficiaries to shoulder more risk in order to earn potentially higher returns.

Injecting risk into Social Security has profound implications. Today, consciously or subconsciously, Americans consider Social Security payments a low-risk, fixed-income safety net for their retirement. If the market goes south for their other investments, there is still Social Security. If you are fortunate enough to live well into your eighties or nineties, you might run out of your other assets, no matter how well invested, but Social Security will still be there.

Thus, under the current system, two people with similar earnings receive the same retirement benefits. This would not be so with individual accounts. Retirees' benefits—and thus the quality of their retirement—would vary according to how they invested and how the market performed over the years leading up to their retirement. Retire when the stock market is up and you get to cash out on a roll. Retire shortly after a downturn, and you get less. Just think about the difference between retiring on September 30, 1999, versus September 30, 2001 might have made.

Proponents of private accounts say that these fluctuations sort themselves out over an entire working life. A look at history suggests otherwise. At least three times in the 1900s, stock market real returns (after inflation) fell to about zero over a twenty-year period. You would have had nothing to show from 1901 to 1921, from 1928 to 1948, and from

1962 to 1982. Other twenty-year periods had average stock market real returns as high as 6 to 10 percent. This meant that some people earned no real return from investing in the stock market, while others received a real pretax return as high as 10 percent.[4] Thus, for example, with individual accounts invested in stock, a worker retiring in the early 1970s would have a nest egg almost twice as large as a worker ten years younger retiring in the early 1980s.[5]

Now, get ready for the really bad news.

Moving to the Bottom Line

We now get to the part where retirees have to pay someone to manage and administer these new accounts. Most of that money goes to the financial services industry; the rest is simply dead-weight administrative cost. But all of it comes out of your pocket, one way or another. There are five major costs: management fees, trading costs, customer service costs, administrative costs, and the cost of buying annuities. That's five ways to lower your returns.

Management Fees.   As we've seen, active mutual fund management is expensive. Management fees average around 1.3 percent per year. Those administering Social Security privatization should be able to do better in negotiating fees than individual investors but don't count on doing a lot better, unless the government strictly limits your choices of accounts. A look at the fees other institutions pay for active management may provide a clue.

- According to Morningstar data, the average expense ratio for institutional shares of domestic equity mutual funds is 0.91 percent.[6]
- The fifty mutual funds with the most 401(k) assets had an equally weighted average expense ratio of 0.96 percent.[7]
- The average expense ratio of actively managed state-sponsored college savings plans looks to be in the same range. It ranges from 0.6 to 1.3 percent in most states.

Thus, we think it's fair to assume that with privatization you'll be paying out about 1 percent of your Social Security savings each year in management fees. *That 1 percent equates to ¾ of a billion dollars in fees to* *the mutual fund industry in the first year alone. It could rise to $10 billion per year within a decade.*

Trading Costs.   Don't forget the cost of turning over the stocks within those actively managed accounts. Brokerage commissions and bid/ask spreads are paid on every trade.

Trading costs average about 0.5 to 1.0 percent per year for actively managed mutual funds. In the Social Security world, we know that trading isn't going to earn the system *as a whole* any higher returns. In many cases, one Social Security mutual fund may actually be selling stock to another Social Security mutual fund! Remember, given Social Security's sheer size, the aggregate pretrading cost returns of $1 trillion in Social Security funds will be the same whether those funds never trade or trade daily.

What that means, of course, is that every single trade by a mutual fund will drive down the total returns of retirees by the cost of those trades. While some beneficiaries may benefit from trading if they pick the right fund, others will suffer if they pick the wrong fund. It's a zero-sum game. And so in ten years about $5–$10 billion more would be going down the drain each year.

Customer Service Costs.   Imagine what it takes to service your mutual fund account each year. Mailing account statements out monthly; running a friendly customer call-in center; allowing you to switch investment options on a regular basis; keeping track of your interest, dividends, and capital gains; keeping all of the accounting straight—all these services require substantial resources. More precisely, it costs funds between $25 and $50 an account per year. This is about what state-sponsored college savings plans charge as well.

Providing customer service for individual Social Security accounts would cost no less. We looked at this issue during the Clinton administration, asking consultants and large fund companies to price customer services for Social Security. The costs were about the same that the industry pays, with our best estimate being around $30 per year. In total, these costs could be staggering. There are over 155 million workers paying Social Security taxes in America. If all of them were eligible for a new private account, someone would need to pick up a cool $5 billion in new costs.

These costs would fall equally on all participants, but would be proportionally higher for the poor. Customer service costs basically do not vary by the size of the assets in an account. People with $5,000 in their account require the same monthly statement as people with $1 million in their account, and phone the call-in center just as frequently. For small savers, that full $30 will eat at returns. With the average 401(k) account at $55,000,[8] that $30 fee does not look so big, and minimum account balances prevent it from ever becoming a significant percentage of an investor's assets. But even $30 per year would represent a high proportion of the assets of the very lower income workers that Social Security was designed to protect.

The Social Security Commission seems to have recognized this problem. They proposed requiring participants with less than $5,000 in their accounts access to an investment plan similar to the low-cost Thrift Savings Plan that serves as the 401(k) for federal workers. They would further try to control costs by providing a limited menu of funds and allowing participants to change funds only once a year.

Administrative Costs. With a partially privatized system, payroll taxes would have to be divided in two. In the leading option, roughly five sixths would go to the Social Security Trust Fund. The other one sixth would go to whatever mutual fund you chose for investment. As with any payroll deduction, your employer would most likely need to perform a lot of behind-the-scenes accounting and record keeping to make the system work properly. In addition, your employer would most likely need to be able to answer your many questions about these new deductions. Those pushing private accounts generally ignore the considerable administrative challenges and costs for employers that would come with private accounts.

Many just assume that employers will simply take care of these new duties. This is how 401(k) plans are administered. *It is also why many small employers, though, find it prohibitively expensive to administer 401(k) plans.* According to Frank Cavanaugh, a former Treasury official and director of the federal government's Thrift Savings Plan, employers incur a minimum of $3,000 per year in administrative expenses for 401(k) plans, even for plans with only ten employees.[9] Given that the average U.S. employer has fewer than ten employees, this means that the annual expenses for tens of millions of individual Social Security accounts may be more than $300 per person. For the 37 percent of businesses with fewer than four employees, expenses could be more than $1,000 per employee. That's why providers of 401(k) plans, such as Fidelity Investments and T. Rowe Price, actually advise against 401(k)s for businesses with fewer than ten employees.

Of course, if employers actually absorbed these costs, Social Security benefits would not decrease. But as a political matter, there is no way that small businesses will readily absorb these costs. During Gary's service in the Clinton administration, he debated this problem during Social Security planning meetings among the president's most senior economic advisers in the West Wing. All recognized that a similar "employer mandate" had sunk health-care reform in the first years of the administration. No one was eager to relive that experience. That's just one of the reasons the Clinton administration concluded that we needed other solutions for the Social Security problem.

Buying Annuities. Like a pension, the current Social Security system pays you a fixed stream of income during your retirement. Better yet, that income is indexed to account for inflation; even better, it is actually indexed to keep up with wage inflation rather than just cost inflation. That means that during retirement, you keep up with the working public's increasing standard of living.

Unfortunately, an individual Social Security account couldn't do that. It's just a basket of stocks and bonds that you'll be presented with upon retirement. Your basket will probably yield you less in annual income than what you will then depend upon to live. Therefore, either you or the government will have to pay someone—probably an insurance company—to convert your individual account into a stream of annual payments.

This process can be very expensive. Basically an insurance company calculates what income it can count on from taking your account and reinvesting that money for itself. It then charges you a premium to account for risk and a further premium to make a profit. A recent study concludes that converting your 401(k) or Social Security account into an inflation-indexed annuity will end up costing you *between 10 and 25 percent of your savings.*[10]

Isn't that boring old Social Security system starting to look a lot better now? A feature that you took for granted would end up costing you at least 10 percent of your savings under a substitute plan.

The Much Diminished Bottom Line

The costs and risks we've seen above would destroy any reasonable chance of the average American doing better by investing their Social Security taxes in the stock market. It's just too expensive.[11] Worst yet is that the very people who most need Social Security would be hurt the most. For low-income workers, the very old and the disabled, a substandard Social Security can mean a retirement in poverty. The very old would suffer most from the loss of annuities tied to wage inflation. These retirees are the most dependent on Social Security, as their other savings have been exhausted during their long retirement.

Of course, the government could agree to eat these costs instead of passing them along to you. But all of this would have to be funded in some way. It might mean lower benefits from the nonprivatized portion of social security or higher taxes, or both. Alternatively, the government could try to impose these costs on employers—but we know that's not going to really happen. After all, the major reason that many policymakers have turned to individual accounts is to avoid facing these hard choices.

A Better Way

If Congress and the president decided that investing in the market were still worth the risk, there is a simple, lower-cost alternative. It's not likely to happen though, and we'll tell you why.

Higher Returns, Lower Costs

The government could simply invest the designated portion of Social Security funds in a total stock market index fund on behalf of beneficiaries. Doing so would have advantages over the system we just discussed.

- The government could negotiate an incredibly low price for the management of this pool of assets. Indeed, when we looked at this as Clinton administration officials we learned that it might even be possible to find a company willing to *pay the government* for the right to manage the funds. This payment would not reflect patriotism but rather (1) the very low costs of indexing, and (2) the potential profit from being able to lend out the securities in the portfolio. Even assuming that the government wished to keep all of the stock loan profits for Social Security funds, we estimated that the management expense ratio would be about 0.01 percent, or one hundredth of 1 percent, of the assets under management.

- The government also could use its bargaining power to negotiate low prices for annuities that would be available to any worker who, upon retirement, wished to convert an individual account to a fixed income stream.
- All beneficiaries would receive the same rate of return, which would be the rate of return of the market as a whole, less expenses. Thus, no beneficiary would be disadvantaged relative to others of the same age.
- Because all beneficiaries would be receiving the same rate of return, calculating returns and providing statements would be made a bit simpler. Administrative costs would be relatively small.
- Some would object that the government's investing in the stock market, even as an agent, runs the risk of picking winners and losers or timing the market. In general, we would agree. It's difficult to see, though, how passively investing in the broad market as a whole, without favoring any particular stock or category of stocks, is more disruptive than the government's selecting a series of mutual fund managers, each with a known style of investing.

Even with this approach to private accounts, there still would be significant administrative and annuity costs and risks. All the larger questions about the viability of a partially privatized system also would remain. There's just about no getting around these problems. But it sure would be better than the mess we just saw.

One irony is that even with the individual accounts envisioned by President Bush, some sort of centralized investment system will still probably be necessary. The Commission recognized this reality for small savers. Others will want to check a simple box on their yearly tax form to get going with an account. No doubt, there will be many others who won't even respond to the offer of a new account. For them, the government will need to provide some default option in which to invest. Someone will have to manage all of this money. Then all those statements about the evil of the government's investing retirees' money are going to look a little funny.

Why the Best Outcome Is Difficult to Achieve

But a comprehensive indexing program is not likely to happen. A fully indexed system blows a wonderful opportunity for the financial industry in at least three ways. First, it diminishes the fees that the mutual fund industry could charge for the task. (So, too, does the Commission's plan to index balances below $5,000, but those balances will eventually grow, and Wall Street is patient.) Second, the fees would not be shared throughout the mutual fund industry, as indexing would likely require fewer firms. Third, as index funds have much lower turnover rates than actively managed funds, trading fees to be earned by the brokerage industry would be significantly lower. Clearly, this is not going to work from Wall Street's point of view. But how to convince Congress to go the other way?

In pushing individual accounts, privatizers have focused their message on two of the most popular themes in American life: trust in choice and distrust of government.

"It's your choice, your money, your future," reads the banner across the top of the Cato Institute's website promoting Social Security privatization. Consider the alluring rhetoric available to those promoting active investing.

- We favor *choice* for individual investors whereas our opponents *oppose choice.*
- We believe that Americans are *smart enough to make their own choices,* whereas the indexers and other opponents believe that Americans are *too dumb to make their own choices.*
- We support *Americans deciding where their own retirement money is invested,* whereas the indexers favor *government making that decision for investors.*
- We want to treat Social Security accounts *just like 401(k) accounts.*

Or to quote candidate Governor George W. Bush, "There is a fundamental difference between my opponent and me. I trust individual Americans. I trust Americans to make their own decisions and manage their own money." (You've recently heard the same refrain when the Bush administration opposed limiting the percentage of company stock in 401(k) plans.)

During the Clinton administration, we envisioned being bombarded by new industry-sponsored commercials similar to those that featured "Harry and Louise" during the health-care debate. These showed a couple sitting at the dinner table decrying the possible government role in health care. Playing on Americans' distrust of government, they were very effective for industry and devastating for the policy. In the Social Security debate, you might prepare yourself for a series of TV advertisements featuring people like Peter Lynch, promising that they'll take care of your money much better than some government bureaucrat will. Such a campaign is quite likely to resonate with investors, as it feeds into Americans' love of picking stocks and mutual funds.

If you think about it, though, choice is a very odd, even perverse, rallying cry when it comes to Social Security. Allowing each worker to choose his or her own mutual funds will result in some workers having a better retirement than others would. Privatizers might call those who do well with actively managed funds skillful and those who do poorly unskilled. We would call them lucky and unlucky. Regardless, though, since when should one's Social Security benefits depend on being lucky? We thought Social Security was at least in part supposed to be a safety net for Americans, especially the unlucky and unskillful. If you lose an arm at the factory, should your insurance benefits really depend on whether you recognized that there was a bubble under tech stocks?

Conclusion

President Dwight Eisenhower once described the purpose of Social Security: "The system is not intended as a substitute for private savings, pension plans, and insurance protection. It is, rather, intended as the foundation upon which these other forms of protection can be soundly built. . . . Hence, the system both encourages thrift and self-reliance, and helps to prevent destitution in our national life."

The privatization plans under consideration by the Congress are a refutation of everything Eisenhower said. They will lead workers to see Social Security as a substitute for private savings. They will erode Social Security's role as a low-risk foundation upon which other investments can build. They will diminish benefits for those most likely to face destitution in their old age. Robert Johnson, a member of President Bush's Social Security Commission, encapsulated the whole mindset of these privatizers when, in describing why Social Security beneficiaries must be allowed to withdraw their money from individual accounts prior to retirement, he said, "What's wrong with taking $200,000 and running a nice bed-and-breakfast inn or buying a boat?"[12]

Doing right by America's retirees will require those in power to buck America's love affair with the markets, ignore a very powerful industry, and make hard choices. It's a challenge worthy of Lincoln. We'll see whether our leaders are equally worthy.

Part VI

The Rest of the Picture

There's no secret to winning the Indianapolis
500. You just press the accelerator to the floor
and steer left.
—*Bill Vukovich*

T hus far, we have focused on one important part of investing: how to achieve the best returns from investment in the U.S. stock market. We have emphasized U.S. stock investing because that is where investors have the most money and where the best performance data exist. But the lessons learned in U.S. equity investing are readily transferable to other assets.

We will now touch on some of the other major subjects of personal investment, using the common sense and objective analysis that have guided previous chapters. We start with asset allocation and then turn to investing in bonds and international stocks. We then review the various investment vehicles that our government subsidizes through tax breaks, with special focus on three that present the greatest opportunities and risks: employer-sponsored retirement plans, variable annuities, and tax-exempt education accounts (better known as "529 plans").

We will summarize the major questions to consider as you make decisions in these areas, offer you some general advice, and point you toward other sources of information. While we won't get you all the way down the road, we will show you the path and light the way.

Chapter 20

Asset Allocation: A Subject Truly Worth Your Time

*Perennials are the ones that grow like weeds, biennials are
the ones that die this year instead of next, and hardy
annuals are the ones that never come up at all.—Katharine
Whitehorn, Observations*

W elcome to the world beyond U.S. equity investing. We'll now
take a look at how much you should invest in other types of
assets, and how best to make those investments. It's time to
get some new colors in our little investing garden.

Asset Allocation

Perhaps the most important question you face in investing your money
is how to allocate your investments among different types of assets—
stocks, bonds, cash, insurance, and real estate. Given that most Americans carry insurance and try to own a home, the question of asset
allocation will generally relate to the remaining three categories: stocks,
bonds, and cash.

Each type has subcategories. Stocks can include domestic and international stocks. Bonds can include Treasury bonds, municipal bonds,
investment-grade corporate bonds, and high-yield (junk) bonds. Cash
is not just the green stuff that comes out of the ATM, but also includes

other short-term liquid assets that carry little or no risk, such as short-term Treasury securities (T-bills), money market funds, and bank certificates of deposit.

Why would you wish to allocate some of your savings into each type of asset? First, holding different types of assets is a form of diversification. When one goes down, the others may go up or go down less. Second, each type of asset promises different risks and rewards. Stocks generally offer the greatest risks and rewards, cash the lowest, and bonds somewhere in between.

Thoughtful asset allocation means finding the right balance between risk and return. If you have a mortgage payment due at the end of the month, you would not want to have the money for that payment invested in the Nasdaq and would prefer to hold cash. Similarly, if your children are starting college in two years, you may want to have the upcoming tuition payments in bonds. If you are saving for a retirement that is still thirty years away, you may be willing to accept the risks that go along with the potentially higher returns of stocks.

Regardless of your time horizon, your own peace of mind is critical to your health and your asset allocation decisions. How bad would you feel if your mutual funds went down by 20 percent, the amount considered to define a bear market? How about the 60 percent drop that was experienced by the Nasdaq in 2001? Your personal tolerance for risk is not something we can know. As you have learned more about risk and returns, though, we hope your personal tolerance will be an informed tolerance.

To assist in that process, here are a few guidelines when it comes to asset allocation.

1. *Asset allocation should be a conscious choice, not a happenstance.*
   You should consciously decide how to allocate your assets. Don't just let allocation happen according to what looks good at the time or be due to the vagaries of your own returns or cash situation. You should not increase your stock allocation, for example, because your brother read a really cool article about a biotechnology company in an airline magazine.

2. *Help on asset allocation is readily available.* One rule of thumb with which most financial advisers start (and some, unfortu-

nately, finish) is that your stock investments should be a percentage of your assets equal to 100 or 110 minus your age.[1] More sophisticated asset allocation models are freely available on the Internet. These models will ask you questions about your time horizons (upcoming educational or medical expenses) and risk tolerance, as well as the size of your assets (including pensions), and whether you have equity in a home.

Finally, there are good books on asset allocation. The latter chapters of Burton Malkiel's *Random Walk Down Wall Street* are a wonderful introduction to the subject. If you read even one book on asset allocation, you probably know 80 percent of what a private banker, financial planner, or full-service broker would tell you.

3. *If you belong to an investment club, shift its focus to asset allocation.* Investment clubs are a poor mechanism for picking stocks. On the other hand, investment clubs could serve as a wonderful resource for asset allocation. Research tasks could be shared, and members could offer mutual advice and support when it comes to choices.

4. *Never pay anyone a percentage of your assets to advise you on asset allocation.* The one place you do not want to allocate your assets is into the account of your financial adviser. If a rule of thumb, allocation models, books, and investment clubs are insufficient to make you comfortable with your choices, that's okay. You can get some personal advice. Just get it from someone who charges by the hour.

5. *Never confuse asset allocation with market timing.* When you hear a Wall Street economist on CNBC advising investors to increase their stock allocation from 60 to 80 percent, that economist is not taking into account your time horizons or tolerance for risk. That economist is simply using allocation percentages as a way of expressing a market timing prediction. The economist is predicting that stocks are due for a big price increase. Ignore this advice completely. Market timing is a failed concept. Asset allocation is an important concept. Don't confuse them.

6. *Do not buy any mutual fund that lists asset allocation as one of its*

objectives. According to Morningstar, there are over 150 such funds sold to individual investors. Again, these funds generally are not shifting asset allocations based on your time horizon, but rather are engaged in market timing. They should be called "market timing funds." Their performance is lousy. Over ten years, their performance trails the S&P 500 by 4.3 percent annually. You may think that comparison unfair, because these funds invest in bonds as well, bringing their average returns down a bit. But they lead the Lehman Brothers Bond index by only 1.5 percent! And that's before considering their tax impact.

7. *Don't forget about asset allocation when making decisions about your retirement accounts.* Your 401(k) plan or IRA is likely to be a significant part of your savings. Include these funds in your decisions. Also, be cautious regarding company stock in these funds. Where company stock is allowed in the plan, studies show that the average 401(k) participant holds one third of her retirement assets in that stock.[2] This is like doubling down at Vegas. If your company does poorly, not only does the stock go down, but your salary or job is also on the line. Diversify the risk by selling the company stock as soon as possible. Remember Enron!

8. *Don't spend time or money trying to allocate within your U.S. stock investments.* Over time the best returns at the lowest risk will come from passively investing in the broad stock market. Breaking your U.S. equity investments down into buckets based upon company size, style, or sector will only make the financial community richer and your family less so.

9. *Periodically—but not frequently—reconsider your asset allocation strategy.* Not more than once a year, you should examine your asset allocation and make certain that it is still consistent with your time horizons and risk tolerance. *You should not base this reexamination on how the various asset classes have performed over the previous year.* If stocks (or bonds) have had a bad year, then you should not buy (or sell) stocks based on that performance. Only if past market performance has affected your tolerance for risk—for example, by reducing your assets to the point that

some short-term expenses are imperiled—or caused a significant change in the risk level of your portfolio should you allow it to change your allocation.

10. *Don't forget to manage your cash balances.* Don't forget that money in your checking account could earn more for you just about anywhere else—the stock market, the bond market, a money market fund. Last year, the New York newspapers reported that a customer who used an ATM just after former President Clinton had used it found the president's receipt, which revealed a balance of over a million dollars in his checking account. If true, this story is an extreme example of a mistake many people make. If you have cash you're keeping for a rainy day (or for a particularly bad credit card bill), then consider investing it in bank certificate of deposits or in a money market account. Transfer it to a checking account only as you need it. But be careful: one bounced check charge will wipe out a year of interest savings.

Chapter 21

Bond Investing

Out of this nettle, danger, we pluck this flower,
safety.—*William Shakespeare*, Henry IV, Part I

Almost all investors should end up allocating some of their assets to bonds. Bonds help diversify the risks of stocks. They also produce more stable and predictable income than stocks.

We'll see, though, that the great mutual fund trap applies with even greater force to actively managed bond funds than it does to actively managed stock funds. Interestingly, though, the escape route is a little different. Index bond funds can be a good alternative, but if you've got a lump sum to invest, buying bonds directly often makes much more sense than buying any fund.

Types of Bonds

All bonds share certain traits. Absent default by the issuing company or government, a bond returns a fixed stream of interest income. Holders always have the option of holding the bond until maturity—that is, until the principal is returned. Thus, with bonds you can know how much you will have on hand in order to cover a future expense.

Most bonds can be traded in the marketplace. Their value will be determined by several factors—the coupon interest on the bond, its maturity date, the perceived risk of the issuer's default, and the overall level of interest rates in the economy.

You will need to determine what type of bond is best suited for you:

- U.S. Treasury securities have no practical risk of default and interest is exempt from state and local taxes. They generally pay a lower interest rate, however, than other types of bonds. Treasury securities vary in maturity from Treasury bills (maturing in less than one year), Treasury notes (maturing in two to ten years), and Treasury bonds (maturing in more than ten years).
- Municipal bonds have an extremely low risk of default, and interest is exempt from all federal taxation. Interest is also exempt from state and local taxes when the bond issued by your state of residence or a city within that state. When considered on an aftertax basis, they earn higher returns than Treasury securities of comparable maturities. The higher your tax bracket, the greater the attraction of municipal bonds.
- Investment-grade corporate bonds and bonds issued by government-sponsored enterprises carry a modest risk of default and generally offer less liquidity than Treasury securities. Accordingly, they pay a higher interest rate than Treasuries. Interest and other earnings on these bonds, however, are fully taxed.[1]
- High-yield bonds (also known as junk bonds) are issued by companies with higher risks of default and therefore offer higher potential interest rates. They carry no tax advantages. The risks and returns of high-yield bonds are akin to those of stocks. Individual investors willing to shoulder this level of risk should probably hold stocks instead.

Picking a Structure for Bond Ownership

Generally, regardless of the type of bond you favor, you will face three options for owning that bond—indeed, the same choices you faced with stocks. These are actively managed bond funds, indcx bond funds, and direct purchases. While we'll go through each in turn, the bottom line is we are not fans of bond funds—even of index bond funds (though they are far better than actively managed funds).

Before analyzing each structure, it is helpful to understand more about how bond prices behave. Bonds generally have lower volatility (risk) and returns than stocks. While this stability is one of the reasons bonds are useful assets, it also means that there is less chance, on average, for a bond investor to beat the market by any significant amount. Winners and losers in the bond world don't win or lose by very much. Thus, of the 224 corporate bond funds in existence for the five-year period ending in 2001, the top-performing fund recorded an annual gain of 9.2 percent while the worst performer posted a gain of 2.0 percent.[2] That's a lot narrower range than the 35.9 percent to -27.4 percent range for domestic stock funds over the same period. In other words, you're paying a bunch of money for investment advice that, whether by design or good fortune, is not going to make much difference.

With these facts in mind, let's look at our three structures.

Actively Managed Bond Funds

Because bond performance varies less than stock performance, it is even more difficult for bond funds to overcome the ankle weights of high fees and transaction. And weights there are.

- The average actively managed corporate bond fund has an expense ratio of 0.9 percent—lower than stock funds but extremely high given that average five-year, load-adjusted performance was 5.9 percent. The annual fee represents a substantial proportion of the gains of even the best performing bond funds.
- The median bond fund also had a turnover ratio of around 80 percent. So, you'll be paying taxes on any capital gains early and often.[3]

We compared the returns of actively managed corporate bond funds to the Lehman Brothers Aggregate Bond Index (the bond world equivalent of the S&P 500 Index), and you won't like what we found.

- Only 21 percent (58 of 273) of actively managed bond funds out-performed the index over a twelve-month period.
- Only 9 percent (23 of 247) of actively managed funds outperformed over a three-year period.
- Only 3 percent (6 of 213) of actively managed funds outperformed over a five-year period.

**Performance of
Ten Largest Corporate Bond Funds Versus Market**

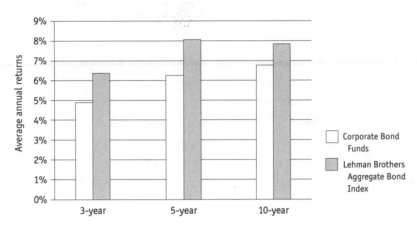

We looked at the five largest actively managed corporate bond funds to see how they did.

Load-Adjusted Performance of Five Largest Corporate Bond Funds

Fund	Size $BB	Average annual return (3-year)	Average annual return (5-year)	Average annual return (10-year)
American Funds Bond Fund of America A	11	3.9%	5.2%	7.0%
Vanguard Short-term Corporate	7	6.5%	6.6%	6.4%
Fidelity Intermediate Bond	5	6.4%	6.8%	6.6%
Fidelity Investment Grade Bond	4	6.0%	7.0%	7.1%
Vanguard Long-term Corporate Bond	4	4.7%	7.4%	8.1%

Load-Adjusted Performance of Five Largest Corporate Bond Funds

Fund	Size $BB	Average annual return (3-year)	Average annual return (5-year)	Average annual return (10-year)
Average	6	5.5%	5.5%	6.9%
Lehman Brothers Aggregate Bond Index		6.3%	7.4%	7.2%

Source: Morningstar Principia Pro, data through December 31, 2001.

Even aside from performance, there is another significant reason why you may wish to avoid actively managed bond funds. One of the advantages of bonds is that they allow you to earn a predictable stream of income, and thus plan for upcoming expenses. For example, if you have an $11,000 tuition payment due in two years, and you can buy a $10,000 two-year bond with an interest rate of 5 percent, then you know that you'll have enough to make the payment. *Bond funds, however, deprive you of this predictability.*

Bond funds lack this predictability for two reasons. First, as the turnover ratios demonstrate, active bond funds often do not hold their bonds to maturity. Instead, they are constantly buying and selling bonds. The interest rates on the new bonds may differ from the old, and capital gains and losses may be incurred in the sale.

Second, even if a fund does not churn its holdings, something rather unattractive can happen to a bond fund when market interest rates decline. As market rates decline, new investors are likely to be attracted to your bond fund as long as it continues to hold some of the older, higher yielding securities. There will thus be cash inflows into the fund. The fund must then invest this cash in more bonds—at the new, lower rates. This influx of new bonds drives down the average yield (interest rates) of the bonds in the fund's portfolio.

Think how perverse that outcome is. You find a bond fund with an average yield of say 6 percent, counting on your money growing at that rate in order to meet a future obligation. In fact, the very thing you fear occurs, and interest rates drop to 4 percent. You are feeling good about your decision—until a bunch of new money flows into your fund. That new money is reinvested at 4 percent, and you and a bunch of new-comers—free riders—all share in a new interest rate of 5 percent.

There is no greater predictability in a rising interest-rate environment. If you buy a bond fund and interest rates rise, then the value of the fund's holdings falls. When you go to sell the fund, it will be worth less than when you bought it.

Index Bond Funds

In the stock world, index funds cure most of the ills of actively managed stock funds. In the world of bond investing, index funds are still good medicine but can't fully cure the patient.

When it comes to fees, transaction costs, and taxes, index bond funds offer all the advantages of their stock counterparts. By far the largest bond index fund is the Vanguard Total Bond Market index fund, which is five times the size of its closest competitor. As we've come to expect from Vanguard, the expense ratio is 0.22 percent, with no loads. The fund is as diversified as its name suggests, holding about 4,800 bonds. Turnover is higher than its stock fund siblings, however, at an actively managed–like 53 percent. The Total Bond Market index fund sometimes beats the index and rarely trails by very much. Other bond index funds fall a bit farther behind. Thus, we believe that the Vanguard index bond fund or another index fund with a similar record is a clearly superior choice to actively managed bond funds.

That said, index bond funds suffer from the same problem of unpredictable returns as actively managed bond funds. You'll also confront other issues we didn't face in the stock world.

1. Index bond funds do not provide the predictable income or fixed date for return of your principal that direct bond ownership does. By buying a "ladder" of bonds—that is, buying bonds of varying maturity dates—you can receive your principal back at regular intervals, for example, timed to coincide with a series of tuition bills. In other words, investing in a mutual fund means giving up one of the central attributes of bond investing. There is no similar sacrifice in the stock world.

2. Index bond funds have high turnover, incurring transaction costs

and generating capital gains liabilities that direct ownership does not. Turnover is far higher than with stock index funds or ETFs.

3. Bond funds bring you only modest diversification benefits. Only a handful of high-quality bonds is necessary to achieve diversification, since bonds are much less volatile than stocks. Also, the default rate on high-grade corporate and agency bonds is small; municipal bonds carry even less default risk; and Treasury securities are riskless.[4] Thus, whereas we would advise against your holding only a handful of stocks, we see nothing wrong with holding a handful of high-quality bonds.

4. There are no index bond funds that focus on municipal bonds. (While there are numerous actively managed funds covering larger states like New York and California, they charge an average fee of 0.8 percent, and almost all charge a sales load. For smaller states, there may be no municipal bond fund at all. Moreover, the extremely low default rates for highly rated municipal bonds make direct ownership of such bonds very low risk.)

Direct Purchases

The good news is that discount brokerages and the Internet have democratized the process of purchasing bonds directly. For a long time investors could not buy bonds for a reasonable price on understandable terms. Investors had to work with a full-service broker, which charged a significant commission and markup on the price of the bond. Thanks to recent innovations in the bond business, you can now buy Treasury, municipal, and even some corporate bonds at low prices.

When it comes to Treasury securities, however, individuals can now purchase securities directly from the Treasury Department at the same cost as Wall Street dealers in these securities. That program, Treasury Direct (which Gary oversaw and enhanced during his time at the Treasury Department) offers investors with as little as $1,000 the opportunity to invest in Treasury securities over the Internet or the telephone (1–800–722–2678 or www.publicdebt.treas.gov/sec/secdir.html). You can buy savings bonds in even smaller amounts. For those interested in protecting against inflation risk, you also can buy Treasury Inflation-Protected securities or savings bonds. Given these options, we can think of no reason to pay a mutual fund to buy Treasury securities for you. (If you really don't have the time, Vanguard does offer a very low-cost Inflation-Protected Securities Fund.)

The news is also pretty good when it comes to municipal and corporate securities as well. With respect to municipal securities, a new broker, munidirect.com, offers both good tutorials on bond investing and transparency with respect to markups and commissions. Its website pledges that you will never pay a commission or markup greater than $5 per $1,000 bond, with a $50 minimum fee per order. Most discount brokers carry an inventory of bonds and have tools for selecting the one that works best for you. We've used TD Waterhouse (www.td waterhouse.com), which generally charges lower commissions than firms such as Schwab or Fidelity.

Furthermore, there are companies selling their bonds to the public through programs akin to Treasury Direct. The LaSalle Broker Dealer Services division of ABN Amro has initiated a program that allows individual investors to buy what it calls Direct Access Notes in amounts as small as $1,000. Companies offering their bonds to the public through LaSalle include General Motors Acceptance Corporation, UPS, and the Tennessee Valley Authority. While the program is not truly "direct," as there is an intermediary, investors don't pay a commission or a dealer markup. The program sold more than $10 billion of bonds in 2001.

Similarly, Incapital, an investment bank, offers "InterNotes" issued by Household Financial Corporation, Bank of America, Daimler-Chrysler North America, and other companies with highly rated bonds. For further information on how to buy bonds, we recommend you look at www.investinginbonds.com, sponsored by the Bond Market Association. To purchase bonds, other good sites include tdwaterhouse.com and tradebonds.com.

Given all these options, we believe that the case for direct purchase of bonds is much stronger than it was for stocks. The conventional advice is that you should have at least $10,000 to $25,000 to invest in bonds before forgoing a fund.

Defenders of bond funds assert that they have a substantial advantage over individual investors when it comes to minimizing bid/ask spreads. Bond funds argue that they make up for their fees by negotiating better spreads. With respect to actively managed bond funds, the easy answer to this argument is the woeful performance described above. The difference in spreads is insufficient to overcome fees and other trading costs. Index funds may be a different matter, though. We believe that the case for direct bond purchase rather than index fund purchase is not solely based on cost. Rather it is due to the certainty of income and maturity dates and the relative ease with which you can purchase two important categories of bonds, Treasuries and municipals.

We have two caveats with respect to holding your own bonds. First, you must have a plan for the interest payments. Allowing that money to lie idle in a money market or checking account isn't the best thing. The easiest way to go is simply to reinvest those earnings in one of your index stock funds every month or quarter. Second, if you plan to move states in the forseeable future, you may wish to defer direct purchases of municipal bonds.

Summary

Our advice on bonds is as follows. Determine the percentage of your assets you wish to allocate to bonds. If you have a significant amount to invest, say $10,000 or more, invest directly by purchasing a few high quality corporate bonds or municipal bonds—with municipal bonds *from your own state* the first place to look. If you have smaller amounts to invest and won't be able to afford a handful of individual bonds, use an index bond fund. If you wish to invest in Treasury securities, wait until you have $1,000 and use Treasury Direct.

Chapter 22

The Benefits of International Stocks

I love America more than any other country in this world,
and, exactly for this reason, I insist on the right to criticize
her perpetually.—*James Baldwin*, Notes of a Native Son

M any asset allocation models and financial planners suggest that
you put some money in international stocks (shorthand for
stocks whose companies are headquartered outside the United
States). We want to introduce you to the debate about whether and
how much to invest in international stocks. We'll then describe the best
structures for doing so.

To Invest in Overseas Companies or Not?

The decision to invest in overseas markets comes down to a tradeoff:
added diversification versus higher risks and costs than with domestic
investment. While we would recommend that investors have some international exposure, smaller savers may find it a closer call.

Upside: Diversification

Those who advocate international investing have a simple point. It is arrogant to assume that the U.S. market will always outperform all other markets, and foolhardy not to diversify the risk that the U.S. markets may underperform. As we go to print, the five largest stocks in a broad-market international index are BP Amoco, GlaxoSmithKline, Vodafone Group, Novartis, and Royal Dutch Petroleum. Who's to say that those stocks will not sometimes outperform the largest U.S. stocks?

History seems to validate this view. While the U.S. market outperformed world markets in the 1990s, the reverse was true in the 1970s. (The 1980s were about a draw.)

A graph provided by Barclays Global Investors best summarizes the diversification benefits of international stock investing for the twelve-year period 1988–2000. The graph shows the risk (as measured by standard deviation) of holding various levels of international stocks over the period from 1988 to 2000. The graph suggests that the first 15 to 20 percent of your assets invested internationally bring substantial diversification rewards. The lowest risk stock portfolio would have included between 20 and 30 percent international stocks. Still, some of the increased gains from 15 to 30 percent may be offset by costs, and the benefits are clearest up to about 20 percent.

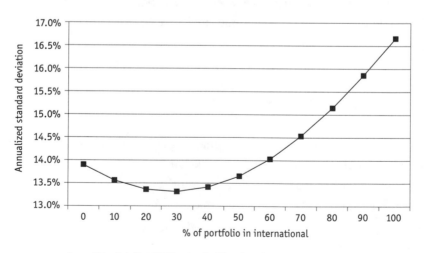

Source: BGI analysis (Russell 3000 as proxy for U.S. equity and MSCI ACWI [ex-U.S.] for international equity).

Still, there are some downsides to international investing that must be weighed against diversification gains.

Downside: Cost

International investing is more expensive. International mutual funds charge higher management fees than their domestic counterparts, actively managed or index. The average expense ratio for all domestic stock funds, actively managed and passive, is 1.3 percent. The average expense ratio for equivalent international stock funds is 1.7 percent, with higher average loads as well.[1] In addition, bid/ask spreads are higher in foreign markets, imposing higher costs on trading and further driving down returns.

Fortunately some international index funds and ETFs carry much lower costs than actively managed funds. Barclays's broad-market international ETF, the iShares MSCI EAFE Index fund (ticker: EFA), has an annual fee of just 0.35 percent. Still, while that fee is much lower than those charged by actively managed international funds, it is still higher than those for domestic stock ETFs. Thus, for overseas investment to make sense, you must receive higher returns or better diversification.

Downside: Risk

The primary risk of investing overseas is currency risk. We live in a land of U.S. dollars. While about 12 percent of the nation's consumption does come from imported goods and services, you will most likely be paying your tuition, mortgage, and medical bills in U.S. dollars and living out your retirement in this country. When you invest overseas, however, you must do so, indirectly, in the local currency. If the U.S. dollar subsequently strengthens, those local currencies will be worth less in terms of the U.S. dollars they will buy. Because currency markets can be as volatile as stock markets, this risk may be considerable.

There are other risks associated with overseas investing. Enron notwithstanding, securities laws and accounting rules are sometimes not as well developed in other countries as they are in the United States. There are also greater political risks in emerging markets. Modern portfolio theory would generally say that these risks should come with higher reward. However, you probably will not receive full compensation for these risks—through higher returns—because other investors, namely those in the country where you are investing, are more able to shoulder these risks.

How to Invest in Overseas Companies

If you have decided to invest in international stocks, the question is how best to do so. There is no reason to believe that the lessons from the U.S. stock market about active versus passive investing would not hold true in foreign markets as well. Determining how well actively managed international funds perform on average can be difficult, though, because there is so much variety in where they invest. Exposure to emerging markets or Japan can have a dramatic effect on a fund's volatility and performance. One rather clearly defined group of funds, though, is Europe. We used Morningstar to compare the performance of actively managed Europe funds to the MSCI-Europe Index over the five- and ten-year periods ending December 31, 2001.

Actively managed Europe funds earned 8.6 percent annually over ten years, trailing the index (11.3 percent) by 2.7 percentage points per year. At five years, the European funds trailed by 4.8 percentage points per year (3.8 percent to 8.6 percent). As for Pacific/Asia, the results were similar. Eliminating survivorship bias would significantly increase the margin of victory for the indexes.

These results are not surprising. Management fees, bid/ask spreads, and sales loads are higher with actively managed international funds than with actively managed domestic funds. Since the ankle weights are even heavier, international fund managers have to run that much harder to outpace the market. At home or abroad, the song remains the same.

Thus, we turn to indexing. There are various indexes that track the overseas market. Morgan Stanley and Capital International (MSCI), an affiliate of Morgan Stanley, operates the best known indexes. MSCI estimates that there are over $300 billion invested in index funds tied to its index, plus another $1.7 trillion in actively managed funds that use its indexes as a benchmark. MSCI's indexes include:

- the MSCI-EAFE, tracking Europe, Australia, Asia, and the far East, which holds about one thousand stocks in 21 countries
- the MSCI-ACWI ex U.S., or All-Country World Index, which holds about nineteen hundred securities in 48 countries
- the MSCI-EMF, or Emerging Markets Free Index

MSCI also publishes indexes for numerous countries. As global markets grow, however, a new index seems to pop up every day. So, if you do buy an international index fund, you will need to inform yourself about the index it is tracking.

Here are the five largest international index funds, the indexes they track, and their costs. All are no-load.

Fund	Size $BB	Index	Expense Ratio
Vanguard European Stock	4.4	MSCI-Europe	0.29%
Vanguard Total Int'l Stock	2.9	MSCI EAFE	0.35%
Vanguard Pacific Stock	1.3	MSCI-Japan	0.38%
Vanguard Emerging Market	0.8	MSCI-Emerging Markets	0.59%
Schwab Int'l Select	0.7	MSCI-EAFE	0.47%

Source: Morningstar Principia Pro, data through December 31, 2001.

Vanguard again dominates the field, and offers very low fees. As was also true with its domestic index fund, Schwab's international fund carries a minimum purchase requirement of $50,000.

There are now international ETFs, as well. Currently the ones with the largest coverage are all offered by Barclays, under its iShares brand. These include the MSCI EAFE index fund (expense ratio of 0.35 percent); S&P Global 100 index fund (expense ratio of 0.40 percent); and the S&P Europe 350 index fund (expense ratio of 0.60 percent). More broad market ETFs should be coming on the market all the time.

A New Option?

A new option for diversifying internationally comes through a series of indexes and linked index funds that track the world's largest global companies.[2] For instance, the iShares S&P Global 100 ETF tracks the one hundred largest companies in the world, holding about 60 percent U.S. stocks. Also, FOLIOfn offers a preselected portfolio of the world's largest companies. While it is too soon to know how well these indexes will perform, they may offer the potential for capturing some of the diversification of overseas markets without taking on all of the higher risks and costs of overseas investment. Because the underlying companies generally trade on major exchanges in the United States and Europe, trading costs should be lower. Because the companies they track operate primarily in the United States and Europe, currency risk may be reduced as well.

On the other hand, all of these new funds have at least two drawbacks. First, they are the equivalent of a large-cap fund entirely invested in large multinational companies. Second, a majority of their holdings are in the United States, where you probably already have stock holdings. While you may wish to consider these funds, we would be cautious with regard to what they really offer you.

Conclusion

Investing between 15 and 20 percent of your stock portfolio in international stocks can bring you clear diversification benefits. Our general advice would be to put these dollars to work as you would here in the United States. Buy an ETF or index fund that represents the broad market rather than one particular region, sector, size, or style.

Chapter 23

Tax-Advantaged Retirement Investing—Putting Uncle Sam to Work for You

> "Anyone may arrange his affairs so that his taxes shall be as low as possible; he is not bound to choose that pattern which best pays the treasury. There is not even a patriotic duty to increase one's taxes. Over and over again the Courts have said that there is nothing sinister in so arranging affairs as to keep taxes as low as possible. Everyone does it, rich and poor alike, and all do right, for nobody owes any public duty to pay more than the law demands."—*Judge Learned Hand*

You might be surprised at how many opportunities there are to shelter your investment income from taxes. Members of Congress have a legitimate desire to increase the national savings rate. They also like to greet voters on election day with some tax breaks in hand. Among the most forceful lobbyists for such breaks is Wall Street, which looks at a new investment tax deduction like an orthopedist looks at a skateboard: it's certain to send more business his way. There's currently close to $2.5 trillion dollars in tax-advantaged retirement accounts. Managing those accounts—for the standard compensation, of course—represents big money to Wall Street.

Once your investments are sheltered from taxes, you may wonder whether you should go ahead and pay for them to be actively managed. After all, you'll no longer pay annual taxes even when your mutual fund manager or broker churns the account. The problem, though, is that you will still pay high management fees, commissions, and bid/ask spreads. You'll also fail to get the full benefits of diversification. Believe us, active fund management is no bargain in the tax-free world either.

Indeed, you will see that the insurance industry has counted on your dropping your guard as soon as you enter the tax-free world. They see it as an ideal place to slip in more fees under the invisibility cloak of tax-advantaged accounts. You need to see it as a place to remain vigilant.

In this chapter, we'll describe the major retirement savings vehicles. We will look at the government's employee retirement savings plan, which offers a nice case study on exactly how you should be taking advantage of these vehicles. Last, we'll give you some general advice about how you can marry Uncle Sam's generosity with passive investment and live happily ever after.

The Different Plans

Employer-Sponsored Plans

About one-half of U.S. workers are covered by an employer-sponsored retirement plan. Many are defined-benefit plans, where you receive a fixed pension from your employer and have no investment decisions to make. They will not be our focus here. Instead, we will focus on the area where the greatest growth in retirement plans has come: defined-contribution plans—better known as 401(k)s and 403(b)s. (Section 401(k) of the tax code covers corporate employees, while section 403(b) covers employees of tax-exempt organizations and public schools.)

Defined-contribution plans are an attractive option. All contributions are deductible from your earnings when computing your taxes. All earnings compound tax-free until retirement, when you must begin withdrawing the money and paying taxes on it.[1] The benefit of these plans is that you get to invest until retirement the money you otherwise would have paid in taxes. You do end up paying ordinary income taxes, however, on your earnings. While income tax rates are generally higher than capital gains rates, you will at least be paying the lower income tax rates associated with retirement rather than the higher rates of your prime earning years. Moreover, employers often match your contributions, and those contributions compound tax-free as well.

The amounts involved can be substantial. One survey shows that the average 401(k) account balance is already $55,000. Even though some large accounts may skew the average, close to 60 percent of accounts are larger than $10,000.[2]

As of 2002, you can now contribute up to $12,000 a year to a 401(k) account. This limit will grow to $15,000 per year by 2006. If you are over fifty years old, you can contribute an additional $1,000 more per year, growing to an additional $5,000 by 2006. Thus, as more of the baby boomers turn fifty, they will be able to contribute $20,000 a year to tax-advantaged savings accounts sponsored by their employers. This type of investment is well worth your time.

Individual Retirement Accounts (IRAs)

Since 1975, investors have been permitted to establish individual retirement accounts, popularly referred to as "IRAs." IRAs are simplified versions of 401(k)s, with greater benefits for those with lower incomes. Contributions are tax deductible if you are not part of a 401(k) or 403(b) plan and you earn less than various limits as set forth in the tax code.[3] Earnings are compounded tax-free until withdrawal, which must begin by age 70½.

As of 2002, eligible individuals may contribute $3,000 per year to these accounts. The maximum allowable contribution will grow to $5,000 per year by 2008. Married couples get to contribute twice these amounts even if only one is earning a salary. The fifty-plus set gets to add $500 per year to these amounts through 2005 and $1,000 per year thereafter.

Roth IRAs

In 1998, Congress set up an additional retirement vehicle, Roth IRAs. These accounts offer a twist on the tax treatment of traditional IRAs. Contribution limits are the same as for traditional IRAs, but contributions are not tax deductible. On the other hand, earnings on those contributions not only compound tax-free, *but also can be withdrawn tax-free.* You only need to keep the account for more than five years (and meet the usual 59½ age requirements) to begin withdrawing earnings. There also is no requirement that you begin to withdraw your money by age 70½ with Roth IRAs.

Picking between these IRA options depends on your personal tax situation, your age, and whether your employer offers you a 401(k) plan.

If you are young and still in a low tax bracket, Roth IRAs can be very attractive. In addition, Roth IRAs are open to more people than traditional IRAs. The income limits are higher and are not affected by your participation in a 401(k) plan.

Self-employed and Small Business Plans

There also are a variety of programs to encourage retirement savings for the self-employed and those working for small businesses. While there are modest differences with each kind, they generally are very similar to 401(k)s. They offer you or your employer the ability to contribute tax-free to a retirement account. Investment earnings build up tax-free until your retirement as well. These plans go by names such as Simplified Employee Pension IRAs (SEP IRAs), Savings Incentive Match Plan for Employees IRA (SIMPLE IRAs), and Keogh plans.

Investing All That Tax-Free Money

Now that we've seen all the tax-free retirement vehicles, the next question is how to fill them up with the maximum allowable amount of passive investment. After all, compounding isn't as significant if there are only meager earnings to compound.

For IRAs, traditional or Roth, the answer is very simple. By law, you can invest your IRA money anywhere you want. You should invest the equity portion of that money—which should be the substantial majority—in index mutual funds or ETFs. If it's currently invested in actively managed mutual funds (or stocks, for that matter) sell it and buy an index fund or ETF. There's no penalty. Enough said.

We'd like to be able to give you the same advice when it comes to investing in a defined-contribution plan like a 401(k). Unfortunately, your employer may have made it a bit more complicated. As an employee you rarely get to choose the mutual fund companies in which your retirement savings are invested. Your employer does. Worse yet, the company's human resources department often selects the fund options. HR departments generally lack financial experience. The old glossy brochure and sleeve of golf balls might have more effect on your retirement security than you realized. Second to none in this area, the mutual fund industry has gotten the lion's share of the business.[4] The result: an overemphasis on actively managed funds. Frequently there is an outright exclusion of passively managed funds. Vanguard just doesn't hand out the golf balls like the other guys.

There is one place to put your 401(k) assets that's worse than an actively managed fund or variable annuity: your own company's stock. The company certainly has every interest in encouraging employee ownership: it increases demand for the stock, creates a loyal set of investors unlikely to sell in bad times, and ties employees closer to the company. Your interests clearly lie elsewhere—in diversifying your financial picture so that hard times at your employer will not cost you both your salary and your savings. The bankruptcy of Enron and financial decimation of many of its employees have made this point crystal clear.

And Enron is not the only company where employees are running these kinds of risks. In 401(k) plans that allow investment in company stock, employees hold one third of their assets in such stock on average. At Procter and Gamble, Dell Computer Corporation, Coca-Cola, and McDonalds, employees hold over 70 percent of their 401(k) assets in company stock on average.

You will not earn success at your workplace by buying company stock. Your supervisor is not checking to see how much you actually own, and probably couldn't care less. We've never heard of anyone getting promoted (or avoiding a layoff) by being a loyal shareholder. On the other hand, you and your family may suffer irreparable financial harm from placing a considerable percentage of your investments in the company that pays your salary. It's not a difficult decision, really.

The Right Way to Do Things—The Thrift Savings Plan

What should your 401(k) options look like? Believe it or not, the best example is the defined-contribution plan operated by the U.S. government, known as the Federal Thrift Savings Plan (TSP). Set up in 1986 for civilian employees, it now includes military employees as well. As of late 2001, the plan held over $100 billion in assets, with over half of it invested in the stock market.

Over the ten-year period 1991–2000, the Thrift Savings Plan's return on stock investments was a 17.43 percent compound annual rate of return, *including all expenses*.[5] That compares to a 17.46 percent return for the S&P 500 Index and exceeds the returns of the average actively managed stock fund by over *4 percent per year*. The return on bond investments was 7.87 versus 7.96 percent for the Lehman Brothers U.S. Aggregate bond index. That too far surpassed the average bond fund for that period.

So how were the government managers of the Thrift Savings Plan able to achieve such stupendous returns? Tech heavy? Early in biotech? Much simpler: the Thrift Savings Plan decided to (1) index and (2) bargain for the lowest possible cost. The government puts the Thrift Savings Plan contract out for competitive bid every three years. Barclays Global Investors is the current investment manager. The TSP's administrative costs plus Barclays's management fees *currently total only 0.03 to 0.09 percent*, depending on the fund.

Judging from the average expense ratios of 401(k) assets in mutual funds, corporate America could learn a lot from the TSP. In particular, corporate America (1) does not generally index, and (2) does not bargain for the lowest possible cost. When the SEC studied mutual fund fees, it found that 401(k) participants pay significant expense ratios. A sampling of retirement-oriented funds found that their fees averaged 0.96 percent per year. While that number is lower than the fees of the average actively managed stock fund, the SEC found that this was primarily due to their size, as the average retirement-oriented fund in their sample had $20 billion in assets. These fees are actually in line with other large actively managed mutual funds.[6]

The sad fact for most workers is that the government probably does a far better job with its employees' savings than your employer does with yours. Keep in mind, too, that most pension funds in the country now have a significant portion of their assets in index funds. The failure of many employers to allow employees the same option is therefore inexcusable.

Now That You're Really Mad, What to Do About It

So, what should you do when it comes to your own 401(k) or 403(b)? Here are a few thoughts:

- If your plan contains a total stock market index fund, transfer the equity component of your savings to those funds, and consider yourself lucky.
- If your plan offers a "brokerage window" that allows the purchase of individual stocks, consider yourself very lucky. Go to the window and buy total market domestic and international ETFs. Pity any of your fellow employees who are using this window to purchase a risky, nondiversified handful of stocks.
- If your employer offers only an S&P 500 equity index fund, buy it and move on. (We'd prefer to see a broader fund, but, as they say, life is not a game of perfect.)
- If you are switching jobs, consider moving your 401(k) or 403(b) to one of the index funds or ETFs profiled in Part IV. You don't have to leave your retirement assets with your old employer's plan or move it to the new one's. You get to pick, tax-free. You'll probably want to participate in your new employer's plan going forward, particularly if it includes matching contributions, but your prior investments can be set free.
- If your employer doesn't offer an equity index fund as a 401(k) or 403(b) option, get politely angry. Talk to your HR department or corporate treasurer about it. Mention the words "fiduciary duty to maximize returns."

As we saw with our attempts to reform the Pension Benefit Guaranty Corporation, though, change won't come easily. You're going to have to make nice and recruit allies. You'll need to work with the benefits people at your employer over time to get this fixed. That may be difficult. Most likely, someone senior in your organization likes the plan just the way it is. The company may be getting back a share of the fees charged against your account. They may even view your recommendations as a challenge to their competence. You may need to work with other employees or, if you have one, your union, to document carefully just how poorly your

401(k) or 403(b) has performed. Send along a copy of this book if you think it will help. We're not just saying that for our publisher. Your HR department will need it to combat the industry rep telling them the virtues of active management and demeaning passive management. Your theme should be, "Just give us the choice."

Variable Annuities:
The Wrong Way to Prepare for Retirement

While 401(k)s and IRAs are of relatively recent vintage, the insurance industry actually possesses one of the oldest retirement tax breaks of the bunch: the variable annuity. Here's a quick preview of this section: don't buy variable annuities.

An annuity is a product designed to pay a regular income stream upon retirement. With traditional annuities, you purchase and contribute to an annuity during your productive years, and then begin receiving prefixed payments in retirement. With variable annuities, your retirement payments depend on your investment returns. The size of those payments can even continue to rise and fall during your retirement, depending upon returns.

Variable annuities offer many of the same benefits as 401(k)s because earnings on your investments compound tax-free. You don't pay taxes on your yearly investment income and only begin paying taxes when you start receiving payments upon retirement.

When you reach retirement, between ages $59\frac{1}{2}$ and $70\frac{1}{2}$, variable annuities give you a choice. You can take your money in a lump sum, or you can buy an annuity and receive payments over a specified number of years. These payments may be fixed, or continue to vary depending upon market returns.

Thus, variable annuities are akin to 401(k)s, albeit without qualification or contribution limits. These advantages have been enticing enough for the insurance industry to capture over $800 billion in retirement savings through variable annuities.

Don't confuse these products with life insurance, though. There's only the tiniest bit of insurance in them. When the owner of a variable annuity dies, the estate or beneficiary is guaranteed return of the owner's original investment. In some cases, a very minimal return is guaranteed as well. This benefit does not come cheap, however. You pay a mortality and risk-expense fee, generally over 1 percent per year.

So What's So Bad About Variable Annuities?

Why don't we like variable annuities? Let us count the ways:

- You have two sets of mouths to feed. The insurance company wants its take for setting up the plan and giving you a tiny bit of insurance. The investment adviser wants its take for what is usually an actively managed fund.
- As with a 401(k), someone else decides where your money is going to be invested. Instead of a relatively beneficient employer, here it is an insurance company eager to earn fees. For that reason, variable annuities are generally invested in high-cost mutual funds. The insurance company takes a part of those fees either by operating the fund or by sharing a sales load with the fund company.
- You get practically nothing in return for the fees you pay the insurance company. You might think you are buying insurance, but the value of the insurance component in variable annuities is very small. The insurance companies are charging well over ten times the value of that death benefit, according to a recent study. The median mortality and expense risk charge was 115 basis points per year, while the insurance value of the death benefit was worth between 1 and 10 basis points per year.[7]
- When shopping for a variable annuity, it's hard to determine how much you'll be paying in fees. Review the annual report or prospectus for a variable annuity and you will see nothing akin to the standard disclosures of the mutual fund industry.

    Economically, there is not much difference between mutual funds and variable annuities, especially when an annuity is invested in mutual funds. As a regulatory matter, however, the products differ a great deal. The Securities and Exchange Commission strictly regulates the mutual fund industry. They require a host of disclosures. There's no federal regulator, however, of the variable annuity industry. Any disclosures depend on in which of the fifty states the insurance company operates. (Memo to Congress: Isn't this a little silly?)

- If for some reason you need to take your money out prior to reaching retirement, you must pay a heavy 10 percent tax penalty. This, though, is similar to other retirement accounts.
- To discourage you from recognizing the error of your ways and fleeing to a better investment, annuities frequently have "surrender fees" of up to 7 percent. While these fees generally come down over time, they are just like sales loads on mutual funds. And you know what we think of them—avoid them.
- All of your earnings will be taxed in retirement at ordinary income tax rates. While you get a tax deferral, you may eventually pay at higher rates than capital gains tax rates. This is also similar to most 401(k) plans.

Amazingly, in recent years, over half of all variable annuities have been sold within 401(k) or other tax-sheltered retirement plans, where the annuity's tax benefit is entirely superfluous—that is, worthless. That is a crying shame (particularly if one of those plans is yours).

Annuities Exposed

Often, numbers speak louder than words. Morningstar tracks the performance of variable annuities as well as mutual funds. What did we find when rooting around in their data?

Using Morningstar, we examined the performance of variable annuity subaccounts (basically, the insurance equivalent of a fund) that were invested in equities.[8] Looking at 7,645 such subaccounts, the average expense ratio for the underlying fund is 0.88 percent. If that wasn't enough to worry about, the insurance company gets its take as well. Usually called a "mortality fee," the average insurance expense was an additional 1.29 percent per year. Thus, the average fund deducts 2.17 percent of your savings each year.

What kind of effect does this have on returns? You guessed it. Over a ten-year period ending June 30, 2001, such variable annuity subaccounts trailed the S&P 500 by 2.4 percentage points per year; over a five-year period, they trailed by 4.2 percentage points.

There is one island in this ocean of fees. TIAA-CREF is the Vanguard of the annuity world. A look at the TIAA-CREF stock subaccount is instructive. The underlying fund expense is only 0.09 percent, and insurance expense is only 0.23 percent, for a total of 0.32 percent.[9]

Chapter 24

Saving for College—Tax-Free

Taxation WITH representation ain't so hot either.
—*Gerald Barzon*

G et ready for some unequivocally good news.

If you're saving for college, you can do so tax-free. Not just tax-deferred, but tax-free. Regardless of whether you're saving for your own education or that of your kids, grandkids, or just about anybody else. Let's look at two options: "529 plans" and Education IRAs.

529 Plans

The single best way to save now for college is through a so-called "529 plan," which derives its name from the relevant section of the Internal Revenue Code. In effect, Congress chartered each state to operate a tax-free family of mutual funds dedicated to college savings. It's a bit of federalism our founding fathers would have liked.

Congress then did some other good things to help spur competition. It allowed each state to accept savers from any other state. Most do. Investors also can change from one state plan to another, every year if they desire. In addition, Congress required that money from 529 plans can be used at any college in the country (and many overseas as well), rather than just at a college in your home state or the home state of your chosen plan. Starting in 2002, colleges and universities are able to set up prepaid tuition plans as well. You can shop around the country for the best plan, get the best returns, and send a family member to school anywhere in the nation.

There are two basic types of 529 plans: savings plans and prepaid tuition plans. Savings plans allow you to contribute money to an account, earning tax-free returns for a portion of future college expenses. Prepaid tuition plans generally allow state residents to guard against inflation by prepaying future college tuition today.

There are many similarities in the two plans. The key difference boils down to how much risk you wish to bear. Prepaid tuition plans guarantee you the funds to pay for college in the future. You pay for this, however, by receiving a lower return on your money. Savings plans, on the other hand, allow you to invest your money in the market for the potential of higher returns. Prepaid tuition plans are like buying a bond with a fixed set of payments in the future. Savings plans are more like buying a mix of stock and bond mutual funds through an IRA or 401(k), but even better. We generally like savings plans better, as they offer higher rates of return.

As good a deal as 529 savings plans are, you may wonder why you haven't heard much about them. First, they are relatively new. While they have existed since 1996, Congress significantly expanded them for tax-year 2002. Second, states generally don't have big advertising budgets to promote them. Third, many of the big-name mutual fund companies are sponsors of 529 plans, they would probably prefer that you use their regular line of products, which earn them higher fees. Last, the brokerage industry has far more to lose than gain from 529s.

The Benefits

Here are the myriad benefits of these new plans:

- As with a retirement savings account, you can invest money without paying federal tax on each year's realized capital gains or interest income.

- Better than a 401(k) or traditional IRA, though, you can withdraw the money tax-free when the beneficiary goes to college. In other words, you don't just defer capital gains taxes, you eliminate them entirely. The best analogue is a Roth IRA.

- The annual limit on contributions is $10,000 per year, many times that of an IRA. If you have $50,000 on hand, you can even invest that immediately. You then simply need to wait five years for your next investment, rather than investing $10,000 per year. Together with your spouse, you could actually contribute $100,000 all in one shot, if you had it. There are caps on the total amount you can invest, which represent each state's estimate of what four years of college will cost (generally in the $100,000 to $150,000 range).

- Contributions are not limited by your age or income, as they are with an IRA. Anyone can participate. Indeed, the benefits of the 529 plans grow along with your tax bracket. The higher your tax rate, the greater your savings. Just about anyone who can envision college expenses should participate, though, and the sooner the better.

- You can make anyone you want the beneficiary of a 529 account—your children, your grandchildren, a cousin, a friend, or even yourself. The tax code simply requires that the beneficiary be living. Hey, there had to be some restriction. . . .

- Actually, there's even a way around that living restriction. If you wish to get going even before your children or grandchildren are born, just name another family member on the account. When the bouncing baby comes along, change the name on the account. Perhaps more important, as one child finishes school or no longer needs the funds, you can transfer the funds to another child.

- Funds can be used for any college-related expense, not just tuition. That includes fees, room and board, books, supplies, and equipment.

- The plans prohibit you from picking individual stocks. Not that you'd be tempted, but it makes us feel much better.

- Most state plans allow you to make contributions through payroll deductions.

- Once you have put money in a 529 plan it is considered out of your taxable estate in case you die. This is true even though you continue to own and control the account.

- In some states, you may also get a modest tax deduction for investments in your home state's plan.

The definitive source for information on 529 plans is savingfor college.com, a website operated by Joseph Hurley, who has also written a comprehensive book on 529 plans. Count on the website for basic education, the most current information, and a handy tool that allows you to compare plans.

Two words of caution, however, are appropriate on 529 plans. First, your 529 contributions count against the annual $10,000 gift limit for tax purposes, if that's relevant to you. Second, as you know, at times Washington politics can lead to strange and confusing outcomes. That is what happened with the tax bill passed in 2001, which included many of the most generous features of 529 plans. To meet budgetary constraints, Congress included a provision that sunsets the entire legislation after December 2010. That means that sometime prior to then, Congress will have to debate the program and decide how to extend it or modify it. Though it is very unlikely, Congress could even revert to earlier tax law, whereby the earnings would not be tax-free, but simply tax deferred.

The 529 Gold Rush and Where to Plan

Once you decide to use a 529 plan, you are in the happy position of having states compete for your business.[1] They've all got websites and brochures and have even come up with catchy, Dr. Seuss–type names for their plans. Let's see, there's GET, MET, and CHET and BEST, VEST, and EdVest and even a chance to START, TAP, and ACT. For those looking for more, there's also MO$T.[2]

As you might expect, almost all state governments decided to hire someone to manage their mutual funds for them.[3] Sensing an opportunity, mutual fund companies and money managers rushed to sign up as many states as possible. They generally sought an exclusive deal where only their own funds would be eligible for investment. Thus, as you look at each state, you see an associated fund or fund company.

TIAA-CREF has been by far the most successful company in the 529 gold rush. They have signed up a dozen states, including both California and New York. Fidelity, Mercury Advisors, Salomon Smith Barney, Strong Capital Management, T. Rowe Price, and Vanguard have each signed up two or three states. There are at least a dozen other mutual fund companies that have signed up one state.

The Active Versus Passive Thing Again

The quality of a given state's plan is generally a reflection of which company it has chosen to operate it. Unfortunately, the vast majority of 529 plans have signed up active mutual fund managers. This makes no sense. State Treasurers should know this by now. Many invest their own state pension funds passively, yet refuse to let you do the same with your college money. California and Connecticut are examples of this mixed-up world of investing. Both have signed up TIAA-CREF to offer actively managed funds for their college savings program. Their own state pension funds, however, are both invested more than 75 percent in index funds, presumably because they (correctly) believe that indexing will yield the highest returns for retired state employees. Do we hear "referendum"?

The plans are too new to have established track records, but you can expect the song to remain the same. As in the taxable world, active fund managers who control 529 plans charge you high fees (albeit somewhat lower fees than for their regular accounts). Their funds also have high turnover, raising trading costs. Passively managed plans, on the other hand, have low fees and low turnover.

Some plans also require out-of-state residents to pay sales loads or purchase through a broker. This makes life simple: don't buy these plans. Also, don't pay a financial adviser who is most likely just spending time at www.savingforcollege.com. Trust us: decades of tax-free earnings are worth a day or two of your time.

A Little Something for the State

In addition to the management fees charged by the fund manager, most states charge an administrative fee. Arkansas, Nebraska, and Wyoming seem to be the least efficient with this, all taking 0.60 percent annually out of your money for program management. Many states require the fund manager to provide the program services out of their take. Connecticut charges only 0.02 percent annually for the services. The total annual cost of a plan is basically the administrative fee plus the underlying management fees.[4]

And the Winners (and Losers) Are . . .

529 plans are proof that not all states are equal. Or maybe it's that not all states' treasurers and education secretaries are equal? We'll walk you through the plans we think are best and worst.

The Best

The Champion: Utah.   The best plan we've seen is the Utah Educational Savings Plan. It offers low-cost broad-based passive investing for your 529 account. The total annual fees are between just 0.20 and 0.35 percent plus up to a $25 maintenance charge.

The Utah plan is a pure index investing plan as follows:

- Equity assets are invested in the Vanguard Institutional Index Fund; bond assets are invested in the Vanguard Total Bond Market Index Fund. Vanguard charges fees of only 0.06 to 0.10 percent.
- Utah charges its own 0.25 percent management fee on top of what Vanguard charges. As we have seen, that's low relative to other states.

For further information, you can visit www.uesp.org.

New Jersey, for New Jerseyans.   New Jersey actually manages its NJBEST plan itself, through the State Treasurer's office, the same office that manages the state pension fund. The Treasurer's office buys stocks directly, with the goal of tracking the overall market. Management fees total 0.50 percent, which is good. Unfortunately, either you or the beneficiary must reside in New Jersey at the time of enrollment in the plan.

Honorable Mention.

Looking at the many 529 plans managed by TIAA-CREF, New York appears to have bargained hardest. Total fees were reduced to 0.60 percent in late 2001. Michigan and Missouri both look to have total annual fees of 0.65 percent. The domestic stock, international stock, and bond funds in which the plans invest, though, are all actively managed. That said, TIAA-CREF's Growth Fund—the one in which the Michigan, Missouri, and New York plans invest—is pretty good on turnover (only 21 percent) and cash holdings (0.6 percent).

The Worst

Maine.   Maine's coastline is beautiful, but its 529 plan is not. Maine cast its lot with Merrill Lynch, which offers two options. There's a "Client Direct" plan open to all investors and a "Client Adviser" plan that can only be purchased from a Merrill Lynch or another participating broker. The total annual fees range from 1.3 to possibly 2.7 percent. You're looking at annual fees four to eight times what you'd pay with Utah.

High fees in the middle and round on both ends.   Ohio is also a pretty ugly scene for college savings. Putnam Investments has managed to institute the old sales load gambit. Annual fees are 1.05 to 1.22 percent. Nonresidents must purchase through a broker and pay a 3.50 percent front-end load, a 2.50 percent back-end load, or higher management fees throughout. Rhode Island may have done Ohio one better. Partnered with Alliance Capital Management, it too has an alphabet menu of choices. They charge annual fees of 1.15 to 1.35 percent. On top of this they have sales loads of 3.25 percent. Now, if you want to lower the sales load, you can add to the annual fees and make it a cool 1.4 to 1.6 percent annual charge, or take on a back-end load and add even more to your fees. Next!

Wyoming.   Wyoming teamed up with a Merrill affiliate, Mercury Asset Management. It didn't surprise us to see them come in with total fees between 1.35 and 1.83 percent per year (depending upon your investment selection). That Merrill bull sure does like to graze on your college savings.

By the way, you'll have a hard time finding out about the Wyoming College Achievement Plan on your own. Nowhere on its website will you find a mention of fees. Not under the investment descriptions. Not under the "Frequently Asked Questions." Not anywhere. This is due in part to one of the drawbacks of the regulatory structure for 529 plans. There is no federal oversight of the disclosures required of these plans. The SEC oddly found that these programs should be regulated under the same rules as municipal securities, and thereby exempted them from disclosure rules. If the SEC doesn't take this up in the future, the states, through their own self-regulatory bodies, should do so.

Any time you need more information about a 529 plan, though, we recommend using the 529 Plan Evaluator at www.savingforcollege. com. Then follow up by gathering materials from any plans that look good.

Asset Allocation

Once you have selected a state plan, you generally have an asset allocation choice to make. Most states offer you a choice between all equities or all bonds or let you sign up for what's called an automatic asset allocation program. These programs automatically shift your assets from stocks to bonds as the child ages and approaches the first year of college.

Automatic asset allocation is *not* market timing. The portfolio changes according to age rather than market performance. It assumes that you will have less tolerance for risk as the date of the beneficiary's college enrollment nears. You may be able to ride out a 10 percent market dip when a child is four years old, but the same dip at age eighteen could affect your ability to make a tuition payment.

Automatic asset allocation programs make a lot of sense. This is particularly true if the 529 assets are the only ones on which you're relying for tuition payments. On the other hand, if you have other liquid assets with which to make tuition payments, you may wish to keep a larger percentage of stocks in your 529 plan, getting the tax benefits on the generally higher returns of stocks.

One Complication: Home Sweet Home

Education is not just popular at the federal level. Many states have taken steps to sweeten 529 plans a bit further—albeit only for their own residents (also known as voters). These sweeteners may in some cases justify choosing your home state's plan even if it doesn't have the lowest fees or provide passive investing for its 529 plan.

First, your home state may offer some state tax relief in addition to the federal relief you're already receiving. Some states, for example, allow you to deduct contributions to a 529 plan for state income tax purposes up to certain dollar limits. Thus, you may save on your state income tax by investing at home. Be careful, though, there's often less there than first meets the eye.

Virginia is a good example. You may deduct up to $2,000 from your income for local tax purposes. While that may save you up to $100 in taxes, it will be more than eaten up by high annual fees (0.90%) that are close to three times those of Utah's, plus an $85 enrollment fee. Virginia's active management will also eat at your returns through higher turnover.

Second, some states exclude assets you hold in their own 529 plan from state financial-aid calculations. The federal calculations will be the same regardless of which state plan you use. The assets can reduce your eligibility for financial aid. Of course, so can taking a better job with higher pay or winning Lotto. We wouldn't recommend against either of them. Still, there are some quirks in how financial-aid departments look at 529 plans. This area is one of rapid change, as universities are just beginning to respond to the growth in 529 plans. So, while you should consider this factor before investing in a 529 plan, we don't believe that financial-aid considerations should dissuade you from investing in a 529 plan.

The Other Education Savings Plan: The Education IRA

Education IRAs are another way to save for college. Actually, you can even use an Education IRA for kindergarten through twelfth grade educational expenses at public, private, and parochial schools. While there is no tuition for public schools, you can use the IRA money for tutoring, books, supplies, or computer equipment and Internet access to be used for school.

You can contribute up to $2,000 per year into an Education IRA. Your contribution is not tax deductible, as with other IRAs, but all of the earnings are tax-free. The income limitations are now approaching $200,000 per year for a couple filing a joint tax return. Starting in 2002, you can also make contributions to both a 529 plan and an Education IRA for the same beneficiary.

Like other IRAs, Education IRAs can be set up at any financial company of your choosing. It is best to invest the equity portion of that money in index mutual funds. Given the size of the fund, it is likely that you will also want to invest the bond portion in an index bond fund.

Final Thoughts on College Saving

If you're going to end up paying for someone's college education, we strongly urge you to contribute as much as you can to a 529 plan. If you're able to contribute more than $10,000 per year, throw another $2,000 into an Education IRA, particularly if you are also going to be paying for private or parochial school.

Obviously, you're going to have to do a little research before you make any final decisions. But make no mistake: the tax benefits are so dynamite that failure to take advantage of these opportunities would be a real disservice to the next generation of your family. Make sure to take a serious look at the Utah plan, as it offers the best way to invest.

By the way, if you belong to an investment club, why not take a little vacation from stock picking and devote all of this year's meetings to mastering 529 plans and Education IRAs?

Conclusion

Most investors spend too much time picking stocks and actively managed mutual funds and too little time picking the vehicles through which they are going to invest. Just a few hours spent setting up a 529 plan for your child will do more for your financial well-being than watching CNBC for a decade or reading mutual fund performance rankings every day.

An Investment Recovery Plan

There are just two rules for success:
1. Never tell all you know.—*Roger H. Lincoln*

B ill James, baseball's best-known statistician and historian, released a new edition of his celebrated *Historical Baseball Abstract*
in 2001. Like its predecessor, the new *Abstract* included a ranking of the hundred greatest players in baseball history. Many readers
were surprised to see that the player judged as the best active major lea-
guer and the thirty-fifth greatest player of all time—ahead of people
like Cal Ripken, Sandy Koufax, and Roger Clemens—was . . . Craig
Biggio. You've probably never heard of Biggio, but you can see him
playing next year for the Houston Astros.

Craig Biggio doesn't hit home runs, and never has. You won't see
him interviewed on *Sports Center* or featured on many posters. What
Biggio does well is all the little things. He steals bases and almost never
gets caught. During the 2001 season, he became only the fifth player in
the history of baseball not to ground into a double play. He managed
to get hit by thirty-four pitches, the second-highest total in the twentieth century. In baseball, things like that add up.

As you face financial markets, you'd do well to remember Craig Biggio. Markets are the equivalent of a pitcher's park: their fences are deep,

the ball is dead, and you won't be able to hit many home runs. What you need to do is what Craig Biggio does: get everything else right. Get your costs down, your diversification up, and your assets allocated intelligently. Don't worry about making headlines; just win.

If you want to take that course, here is how we'd start.

1. **Ignore all rankings!** Morningstar's five-star funds perform about the same as its three-star funds. Stocks in the S&P 500 receiving the highest analyst rankings perform no better than those receiving the lowest rankings. *Money* magazine's top-ranked funds for last year are funds you should avoid this year. *Stop thinking all it takes to beat the market is a magazine subscription.*

2. **Watch financial news for entertainment value only.** The financial media and Wall Street depend on each other to promote frequent trading and to make the market look complicated and interesting. Your best interests—a simple buy-and-hold strategy—are contrary to theirs.

3. **Realize that analysts aren't really talking to you.** Analysts give their best advice to the people who pay them—pension funds and other institutional investors. They then go on TV to promote themselves and the stocks they've already recommended. Why do you think they're willing to appear for free?

4. **Never underestimate the power of an index fund.** Viewed by many investors as boring, index funds are a miracle of innovation and efficiency. You can invest $5,000 in hundreds or even thousands of different stocks that will guarantee you a market return, and the cost is around $10 per year. Especially for those regularly investing small amounts, it's the greatest bargain in investing.

5. **Better yet, meet the new, exchange-traded index funds.** If you have more than $5,000 to invest, you can take that cost down from $10 to $5 per year, and forget about having unwanted capital gains distributed to you. There has never been a more efficient way to invest in stocks, and pension funds and other institutional investors are buying them in droves. Most individual investors have yet to hear of them.

6. **If you are paying a percentage of your assets to try to beat the market, stop.** Say good-bye to active fund managers, full-service brokers, and asset-based financial planners. And load funds, of course. If you feel hesitant, try to think of anyone else in your life to whom you pay a percentage of your wealth for services.

7. **Take control of your tax situation.** Every year, ask yourself this question, "Have I sheltered every possible dollar of my investments from taxation?" Take all steps necessary to giving yourself an intelligent answer.

8. **Sit down and draft an asset allocation plan.** If you need help, then get it (for free on-line or in a book, or by the hour with a planner). If you don't know how much of your total net worth is allocated to each asset class and *why*, then you're making about the worst mistake in investing.

9. **Don't try to time the markets.** Markets go up and markets go down. Wall Street pros do a lousy job predicting when the market will do either. You'll do no better than they do.

10. **Take every dollar you intend to save for your kids' or grandkids' education and invest it in a 529 plan.** If you don't know what a 529 college-savings account is, imagine investing in the stock and bond markets and never, ever paying any tax on what you earn. As of 2002, your dream has come true.

11. **Recognize that there is an ongoing revolution in the bond business.** You can now buy Treasury, municipal, and corporate bonds directly from the issuer at wholesale prices. Given that fewer than 10 percent of bond funds outperform the bond market, direct purchases look pretty good.

12. **If your employer does not include index funds among your 401(k) options, then consider it a pay cut.** Work to reverse that pay cut by buying an additional copy of this book and highlighting it for the Human Resources department. (A bit self-serving, but you get the point.) And don't get Enroned by loading up your 401(k) with company stock.

13. **Avoid variable annuities.** Insurance companies will entice you with a tax break and the tiniest bit of insurance. Then they'll charge you many times what it's worth. The only upside: they

make actively managed mutual funds look like a relatively good deal.

14. **Write to your senators and representatives and tell them that if they vote to privatize Social Security funds, then you'll vote them out of office.** Current "reform" plans would allow Wall Street to gain *billions* of dollars in fees and commissions from Social Security every year. We call it the Great Social Security Heist; do your best to thwart it.

15. **Spend more time with friends and family.** Do you really need to check your stock prices that tenth time today? Do you really care what Wal-Mart's next quarter might look like? Focusing on these things isn't making you any wealthier or any more interesting. Get out a little!

How Index Funds Work

ere is a brief look at how index funds operate, and why they are so efficient.

Index fund managers have two basic choices in trying to track an index. The first is to replicate the index by buying proportionate weightings of all the stocks held in the index. If the market capitalization of IBM represents 1 percent of the market capitalization of the S&P 500 Index, then an index fund attempting to track the S&P 500 Index would continually keep 1 percent of its shareholders' money invested in IBM. Such complete replication, however, can bring significant costs if the index includes small capitalization, less liquid stocks, as a total market index would. When small-cap stocks are added to, or removed from, an index, the fund must pay wider bid/ask spreads than it would with, say, an S&P 500 stock—as much as ten times wider.[1]

The alternative to complete replication is sampling, or optimizing; buying a subset of the index that computer modeling indicates will tend to track the overall performance of the index. Thus, the manager of a fund tracking the Wilshire 5000 Index might buy only 2,700 stocks.

Sampling lowers transaction costs, as the fund can purchase fewer stocks, generally focusing on the more liquid ones.

While sampling is a less expensive strategy, it does increase a fund's risk of producing tracking error. Tracking error is the amount by which the precost returns of the index fund differ from those of its underlying index. If you buy an S&P 500 index fund and the index goes up 12 percent, you expect the fund to do the same.

Those hostile to indexing tend to inflate the importance of tracking error. Most index funds state that their goal is to achieve performance correlation with their index of at least 95 percent. Most do significantly better, with the large index funds reaching correlations of more than 99 percent. Note also that tracking error does not always work against you: it is just likely to raise returns above the underlying index as it is to lower them. You can expect any tracking error to even out over time, having no meaningful effect on your returns. In other words, don't stay up nights worrying about tracking error.

As replication and sampling each have their costs and benefits, different funds employ different strategies. With respect to S&P 500 index funds, the largest index funds, like Vanguard and T. Rowe Price, generally employ a complete replication strategy. Other S&P 500 index funds, however, pursue a modified replication strategy, investing in the 500 stocks but only in approximately the amount of their share of the index.[2]

Life for index fund managers became a lot easier with the introduction of index futures contracts in 1982, particularly the S&P 500 Composite Index future. A futures contract on a financial asset is just like a futures contract on a physical asset. (Those who saw Dan Akroyd and Eddie Murphy in *Trading Places* will remember this well.) A soybean futures contract is a promise to deliver a given quantity of soybeans at a future date at a set price. Similarly, an S&P 500 contract is a promise to deliver a basket of the five hundred stocks in the index at a future date at a set price. In both worlds, delivery rarely occurs, as contracts are often settled for cash.

These futures contracts allow fund managers to invest cash in the equivalent of stocks very quickly and at very low cost. Thus, an S&P 500 index fund that receives a cash dividend from any of its stocks is not required to break that dividend into five hundred small parts and buy each of the stocks in the index. With futures, the fund manager can take the dividend and purchase a futures contract on the S&P 500. The index manager can wait until a more general rebalancing is necessary— say, when a component of the index is changed—and then cash in the futures contracts to buy the underlying stocks.

Large index funds can take advantage of their size to protect and even increase their returns. First, because they have large daily cash inflows, they can act as an important source of liquidity to the market. This means leverage with market makers, who often give the funds a better spread than the general or smaller institutional public. Second, index funds can match or "cross" trades with other members of their fund families, thereby decreasing costs. It's all in the family.

The largest funds are also able to exploit occasional arbitrage opportunities between cash prices and the price of the corresponding futures contract. The futures market allows all market participants to observe two prices for an identical basket of stocks: the cash price on the securities exchanges and the futures price on the commodity exchanges. To the extent that the prices drift apart, index fund managers are presented with arbitrage opportunities.

Over time, this arbitrage opportunity has shrunk, as more arbitrageurs and faster computers have exploited differences between cash and futures prices more quickly. For a large index fund, though, even a tiny difference can mean returns, given the size of its purchasers.

A final revenue source for large funds comes from lending their securities out to brokerage companies for use in covering short sales by other investors. Brokers charge short sellers for the use of securities, and index funds can receive a share of that fee. On average, large index funds can earn an additional return of between 0.01 to 0.05 percent on assets per year. That's pennies, but those pennies add up.

While the low turnover of index funds makes them tax efficient, they do sometimes distribute gains. First, any gains on futures contracts must be recognized immediately. Second, when a stock is dropped from the underlying index, the fund may incur a gain from selling the stock. Third, if the fund experiences outflows and must shrink, resulting sales may generate gains. Finally, corporate actions (such as mergers) taken by portfolio companies may yield unwanted gains. Nonetheless, well-managed funds can minimize and offset these gains. Index funds are still far more tax efficient than their actively managed counterparts.

Notes

Introduction

1. For laughs only, see the sports betting tips at www.casino-info.com.

Chapter 1

1. Morningstar Principia Pro, data through December 31, 2001. Funds identified were all domestic stock funds, excluding index funds, exchange-traded funds, funds open only to institutional investors, multiple classes of the same fund, and funds holding more than 20 percent of their assets in bonds.

2. Kornheiser, Tony, "Taking the Plunge," *Washington Post,* March 18, 2001, p. F2.

3. Morningstar Principia Pro, data from September 30, 2001.

Chapter 2

1. *Fortune,* December 18, 2000.

2. Futrelle, David, online chat at www.money.com, 2001.

3. For a chronicle of Mr. Acampora's sometimes hilarious misadventures, see Howard Kurtz's *The Fortune Tellers.*

4. "In Brief: Fund Ad Outlays Rose 22 Percent in 2000," *American Banker* (April 30, 2001), 10 (citing Financial Research Corp. study).

5. Jaij, Prem C., and Joanna Shuang Wu, "Truth in Mutual Fund Advertising: Evidence on Future Performance and Fund Flows," *Journal of Finance* 15 (April 2000): 937.

Chapter 3

1. See Fama, Eugene, and Kenneth French, "The Equity Premium" (July 20, 2000), available at www.ssrn.com. They compared the real returns on the S&P 500 (and its relevant predecessors) to the real returns on six-month commercial paper.

2. McGrattan, Ellen, and Edward Prescott, "Is the Stock Market Overvalued?" *Federal Reserve Bank of Minneapolis Quarterly Review* 24 (Fall 2000): 20–40.

3. Vassal, Vladimir de, "Risk Diversification Benefits of Multiple-Stock Portfolios," *Journal of Portfolio Management* 27 (Winter 2001): 32.

4. Fama, Eugene F., and Kenneth R. French, "The Cross-Section of Expected Stock Returns," *Journal of Finance* 47 (June 1992): 427.

Part II

1. Investment Company Institute Fact Book (2001) (hereafter ICI). We exclude money market mutual funds because they are effectively deposit accounts. During the 1990s, stock funds attracted 83 percent of the net new cash flow to all mutual funds. As of year-end 2001, equity funds held $3.4 trillion, and hybrid funds holding a combination of equity and bonds held another $350 billion. Bond funds held $825 billion. Money market funds held $1.845 trillion.

2. Ibid.

Chapter 4

1. Sharpe, William, "The Arithmetic of Active Management," *Financial Analysts Journal* 47 (January/February 1991): 7–9. Mr. Sharpe also has his own website (just search for his name on www.google.com or some other search engine), which contains a host of good research.

2. Survivorship bias can bring heartache to fund managers as well as to investors. Imagine a fund manager who's ranked in the thirtieth percentile (top 30 percent of funds in their category) and receives a Morningstar four-star ranking. Then, a couple of the lousiest funds in the category get folded up. All of a sudden, with no change in performance, voilà, it's a three-star fund.

3. Malkiel, Burton G., "Returns from Investing in Equity Mutual Funds 1971 to 1991," *Journal of Finance* 50 (June 1995): 549.

4. *Financial Planning* (June 2001).

5. Morningstar Principia Pro (data as of December 31, 2001). Data are for surviving actively managed domestic stock funds, excluding index, exchange-traded, and institutional funds, and multiple classes of the same fund, and funds holding more than 20 percent of their assets in bonds.

6. 399 funds: industry funds, excluding index funds, ETFs, institutional funds, multiple classes of the same fund, and funds holding more than 20 percent of their assets in bonds.

7. Schultheis, Bill, *The Coffeehouse Investor: How to Build Wealth, Ignore Wall Street and Get on With Your Life* (Longstreet Press, 1998).

8. Bogle, John, "The Death Rattle of Indexing," in *Perspectives on Equity Indexing,* ed. Frank Fabozzi (2000): 2.

Chapter 5

1. Carhart, Mark M., "On Persistence in Mutual Fund Performance," *Journal of Finance* 52 (March 1997): 57.

2. Ibid.

3. Brown, Stephen J., and William N. Goetzmann, "Performance Persistence," *Journal of Finance* 50 (June 1995): 679.

4. Wermers, Russ, "Mutual Fund Performance: An Empirical Decomposition into Stock-Picking Talent, Style Transaction Costs, and Expenses," *Journal of Finance* 55 (August 2000): 1,655.

5. Not adjusting for the greater risk of these funds, Wermers found the stocks outperformed by 1.3 percent. Of this total, 0.6 percent was due to the fact that, as a group, mutual funds held proportionally more small-cap stocks, representing greater than average risk.

6. Arteaga, Kenneth, Conrad Ciccotello, and C. Terry Grant, "New Equity Funds: Marketing and Performance," *Financial Analysts Journal* 54 (November/December 1998): 43.

7. Zweig, Jason, "When to Take a Wild Ride . . . On a New Fund Rocket," *Money* (July 1996).

8. Van Kampen American Capital changed its name to Van Kampen Investments. The IDS New Dimensions Fund was acquired by American Express and became the AXP New Dimensions Fund. The Spectra Fund split into two classes, N and A. We tracked the N shares, which are those sold directly to the public.

9. The funds were Fidelity Magellan, American Funds Washington Mutual, American Funds Growth Fund of America, Fidelity Equity-Income, Fidelity Puritan, Vanguard Windsor, Lord Abbott Affiliated A, American Funds American Mutual, Templeton World, and Pioneer Value A. Some have changed names since 1991; we give the current name.

10. Ennis, Richard M., "The Case for Whole-Stock Portfolios," *Journal of Portfolio Management* 27 (Spring 2001): 17.

11. Hulbert, Mark, "No Stars for Morningstar," *Forbes*, December 29, 1997, p. 104.

12. Sharpe, William, "Morningstar's Risk-Adjusted Ratings," *Financial Analysts Journal* (July/August 1998): 21.

13. Chatzky, Jean Sherman, "Money Talk: Seeing Stars: Should Investors Be Weaned from Morningstar Fund Ratings," *Money*, January 2000.

14. *Forbes* 14, August 24, 1998, p. 126.

15. *Forbes* assumed that dividends were reinvested, that the funds were sold when they dropped off the Honor Roll, and that the proceeds were used to make equal investments in each year's newcomers.

16. We hypothetically invested $10,000 in each of the funds picked for 1998, let the money ride on those funds that continued on the list in subsequent years, and (like *Forbes*) liquidated the shares in the non-returning funds and invested it pro rata in the new arrivals. We also invested an equal aggregate amount in the Vanguard Total Stock Market Index Fund. Unlike *Forbes*, we did include loads—we could not think of any reason not to. For ease of calculation, we did not reinvest dividends. It is possible that this led to a slight bias of the results.

Chapter 6

1. Morningstar Principia Pro as of December 31, 2001. Search was for all mutual fund share classes charging a sales load, excluding index funds, exchange-traded funds, and institutional funds—7,389 funds in all. The 4.1 percent came from adding the average front-end and back-end load.

2. Looking solely at diversified funds, Carhart estimates trading costs at 0.95 percent per year. Wermers reports 1.04 percent per year in 1990, dropping to 0.48 percent by 1994. Sector funds have higher turnover than diversified funds, and thus should have higher trading costs.

3. Search includes actively managed (nonindex, non-ETF) funds, excluding institutional funds and multiple classes of the same fund. Stock funds are classified domestic stock by Morningstar, and hold less than 20 percent of their assets in bonds. Data are as of December 31, 2001.

4. SEC Report of the Division of Investment Management on Mutual Fund Fees and Expenses, January 2001. Fee study released January 2001. The SEC found that the average for all long-term (non-money market) funds was 1.36 percent, though this average includes bond funds, which tend to have lower fees. The SEC also measured the average fee weighted by the size of each fund. For this average, they determined that the industry had fees of ap-

proximately 0.9 percent. Throughout the book, we report data on an unweighted basis, as that is how Morningstar presents it. As the SEC numbers show, the average investor may pay a little less than these averages because our numbers count large and small funds equally. Since large funds tend to have marginally lower expense ratios, asset-weighted numbers tend to be lower. On the other hand, some of the largest funds with below average expense ratios are closed to all or new investment, and thus probably should not be included. So the average fees a new investor would pay probably lie somewhere in the middle.

5. Testimony of Matthew Fink, president of the Investment Company Institute, before the Subcommittee on Finance and Hazardous Materials, House Committee on Commerce, September 29, 1998.

6. Morningstar Principia Pro. Data are for mutual funds charging a front-end or back-end load, excluding index funds, ETFs, and institutional funds.

7. Each year there are nearly $1 trillion each in stock mutual fund sales and in redemptions. With about half of these in load funds and the average 4.1 percent total load, that leads to investors paying about $20 billion in sales loads per year.

8. Mark Hulbert, "Do Funds Charge Investors for Negative Value Added?" *New York Times,* July 8, 2001.

9. Morningstar Principia Pro, data through December 31, 2001. The 80 percent figure is a median. Outliers push the mean far higher.

10. For example, see Berkowitz, Stephen, and Dennis E. Logue, "Transaction Costs: Much Ado About Everything," *Journal of Portfolio Management* 27 (Winter 2001): 65.

11. For a good discussion of bid/ask spreads, see Sauter, George, "Medium- and Small-Capitalization Index," in *Perspectives on Index Investing,* ed. Frank Fabozzi, pp. 135, 147 (2000). Electronic trading networks, such as Instinet, can allow a trader to avoid the bid/ask spread by trading directly with another trader, cutting the dealer (and the dealer's spread) out of the transaction. For large funds, however, ECNs generally carry insufficient volume. Similar systems such as the Direct Order Transfer Box and electronic crossing networks also try to match trades, but cannot be used in most cases.

12. Berkowitz and Logue, "Transaction Costs," p. 65.

13. The market effect is a completely invisible cost, as there is simply no way of knowing what higher price a smaller order would have fetched. While the price of the last previous trade may be a good measure, other events may also have affected the price between trades. In any event, mutual funds are not required to estimate or report these costs, so investors have no way of knowing them.

14. ICI, 105.

15. Morningstar Principia Pro average for domestic stock funds, excluding index and exchange-traded funds, multiple classes of the same fund, and funds open only to institutional investors.

16. For a comprehensive look at the ins and outs, see Dickson, Joel, John Shoven, and Clemens Siaim, "Tax Externalities of Equity Mutual Funds," *National Tax Journal* 53 (September 2000): 607. The complications come with how funds treat capital losses, and their ability to deduct the firm's expenses from taxable income distributed to shareholders.

17. Apelfeld, Roberto, Gordon Fowler, Jr., and James Gordon Jr., "Tax Aware Equity Investing," *Journal of Portfolio Management* 22 (Winter 1996): 18. The SEC relied primarily on a study by KPMG Peat Marwick, "An Educational Analysis of Tax-Managed Mutual Funds and the Taxable Investor."

18. Dickson, Joel, and John Shoven, "Ranking Mutual Funds on an After-tax Basis," Working Paper No. 4393, National Bureau of Economic Research, 1993.

19. ICI Mutual Fund Fact Book 2000, 23.

20. Apelfeld, Fowler, and Gordon, "Tax Aware Equity Investing," p. 19.

21. Funds were already required to disclose the tax consequences of your buying, holding, exchanging, and selling fund shares, and whether the fund engaged in active and frequent portfolio trading that might affect fund performance. No specific past performance was reported, though, so the real effects were never quantified for investors. The new disclosures achieve that goal.

Chapter 7

1. Burks v. Lasker, 441 U.S. 471, 484 (1979).

2. Levitt, Arthur, "Opening Remarks at the SEC Roundtable on the Role of Independent Investment Company Directors," February 23, 1999.

3. Brown, Stewart, and John Freeman, "Mutual Fund Advisory Fees: The Cost of Conflicts of Interest," *University of Iowa Journal of Corporation Law* 26 (August 2001): 609–73. Brown is professor of finance at Florida State University and Freeman is professor of legal and business ethics at the University of South Carolina. They examined over thirteen hundred diversified mutual funds and 220 separate pension portfolios. To make a comparable analysis, they looked only at advisory fees, which are paid for investment services and research. They excluded administrative and sales distribution fees, which are largely associated only with mutual funds. So their analysis appropriately excluded fees for customer service, shareholder mailings, and broker compensation.

4. Ibid; see also "Do Fund Management Fees Clip Investors," *The Wall Street Journal,* August 27, 2001.

5. Berkowitz and Logue, "Transaction Costs," p. 65.

6. Investment Company Institute, Understanding the Role of Mutual Fund Directors (2001).

Chapter 8

1. Barber, Brad M., and Terrance Odean, "Trading Is Hazardous to Your Wealth: The Common Stock Investment Performance of Individual Investors," *Journal of Finance* 56: 17.

2. Barber, Brad M., and Terrance Odean, "Boys Will Be Boys: Gender, Overconfidence, and Common Stock Investment," *Quarterly Journal of Economics* 116 (February 2001): 261–92. The researchers wanted to make sure that the transactions, and associated underperformance, were not motivated by liquidity or tax needs. Accordingly, they looked at a subset of the data where buys quickly followed sales (indicating that the investor was not selling because he needed cash).

3. Barber and Odean, "Trading Is Hazardous," 773, 780, n. 7.

4. We used two websites: "Robert's Online Commissions Pricer," which instantly prices any trade (by exchange, shares, price, and means of transmission) across more than 80 discount brokers, and www.cyberinvest. com, which lists commission schedules. We took the median cost rather than the average cost because the average was skewed upward by some very high commissions. The median cost was also closer to the basic commission rates charged by the largest discount brokers such as Schwab and E*Trade.

The Barber and Odean study of discount brokerage customers showed an average trade value of around $12,000, at an average price per share of $31, or around 400 shares. In samples such as these, reported average numbers are generally higher than the median numbers. So, the median transaction size is likely to be even lower than $12,000 or four hundred shares.

5. Hurley, Mark, and Tom Fuller, "Advisors Must Shift to Value-Based Fees," *Financial Advisor* (July 2001).

Chapter 9

1. The study controlled for market risk, size, book-to-market ratio, and price momentum effects.

2. Craig, Suzanne, "J. P. Morgan Wins (by Not Losing as Much)," *Wall Street Journal,* November 19, 2001, C1.

3. Ratings were classified on an eight-class scale: very strong buy, strong buy, buy, outperform, perform, underperform, sell, and strong sell. ("Perform" equates

to the equally common terms "market perform," "hold," and "neutral.") Beginning in January 1997, Investars.com invested a hypothetical amount of money in each stock rated by each of the investment banks. If the rating was a "buy," for example, then Investars.com made a hypothetical purchase of $300,000; an "outperform" equates to a $200,000 purchase; a "perform" equates to no purchase; and an "underperform" equates to a $200,000 short sale. As stocks are upgraded and downgraded, corresponding purchases and sales are made.

4. For this purpose, Investars.com defined a client as a company for which an investment bank had led or co-led an initial public offering.

5. Looking at a broader group of investment banks, the sixty-nine with more than one hundred stocks covered, the results are not much better. Only thirteen of sixty-nine made money. Only one exceeded the returns of the S&P 500 over the same period.

6. The Investars.com data does have some drawbacks that may understate analyst performance. First, the ratings are not weighted by market capitalization, so a bad call on a small stock counts just as much as a good call on a large, widely held stock. Second, because analysts covered a heavy proportion of technology stocks and IPOs over the reported period, the bear market in these sectors over the reported period hit analyst performance hard. That said, we doubt that these factors were so great that, absent their influence, analysts would have been outperforming their benchmarks.

7. The study was conducted by Professor K. R. Subramanyam at the University of Southern California, Fromh Heflin at Purdue University, and graduate student Yuan Zhang at Marshall.

8. These results are for newsletters as a whole over the ten years ending June 30, 2001. If a newsletter contains various model portfolios, their returns are averaged.

9. www.valueline.com/why_use_how.html.

10. For the most recent and comprehensive study, see Choi, James, "The Value Line Enigma: The Sum of Known Parts?" *Journal of Financial and Quantitative Analysis* 35 (September 2000): 485–98. Choi's study also discusses and cites the major studies that preceded it.

11. Barber, Brad M., and Terrance Odean, "Too Many Cooks Spoil the Profits: Investment Club Performance," *Financial Analysts Journal* 56 (January/February 2000): 17.

Chapter 10

1. We tracked the price of each stock beginning with its closing price on the day it appeared in the *Journal* and ending six months, twelve months, and twenty-four months later. We obtained stock prices from Bloomberg and the

Center for Research in Securities Prices (CRSP) and used an on-line database at Columbia University to obtain old ticker symbols (as the *Journal* does not list the tickers for the Darts' picks). If the end date fell on a Saturday, we used Friday's price; if the end date fell on Sunday, we used Monday's price. The *Journal* ends each contest at the end of a month, which may or may not be six months after the beginning of the contest.

2. There's a whole body of research on the Dartboard Contest. See, for example, Greene, Jason, and Scott Smart, "Liquidity Provision and Noise Trading: Evidence from the 'Investment Dartboard' Column," *Journal of Finance* 54 (October 1999); Liang, Bing, "Price Pressure: Evidence from the 'Dartboard' Column," *University of Chicago Journal of Business* 72 (January 1999): 119; Barber, Brad, and Douglas Loeffler, "The 'Dartboard' Column: Second-Hand Information and Price Pressure," *Journal of Financial and Quantitative Analysis* 28 (June 1993): 273.

3. While it did not have a large effect on results, our methodology also differed from the *Journal* in the treatment of corporate events. In acquisitions, we reinvested the proceeds of the sale in the S&P 500 index for the remainder of the contest and combined the performance of the index with the original stock's performance on a compounded basis. The *Journal,* on the other hand, assumed that the proceeds of corporate events were simply invested in cash. Because the Darts' stocks experienced more corporate events, the *Journal's* treatment lowered the returns of the Darts about seven to ten basis points per year versus the Pros.

Chapter 11

1. *New York Post,* May 13, 2001; June 26, 2001.

2. Hirschey, Mark, "The 'Dogs of the Dow' Myth," *The Financial Review* 35 (2000): 1.

3. The Dow Dogs theory is by definition a high-cost, high-tax investing strategy. First, the Dogs by definition pay a high dividend, which is taxed as ordinary income. Second, historically, three to four of the stocks turn over annually, yielding a turnover ratio of 30 to 40 percent. See Hirschey, "The 'Dogs of the Dow' Myth," 13. See also McQueen, Grant, Kay Shields, and Stephen Thorley, "Investment Strategy Beat the Dow Statistically and Economically," *Financial Analysts Journal* 53 (July/August 1999): 66–72.

4. McQueen, Grant, and Steven Thorley, "Mining Fool's Gold," *Financial Analysts Journal* 55 (March/April 1999): 61–72.

5. Fabrilcant, Geraldine, "Talking Money with: Monica Seles," *New York Times,* February 25, 2001.

Chapter 12

1. Bjorgen, Eric, "Why Cashing Out Hurts," *Mutual Funds* (August 2001).

2. Dellva, Wildred, Andrea DeMaskey, and Colleen Smith, "Selectivity and Market Timing Performance of Fidelity Sector Mutual Funds," *Financial Review* 36 (2001): 39–54.

3. Some of the poor timing performance appeared to be attributable to unexpected inflows (share purchases) or outflows (redemptions) that forced the managers to increase or decrease their cash holdings even if doing so conflicted with their timing strategy. In other words, poor market timing by individuals forced fund managers to follow suit. But from the point of view of an investor, the cause of the mistiming shouldn't really matter.

4. Rao, S. P. Umanheswar, "Market Timing and Mutual Fund Performance," *American Business Review* 18 (June 2000): 75.

5. Graham, John, and Harvey Campbell, "Grading the Performance of Market-Timing Newsletters," *Financial Analysts Journal* 53 (November/ December 1997): 54.

6. E. S. Browning, "Strategists Get a New Chance to Get It Right," *Wall Street Journal,* December 10, 2001, C1.

7. See interview with Richard Ferri of Portfolio Solutions LLC in Jim Wiandt and Will McClatchy's *Exchange Traded Funds: An Insider's Guide to Buying the Market* (Wiley, 2001) (noted further in Chapter 15).

Chapter 13

1. Kent, Daniel, and Sheridan Titman, "Characteristics or Covariances?" *Journal of Portfolio Management* 24 (Summer 1998): 24.

2. Barber and Odean, "Too Many Cooks," 17.

3. Kahneman, Damil, and Mark Riepe, "Aspects of Investor Psychology," *Journal of Portfolio Management* 24 (Summer 1998): 52.

4. Kahneman, Damil, and Amos Tversky, "Prospect Theory: An Analysis of Decisions Under Risk," *Econometrica* 47 (1973): 313–27.

5. Shefrin, Hersh, and Meir Statman, "The Disposition to Sell Winners Too Early and Ride Losers Too Long: Theory and Evidence," *Journal of Finance* 40 (1985): 777–90.

6. Odean, Terrance, "Are Investors Reluctant to Realize Their Losses?" *Journal of Finance* 53 (October 1998): 1775.

7. Albright, S. Christian, "A Statistical Analysis of Hitting Streaks in Baseball," *Journal of the American Statistical Association* 88 (December 1993): 1175.

8. Tversky, Amos, and T. Gilovich, "The Cold Facts About the Hot Hand in Basketball," *Chance: New Directions for Statistics and Computing* 2 (1989): 16.

9. Zweig, Jason, "Do You Sabotage Yourself," *Money,* May 2001.

Chapter 14

1. Through 2001, the Wilshire 5000 and Russell 3000 had a correlation of 99 percent, based upon Morningstar Principia Pro.

2. For this reason, we generally have compared the performance of active fund managers to the S&P 500, rather than other broad indexes.

3. Zweig, Jason, "Is the S&P 500 Rigged?" *Money*, July 2001, p. 85.

4. Shilling, Henry, "Investing in Index Funds," in *Perspectives on Equity Investing*, ed. Frank Fabozzi (2000): 226.

5. In this chart and subsequent ones, we exclude index funds open only to institutional investors or retail investors with large amounts to invest.

6. Morningstar Principia Pro. Screened for domestic stock funds, excluding index and exchange-traded funds, and funds open only to institutional investors.

Chapter 15

1. For a detailed discussion of how ETFs work and how they fit into various trading strategies of institutional and retail investors, see Wiandt and McClatchy, *Exchange Traded Funds*.

2. For a good history of the development and legal structure of exchange-traded funds, you should read Gary L. Gastineau's "Exchange-Traded Funds: An Introduction," in the *Journal of Portfolio Management* (Spring 2001).

3. While ETFs generally should have minimal capital gains distributions, one exception came in 2000, when some Barclays's iShare funds actually distributed capital gains. This occurred as those funds were forced to sell some underlying stocks to comply with regulatory limits on concentration. This problem can occur if one stock is particularly large in relation to the overall fund, as in sector ETFs and country ETFs. This phenomenon should not be a problem for domestic broad market ETFs or for a multicountry international ETF.

4. The basis of the shares returned is a matter of indifference to the institutional investor, whose basis is whatever it paid for the basket as a whole, not what the fund paid for each of the underlying shares.

5. For these purposes, we have used a projected equity premium of 3 to 4 percent as most commonly forecast by economists.

6. Gastineau, "Exchange-Traded Funds: An Introduction."

Chapter 16

1. Campbell, John, Burton Malkiel, Martin Lettau, and Yexiao Xu, "Have Individual Stocks Become More Volatile: An Empirical Exploration of Idiosyncratic Risk," Working Paper No. 7590 at National Bureau of Economic Research (2000).

2. This trend holds true even if the volatility of the 1987 market crash is eliminated from the data.

3. Computed by amortizing the initial brokerage costs ($900 to $1,500) over ten years using an 8 percent rate of return. With regard to exchange-traded fund, an up-front brokerage commission of $30 was charged. This resulted in a breakeven of $145,000 to $235,000 per purchase.

4. Discount portfolio companies are similar to electronic communication networks (ECNs) like Instinet and Island. The ECNs have taken market share from the exchanges by allowing traders to transact off-exchange by matching trades. The difference with an ECN is that they attempt to find a matching trade when immediate execution of trades is required. The discount portfolio companies have the advantage of being able to pick through several hours of trades to find a match.

5. Holding trades and later matching them saves money in two main ways. First, it can save considerable labor costs. The discount portfolio companies are all on-line, and you must trade electronically with them to qualify for their low rates. For matched trades, the company doesn't pay anyone to take telephone calls at the front end, to send the order to one of the exchanges, or to execute the trade on the back end. Second, it eliminates "principal risk." This is the risk that the market might move against them after they have sold you a stock, forcing them to cover a trade at a loss. When trades are matched, there is no such risk and no need to pay a market maker a spread to assume such risk.

Chapter 18

1. Morningstar Principia Pro, data as of December 31, 2001. Search of 219 domestic stock funds classified as fund of funds.

2. Fidelity commission schedule as of September 2001.

3. Morningstar Principia Pro. Search was for distinct classes of tax-managed funds, excluding index funds, ETFs, and institutional funds, as of December 31, 2001.

4. Morningstar Principia Pro, data through December 31, 2001, for distinct portfolios of tax-managed funds open to individual investors.

Chapter 19

1. Aaron, Henry, Alicia Munnell, and Peter Orszag, "Social Security Reform: The Questions Raised by the Plans Endorsed by President Bush's social security commission, December 3, 2001 (available at www.socsec.org).

2. May 2, 2001, release from the President's Commission to Strengthen Social Security.

3. ICI Mutual Fund Report, May 2001.

4. Mueller, John, "Three New Papers on 'Privatizing' Social Security, One Conclusion: Bad Idea," paper presented at National Press Club, October 14, 1997.

5. Assuming the retiree invested steadily in the stock market over forty years. The Century Foundation, Issue Brief 10.

6. Data as of December 31, 2001, for domestic stock funds open only to institutional investors.

7. Equally weighted fees based upon the Securities and Exchange Commission Report on Mutual Fund Fees, January 10, 2001.

8. Research released February 7, 2001, by the Investment Company Institute and the Employee Benefit Research Institute.

9. Press conference organized by the Institute for America's Future on August 22, 2001.

10. See Brown, Jeffrey, Olivia Mitchell, and James Poterba, "Mortality Risk, Inflation Risk, and Annuity Products," National Bureau of Economic Research Working Paper 7812 (July 2000). The authors examined how nominal annuities—that is, those not adjusted for inflation—were priced in relation to their true "money's worth," that is, the expected present discounted value of future payouts. The authors estimate that the money's worth ratio (the money's worth divided by the price paid to the insurance company) is 78 to 85 percent for a sixty-five-year-old purchaser and 79 to 87 percent for a typical purchaser. The ratio drops further for an inflation-adjusted annuity akin to the current Social Security system. Only one private company offers such a product in the United States, at a money's worth ratio of 74 to 75 percent.

11. Only once all of the transition costs are incurred and the system is fully up and running—say in fifty or seventy-five years—do some economists suggest that it might work for the majority of retirees.

12. Godstein, Amy, "Social Security Panel Unable to Agree," *Washington Post*, November 10, 2001.

Chapter 20

1. Thus, an eighty-year-old would invest 20 to 30 percent in equities, while a thirty-year-old would invest 70 to 80 percent. This is obviously a bit simplistic, especially if the eighty-year-old has significant resources and will be leaving a sizable sum to a thirty-year-old.

2. The Employee Benefit Research Institute and Investment Company Institute joint study released February 7, 2001.

Chapter 21

1. Two types of agency paper issued by the Federal Home Loan Banks and the Farm Credit System actually are exempt from state and local taxes. This is not the case, however, with other agency bonds (representing the majority of such paper).

2. Morningstar Principia Pro, including funds classified Taxable Bond with a prospectus objective of Corporate Bond, excluding institutional and index funds and funds with 20 percent or more in stocks. We also exclude multiple classes of the same fund.

3. Morningstar Principia Pro, data through December 31, 2001. Funds are taxable bond funds classified as Corporate General or Corporate High Quality, excluding index and institutional funds, multiple classes of the same fund, and funds holding 20 percent or more of their assets in stocks.

4. According to historical data from Standard & Poor's, the likelihood of default over the life of a AA-rated bond is 1.07 percent (or about one in a hundred); for A-rated bonds, still only 1.83 percent. For municipal bonds, the historical default rates are 0.00 percent for AA-rated bonds and 0.16 percent for A-rated bonds. Furthermore, any defaults are generally preceded by several downgrades by the rating agencies, which usually allows a risk-averse investor to sell before default, albeit probably at a loss.

Chapter 22

1. Morningstar Principia Pro, as of December 31, 2001, including all actively managed domestic and international funds open to retail investors, excluding multiple classes of the same fund.

2. Morningstar Principia Pro, as of December 31, 2001. Funds were international funds classified as Europe, excluding multiple and institutional classes and index and exchange-traded funds.

Chapter 23

1. Under these plans, you generally are required to begin withdrawing your money between the ages of 59½ and 70½. With a few exceptions, if you wish to take money out earlier you will pay a 10 percent penalty tax. You'll also owe income taxes on all withdrawals. After the age of 70½, you must take a required minimum distribution every year, usually based upon your life expectancy.

2. Research released February 7, 2001, by the Investment Company Institute and the Employee Benefit Research Institute.

3. These limits phase out the deductibility of IRA contributions between $34,000 and $44,000 for a single filer and between $54,000 and $64,000 for a

married couple, filing jointly for tax year 2002. These limits increase yearly through 2008, when they reach limits approximately 50 percent more than those in 2002.

4. Investment Company Institute report, "Mutual Funds and the Retirement Market," June 2001.

5. Data available on the Thrift Savings Plan website at www.tsp.gov/rates/history.

6. Equally weighted fees based upon the Securities and Exchange Commission Report on Mutual Fund Fees, January 10, 2001.

7. Milevsky, Moshe Arye, and Steven Posner, "The Titanic Option: Valuation of the Guaranteed Minimum Death Benefit in Variable Annuities and Mutual Funds," *Journal of Risk and Insurance* 68 (March 2001): 93.

8. Morningstar Principia Pro, data as of June 30, 2001.

9. Despite its low fees, the TIAA stock fund trailed the S&P 500 over the past five and ten years, by 2.82 percentage points and 1.92 percentage points respectively. This poor performance, though, is probably attributable in part to the subaccount's international diversification, as it holds almost 20 percent of its assets in non-U.S. stocks.

Chapter 24

1. Forty-seven states had plans as of year-end 2001. Indiana had a plan but closed it as of year-end, as the state sought new management. Given time, Georgia and South Dakota are sure to catch up.

2. In order, Washington's Guaranteed Education Trust, Michigan Education Trust, Connecticut Higher Education Trust, Tennessee's BEST Prepaid College Tuition Plan, Virginia Education Savings Trust, EdVest Wisconsin, Louisiana's Student Tuition Assistance and Revenue Trust, Pennsylvania's Tuition Account Program, Alaska's Advanced College Tuition, and Missouri Saving for Tuition Program.

3. As of September 2001, only Louisiana, New Jersey, and North Carolina manage their college savings plans' investments in house.

4. Most states also charge a variety of one-time or annual fees for items ranging from enrollment and annual maintenance to late payment fees and change-in-beneficiary fees.

Appendix

1. Neubert, Albert, "The New Breed of Investable Indexes," in *Perspectives on Equity Indexing*, ed. Frank Fabozzi (2000): 120.

2. Shilling, "Investing in Index Mutual Funds," p. 226.

W e have drafted this bibliography to be of maximum use to individual investors looking for more information on the topics we've discussed. We do not repeat every reference cited in the book but rather include only the most readable and important works. For those of an academic bent, look to the notes.

General Finance

Jagannathan, Ravi, and Ellen R. McGrattan, "The CAPM Debate," *Federal Reserve Bank of Minneapolis Quarterly Review* 19 (Fall 1995): 2 (summarizing competing views on the utility of the capital asset pricing model).

Malkiel, Burton G., *A Random Walk on Wall Street* (W. W. Norton & Co., 7th ed., 2000).

Markowitz, Harry, "Portfolio Selection," *Journal of Finance* 7 (1952): 77.

Mutual Fund Performance

Carhart, Mark, "On Persistence in Mutual Fund Performance," *Journal of Finance* 52 (March 1997): 57.

http://www.quote.com (mutual fund information from Lipper and Morningstar).

Malkiel, Burton G., "Returns from Investing in Equity Mutual Funds 1971 to 1991," *Journal of Finance* 50 (June 1995): 549.

Morningstar Principia Pro Database (available from Morningstar at www.morningstar.com). Much information is also available free on the same site.

Wermers, Russ, "Mutual Fund Performance: An Empirical Decomposition into Stock-Picking Talent, Style, Transaction Costs, and Expenses," *Journal of Finance* 55 (August 2000): 1655.

The Perils of Stock Picking

Barber, Brad, and Reuven Lehavy, Maureen McNichols, and Brett Trueman, "Can Investors Profit from the Prophets? Security Analyst Recommendations and Stock Returns," *Journal of Finance* 56 (April 2001): 531.

Barber, Brad M., and Terrance Odean, "Trading Is Hazardous to Your Wealth: The Common Stock Investment Performance of Individual Investors," *Journal of Finance* 55 (April 2000): 773.

Fama, Eugene F., and Kenneth R. French, "The Cross Section of Expected Stock Returns," *Journal of Finance* 47 (June 1992): 427.

Graham, John, and Harvey Campbell, "Grading the Performance of Market-Timing Newsletters," *Financial Analysts Journal* 53 (November/December 1997): 54.

Kahneman, Daniel, and Mark W. Riepe, "Aspects of Investor Psychology," *Journal of Portfolio Management* 24 (Summer 1998): 52.

Kurtz, Howard, *The Fortune Tellers: Inside Wall Street's Game of Money, Media, and Manipulation* (Touchstone Books, 2001).

Sharpe, William, "The Arithmetic of Active Management," *Financial Analysts Journal* 47 (February 1991): 7.

Passive Investing

Fabozzi, Frank, *Perspectives on Equity Indexing* (2000).

Gastineau, Gary, "Exchange-Traded Funds: An Introduction," *Journal of Portfolio Management* 27 (Spring 2001): 88.

http://www.amex.com (information on ETFs).

http://www.indexfunds.com (information on index funds and ETFs).

Wiandt, Jim, Will McClatchy, and Nathan Most, *Exchange Traded Funds: An Insider's Guide to Buying the Market* (Wiley, 2001).

Buying Bonds

http://www.direct-notes.com (direct sales of corporate bonds).

http://www.internotes.com (direct sales of corporate bonds).

http://www.investinginbonds.com (best introduction to how bonds work).

http://www.publicdebt.treas.gov/sec/secdir.html (Treasury direct sales).

Risk

Bernstein, Peter, *Against the Gods: The Remarkable Story of Risk* (Wiley, 1996).

Taxes

Apelfeld, Roberto, Gordon Fowler, Jr., and James Gordon, Jr., "Tax Aware Equity Investing," *Journal of Portfolio Management* 22 (Winter 1996): 18.

http://www.savingforcollege.com (for everything you'd want to know about 529 plans).

Index